Two Feet, Four Paws

The Girl Who Walked Her Dog 4,500 Miles

Spud Talbot-Ponsonby

SUMMERSDALE

Summersdale Publishers
46 West Street
Chichester
West Sussex
PO19 1RP

Printed and bound in Great Britain by Biddles Ltd.

ISBN 1 84024 002 4

Front cover photo by Gary Anthony, Photonews Scotland Ltd.

Acknowledgements

My sincerest thanks go to the following people, who were all responsible for the success of the Walk: the twenty-seven drivers, whose good humoured patience and unwavering support enabled us to keep going; everyone who put us up, and put up with us en route, and sent us on our way washed, fed and re-charged; the hundreds of people who tended to the Spudtruck, donated food and helped in too many ways to mention; and above all my family — especially my sisters, PC and Charles, and my unique father, Pops, whose staunch belief in me both during the Walk and during the writing of this book has kept me going through the bleaker hours.

My thanks also go to the twenty members of the Walk committee, who helped procure sponsors and get the project off the ground; and to all the sponsors, especially Berghaus, Cable and Wireless, Scottish Communications, Pet City, Travellers Tales (Talking Books), Thistle Hotel Group, Rank Organisation; and to all the many, many people who donated pennies and pounds. I wish I could mention you all.

Finally my thanks go to Ffyona Campbell for her advice and encouragement; and to the following people who have allowed Tess and I into their various homes during the writing of this book — from the Western Highlands of Scotland, to Land's End; Derek and Pamela Powell, Anne Evans, Richard and Shally Hunt, and Sally Stone.

For Mum,
Who showed me the way

Above all do not lose your desire to walk: every day
I walk myself into a state of well being and walk myself
away from every illness: I have walked myself into my
best thoughts, and I know of no thought so burdensome
that one cannot walk away from it . . . but by sitting still,
and the more one sits still, the closer one comes to
feeling ill . . . Thus, if one just keeps on walking,
everything will be alright.

Søren Kierkegaard

Contents

Foreword by Ffyona Campbell 7

Preface 8

1 London to Cromer 9

2 Cromer to Hull 25

3 Hull to Redcar 36

4 Redcar to Edinburgh 48

5 Edinburgh to Fraserburgh 62

6 Fraserburgh to John O' Groats 77

7 John O' Groats to Ullapool 90

8 Ullapool to Glenuig 104

9 Glenuig to Glasgow 117

10 Glasgow to Carlisle 130

11 Carlisle to Liverpool 142

12 Liverpool to Aberystwyth 155

13 Aberystwyth to Carmarthen 169

14 Carmarthen to Bristol 182

15 Bristol to Boscastle 193

16 Boscastle to Plymouth 205

17 Plymouth to Swanage 218

18 Swanage to Hastings 231

19 Hastings to London 243

Epilogue 256

Foreword

The hardest question for any long distant walker to answer is the inevitable *Why?* There is rarely a simple answer. Spud's underlying motives were clearly the cause she was walking for, but as her journey unfolds and her curiosity of the country increases, her journey becomes something much more. Her story illustrates that you don't necessarily need to travel the world to find a diversity and richness in country and culture, as she takes us on a colourful trip ranging from the back streets of Middlesbrough, to the incredible isolation of the Scottish Highlands, to the miles of Britain's promenades.

Walking allows you to see and feel things you miss at twentieth century speed. It is therefore the appropriate way to witness a country and its people, and Spud brings Britain to life in a way which is humorous, yet poignant and refreshingly honest. This book might just make you think twice about fleeing abroad at the first opportunity.

Of course, her journey is also brought to life by the irrepressible Tess, whose role is vital. It is through her ever cheerful nature that many of Spud's encounters are initiated, and awkward barriers removed. Perhaps everyone needs a friend like Tess?

Ffyona Campbell

Preface

Is it true that travellers who set out to explore some part of our globe experience more than their average amount of luck? And is this why they are given shelter by strangers; offered beasts of burden to lighten heavy loads; offered food when their plates are empty; found by guardian angels in the absence of human life; and find more goodness than maliciousness at every turn? Could this all be luck?

Or is it that if you take the risk of the journey and trust whatever fate it holds, you will be shown the inherent goodness which still makes up our world — however hidden it often may be?

Through our journey I came to realise that by making oneself available to that inherent goodness, you will notice that all is not lost in the midst of our consumerist, often selfish, and sometimes violent society. It is important that we realise this, and each of us, in our own way, can make such journeys of exploration; for it is often there on our doorstep.

But there was still an element of luck in my journey.

Three weeks after the walk was completed I was stung by a bee — an insignificant event under normal circumstances — except this time I was to discover I had developed a potentially fatal reaction to bee stings — anaphalactic shock. Within twenty minutes I was fighting for breath, lost my sight, and finally consciousness. The haste with which I was taken to the doctor saved my life. It was a matter of minutes.

The experience left me wondering how I had spent the last ten months of my life in glorious isolation, often miles from habitation, let alone a doctor, and yet had not been stung by a bee . . . ?

CHAPTER ONE

When the alarm went off at 6am on Sunday 1st August 1993 I had no idea that in six hours time I would be setting off to walk the equivalent distance of London to Calcutta. But perhaps Tess had been struck by a moment of enlightenment, and it was for this reason that she was no-where to be found when the back-up vehicle, the Spudtruck, was ready to leave for Tower Bridge.

At this stage I had only belonged to Tess for one month, and we were experiencing the struggle for dominance common at the start of all relationships between man and beast. Tess was winning the battle. I eventually found her in the furthest corner of the house, ignoring my calls and happily shredding a sheepskin rug into tiny pieces. Her bright eyes shone out in victory.

Blackmailing her into following me with promises of a walk was not going to work. She had heard the word so much that she knew it was a waste of energy to rush for the door. In desperation I resorted to the voice intonation favoured by dog owners throughout Britain and, in what is equivalent to 'goo goo, gaa, gaa' in baby language, I cried 'Walkies!' She was soon leaving a trail of wool down the stairs and into the Spudtruck.

We had decided to leave from Tower Bridge for several reasons. I felt that by setting off on the water's edge I would reduce the risk of getting lost; while Shelter's PR team wanted a good backdrop for the photocall. The prospect of this photocall appalled me, inducing visions of armies of pushy reporters amidst the whirr of cameras and large fluffy microphones.

Instead, our allocated quota of small scale fame started with three photographers unsuccessfully attempting to balance Tess on a bollard the size of a football. During those initial painful minutes in front of the camera it was apparent that Tess and I had at last agreed about something. Sitting in contortionist positions, squinting into the sun, wearing fixed smiles for an age, we had discovered something alien at which neither of us was any good. Also during this first photographic ordeal, the tantalising smell of bacon beckoned from within the hotel. Such is the price of small scale fame.

The day was a scorcher. The sun blazed down and there was no wind at all. By 1pm the Tower Hotel room was buzzing with friends, family and sponsors who had come to see us off. At 2pm the coastline beckoned.

I gathered together my array of suburban maps, and changed my boots for the umpteenth time. My father, Pops, raised a toast. 'Ladies and Gentlemen, Spud and Tess are on their way. I'm sure you'll all want to raise a glass to wish them all the luck in the world!'

In response there were shouts and cheers. The surge of encouragement was tangible, and I blundered out of the hotel through a film of tears. On the other end of the lead, Tess set a cracking pace through St Catherine's Docks and down Wapping High Street. Ringing in my ears were the final terrifying words from Rebecca Stephens — 'Whatever you do don't give up!'

But very soon all I could think about was my stomach, which was still complaining that it had missed the full English breakfast. I didn't want to be caught eating our pre-made sandwiches after only four miles, but half way down long, straight Ribble Road I decided that we were safely out of reach of friends. We entered a small park and found a bench.

The paint was coming off the bench in large flakes, and I perched gratefully on the three remaining slats. When I opened my smart new rucksack to find the sandwiches Tess was instantly by my side. Such display of devotion allowed me a momentary warm glow. *Here I am — just me, the road, and my faithful dog,* I thought.

I broke off chunks of crust for Tess. 'Well, Tess. Only 4,496 miles to go!' I began, but in response her large brown eyes remained glued to the sandwich, watching it from hand to mouth as spectators watch a Wimbledon rally. The sandwich finished, she departed to terrorise the first of many unsuspecting toddlers into parting with their ice creams, shattering my warm glow and demonstrating that, at least for now, this was cupboard love.

A little further on we slipped into a cavernous east end pub to answer nature's call. Wearing stout walking boots and carrying a rucksack I could well have been a Martian, as the beery, smoky conversation ceased until we had departed. Outside, while studying my map, one of the customers came out. 'Are you lost, dearie? Where are you going?' he asked.

I looked him in the eye and replied 'Scotland' very seriously. He gave me a disbelieving look before disappearing back into the Nags Head.

In truth my reply had been meaningless. How could I comprehend the scale of ten months of walking, through four seasons, covering 4,500 miles? It was as if the number and noun had been randomly selected. I had no comprehension of what lay ahead. Most of the planning of the last five months had been to raise money for Shelter, and I supposed I would face the walking aspect when the time came — one day at a time.

My walk was the purposeful yet vacant march of a country bumpkin. I stepped blindly off kerbs; walked through pedestrian lights regardless of their colour; wrapped Tess around lampposts; and tripped over uneven paving stones.

Tess was far more streetwise. After the sudden death of my previous dog I had found Tess in an urban dogs' home; and she was the antithesis of me. She was unused to open spaces, chased everything which moved, had never seen the sea, stiles, fences or farmyards, loved rubbish bins, preferred to walk on tarmac instead of grass, and was streetwise to the perils of territorial dogs and traffic pollution.

We came to cross a busy side street, but as I stepped off the kerb there was a sharp tug on the lead. Tess had her toenails dug firmly into the pavement, and her long snout was wrinkled up in disgust. The exhaust fumes are at her nose level, and to this day she will not be persuaded to walk within 8 feet of the rear of an idling car. Ignoring the looks of incredulity from the drivers, I picked her up and continued.

But the streets of East Ham, West Ham, Barking and Dagenham were largely deserted. Cage-like shutters were pulled down over shop fronts, and only the occasional corner shop was open for a slow Sunday trade. The only people on the streets were the largely Asian communities, who eyed Tess with suspicion and often crossed the road to avoid her. I was not sure whether this pleased me or not as, being a social sort of person, I wondered whether I was to spend the next ten months being avoided because of my dog.

After sixteen miles we were plucked from our reverie at a roundabout in Rainham. At the wheel of the Spudtruck was one of my three sisters, Charles, who was the first of a rota of 28 people who had been bullied into driving the Spudtruck. They consisted of family, friends, and friends of friends, most of whom I knew, though many not very well, but some of whom I had never met.

With the aid of a map of Britain, a pin board and a piece of string, I had divided up Britain's coast into forty weeks of 120 miles each, identifying the end of each week by a red pin. Each driver had then put their name down for a weekly or fortnightly stretch, and were expected to turn up in the appropriate place on the appropriate Monday, which would be changeover day and my day off.

Because we had been unable to get a vehicle sponsored, the fifteen year old Ford campervan had only been acquired by us three days previously. Little did I realise the headaches our friend would give us on an almost daily basis — starting with the first night.

I swilled down my aching and dusty body in the cupboard designated for this purpose, but, despite the presence of a gas heater, the water was cold. We then ate pasta in the dark after the auxiliary battery, which was supposed to provide power, followed the example of the shower.

In the morning the toy looking tap rewarded us with a disconcerting gurgle, rather than running water. Still undaunted, we found water for tea and went to light the gas. A small flame ignited and then died. It was clear that of the adjectives used in the advertising of this campervan (budget and reliable), only one was true: its facilities amounted to what we would have had in a tent.

The fact that we had parked amidst the combines and dryers of a farmyard that night didn't mean that we were free from the urban sprawl of Havering. Charles dropped us back at the roundabout and we took to a main road which was to set a precedent for so many more miles.

The verge was thick with dusty crisp packets, and the fume covered grass hid broken bottles. Lorries directed stinking black fumes in our path, and many eyes briefly witnessed our progress from within the clinically cocooned environment of air conditioned coaches. Cars completed the never ending train of automation, glinting a metallic heat in the sunshine which was increasing in strength.

I let Tess off the lead at the first footpath, and she raced off with sheer joy at her freedom, seemingly oblivious to the quality of countryside. The vegetation was comprised of every plant termed 'weed', and even these struggled as they fought with old rolls of wire, ripped corrugated iron, rusted oil drums, plastic containers and sacks. The scene was heightened by the blazing sun, the already scorched soil, and the burnt-off, brown grass whose brittleness scratched and clawed at my bare legs.

For the rest of the morning the footpaths tacked their way across such country, weaving through the margin of human interference which is suitably ignored by the majority of us. It is here, on the junction between urbanisation and rural idyll, that our mess is buried, burnt, dumped or disposed of in some other way.

The wounded landscape of sand and gravel pits give way to rubbish tips. These were overseen by monstrous machines within which no man was visible, so that it appeared we had come across a world which humanity created, but where humanity no longer has a place. The thick stench of rubbish made me feel nauseous in the heat as we followed their decoratively litter-strewn perimeter fences; but I couldn't help but marvel in a miserable way at the scale of services needed to sustain our population and lifestyle.

We then found ourselves in a large patch of wasteland, haphazardly fenced off and containing hundreds of ponies, at the far side of which, like a sleek, glinting and roaring time tunnel from the next century, raced the M25.

In the time it took for one car to come into view from our right, and then disappear from view to our left, we had only taken a few small steps. By the time we reached the motorway that car was at least ten miles away. I felt embarrassed by my slowness, and pleased that I was largely invisible to the drivers who might laugh at our progress; but at the same time ridiculously smug that I was resorting to man's oldest form of transport — a form which placed me firmly back at the starting line of man's existence.

I gave Tess a drink by sloshing water from my bottle into my cupped hand. Her thirst satisfied, she trotted off, panting in the heat and in glorious oblivion to the task ahead. I heeded her advice.

The oil refineries and chimneys of Canvey Island soon joined us to the right, and we sped through Corringham and set off across Fobbing Marshes. Under normal circumstances I would do everything possible to avoid such a sinister stretch of country, as we ducked through the undergrowth and leapt dykes as the day began to close on what, I later gathered, has been the scene of rapes and muggings. But I felt that we were different; somehow untouchable because we were on a specific mission. I was detached from real life — a passer-by who was merely observing.

At six o'clock I turned on the two way radio which had been loaned to us. Because it had to be regularly recharged off the mains, we could only turn it on for five minute stints at pre-arranged times.

It was good to hear Charles' familiar voice. 'Wow! We made contact. How're you?' I said. There was a pause on the other end, then,

'Fine. What about you? Over.'

'It's not very nice out here. Sort of abandoned and eerie. We're nearly at the river.'

There was another pause.

'You must say over! Over —'

'OK! Over!' I laughed at our amateur Anneka Rice impersonations.

'Actually it's bad news,' Charles continued. 'You can't cross the river. You'll have to go round. Over —'

I looked at the map and swore at no one. What I had assumed to be a footbridge was in fact a weir, and we now had a five mile detour, and even longer on these foreboding marshes.

The raised banks disappeared, and the ground underfoot deteriorated until waist high grass camouflaged ground sculpted into deep ruts which tripped me up at every opportunity. It was like walking through deep snow drifts. After 25 miles we reached South Benfleet where, thanks to Charles and Havering's campervan experts, we now had hot and cold water, and gas. It was time to notice the benefits of the space I would call home.

Within 7ft by 9ft by 14ft you have an entire house compact enough to fit into a NCP parking space. Beds, wardrobes, kitchen, ensuite bathroom, and ample storage space are within arm's reach from the kitchen/dining room/dressing room table. Housework is kept to a minimum, window cleaning is easy, you can sleep in your home outside the pub after a boozy night, your phone bills cease, as do electricity bills and rates, unwelcome visitors are rare, and best of all you can enjoy a 180 degree panoramic sea view all to yourself — all at the snip of the price of a house.

I felt myself slipping straight into the spontaneous and transient life — so long as the body would be capable of sustaining a life other than the walking regime. At the end of day two my aching body gave me doubts.

Southend-on-Sea marked our arrival at the seaside, and what better way to be introduced to the Great British Seaside than by garish Southend on a sunny day. Although it was mid summer, the narrow stretch of beach with its forlorn beach huts didn't hold the same attraction as the amusement arcades, novelty shops, burger bars, Postman Pat, candy floss, sticks of rock, or dirty postcards which were clustered around the longest pleasure pier in the world.

Over the next ten months I was to develop a great affection for our piers, and to learn to appreciate them as truly British icons. But in Southend I saw the pier as an anachronism. I watched the families of insistent children, and equally insistent mothers crawling up its length. I watched the patient fishermen. I watched the couples leaning hand in hand over the railings — and I wanted to turn back time. I was being unfair. If I had expected to see the east coast resorts stagnating in Victorian history, I was luckily disappointed.

Drawn to the bright mingle of holidaymakers, we decided on our first attempt at fundraising here. The whole idea of the walk had come about as a result of my disgust at the number of people homeless in Britain.

In January 1993 my life had reached a stalling point. I had only been home from New Zealand for seven months, where I had lived and farmed, at intervals, for four years. Since I had been home, I had been employed in a variety of jobs.

In Torquay I had taught English to European businessmen. In Ireland I had looked after horses and their seventy year old, one armed owner, where I learnt a wealth of equine knowledge, how to *kid*, listen to yarns and sidestep very quickly! During those winter months I had also learnt the number of homeless people dying from hypothermia.

On returning from Ireland I decided that Swindon town needed a wider choice of lunchtime sandwiches, but from the start this venture lost money two ways. One; there is only so much you can charge for a sandwich. Two; a good deal of sandwiches went to people on the streets.

I was finally accepted by VSO to work abroad as a volunteer. On top of all this, I had niggling desires to go back to New Zealand, where I could fall easily back into the life of my dreams. Perhaps this option seemed too easy. In fact my whole life seemed too easy.

The people who died on the streets; the recipients of my sandwiches; and finally the questions asked by VSO as to why one goes abroad to volunteer when we have so many problems in this country, all pointed one way. My conscience had been suitably pricked, and, while mindlessly painting a stretch of wall at home, I had come upon the idea of raising cash and awareness by walking Britain's coast.

But this wasn't the sole reason for the walk. Whether or not I knew it at the time, there was an underlying need for a challenge, and I had found the excuse. Friends and family didn't seem remotely surprised, and when I had sat my father down with a large drink to tell him, he had replied, 'I thought you were going to tell me you were going to walk around the world!'

Like so many other seaside resorts, Southend has a significant homeless problem, but its pier was not a successful first fundraising venue. Several sweaty sponsor forms and leaflets later we were beaten by Postman Pat, and I fled Southend in search of peace.

Between Southend and Colchester, the coast is comprised of endless river estuaries, islands and reclaimed marshes, so that for much of the time the real sea was miles away and our route was circuitous. The O\S map kept me busy through the scattered villages to the River Crouch, where I hoped to find a lift to Burnham-on-Crouch.

The river lay empty except for a solitary yacht. Sitting on a concrete wall was the owner of the yacht, seemingly waiting for just such a damsel in distress. Apart from my knight-turned-ferryman there wasn't a soul in sight, and the exposed, shiny, silent mud flats were left to the feeding birds.

At this stage one end of a bird looked the same as the other, and I couldn't comprehend why they actually liked the stinking mudflats. Tess also treated them with little respect, and always interrupted their feeding in a cloud of legs, feathers and bills. We were a pair of insensitive youths prying into the lives of nature's sensitive equilibrium; we were not in harmony with our surroundings.

Nevertheless, I found an eerie peacefulness on such flat landscape; a peace which was to accompany us on the miles of sea wall we now faced. Stretches of the sea wall were concrete, while others were grazed and the ground was scorched, and hard as rock, so that huge cracks had formed. The only sound was the drone of tractors and combines which worked busily, sometimes seen and sometimes unseen, on the billiard table flatness of meticulous farmland to our left. The delicious smell of slightly musky, ripe corn and cut straw was heightened by the heat, and the sky stretched away, a very pale hazy hue into the distance, where it merged with the corn in a wavering line of heat. To our right, mottled marsh vegetation stretched far out to where I presumed the real sea began.

Like an oasis of shade and water, the Spudtruck was parked in the car park at Colchester station. Tess took on renewed vigour on seeing the correct white van, (she had already been severely disappointed by a laundry van and a roofing van).

Charles was snowed under with Shelter paraphernalia, but gave me a large grin from beneath Tess' vociferous welcome. 'How're you feeling?'

'Weak!' I admitted.

Thanks to some dubious garage water, I had spent the last two days rushing from bush to bush to public loo. You don't have to go to Delhi to get the Belly; Essex does a pretty good variety, as do many other areas of Britain. The effect meant that I was sapped of all energy. Each shadeless mile felt like ten.

Tess, meanwhile, was suffering from the same thing, and was providing more than enough gas to make up for the five gas leaks which Charles now told me had been found in the Spudtruck. The Spudtruck had followed the example it had set the first night. Food had been tepid and eaten by the more reliable candlelight, and the water had been cold.

I collapsed on the seat and drunk several glasses of water, wondering whether this was going to produce the same results, then satisfied my body's carbohydrate craving with plain bread, before stretching out on the floor with my feet sticking into the cab.

Added to Essex Belly was the simple fact that my body hurt. My lower back hurt; my hips hurt; and my legs had pins and needles throughout — as though they were being starved of oxygen. We had only walked eighty miles, and it was impossible not to lie in bed at night, feeling my hurt body trying to relax, and worrying about how I would feel in the morning, and the next morning, and the next . . . Luckily sleep, that great healer, was never far.

I looked up through the skylight to the still cloudless sky. The stationmaster could be heard announcing the imminent arrival of the 2.15 to Nottingham, and a few minutes later there was a squeal of brakes. From now on many a lunch would be eaten in such surroundings. We should really be taking up train spotting.

In the afternoon, we skirted the grounds of Essex University, and passed an empty cottage which drew me to a halt. The paint was peeling off its cream weatherboard and once smart green window frames, and the garden was overrun by waist high ragwort and thistles. But still visible, elaborately painted on a strip of wood, was the name — The Memories.

For all its cosmetic shabbiness, The Memories was still a charming cottage. What blatant neglect and waste! The frustration of others more closely affected was evident in two lines of graffiti:

'Another home wasted, don't let 'em rot
squat the fucking lot.'

In many ways it was easy to walk for homeless people, and to keep walking through the pain. What was my temporary discomfort compared to a lonely life on the street? At least I had a bed at the end of the day; a (sometimes) hot meal; and above all the love and support of friends and family. My determination increased.

Tess was unaware of my temporary metamorphosis. She was more interested in the abundance of sticks which littered the path alongside the River Colne. The half charred sticks came from fires abandoned beneath mangy bushes, where beer cans and gaily abandoned condoms were further evidence of illicit parties.

The River Colne became wider, and the path began to lose its air of the morning after a debauched party. The vegetation grew thicker and the first autumnal signs were evident — polished conkers, and sloes which indicated otherwise insignificant blackthorn bushes. The countryside was turning brown in the British heatwave, and I felt as dehydrated as the country looked.

Respite came after we had walked 130 miles, which was more than I had ever purposefully walked, and we stayed in a caravan park at Point Clear. On Sunday I took my first day off, and we joined the noisy, colourful streets of Clacton.

Here, every shop and business was geared towards the influx of summer visitors, and with the continued good weather the shops groaned and money jingled in as quick succession as the compulsory Postman Pat jingle. Amusement arcades persuaded people to part with their money, or at least persuaded children to persuade their parents to part with their money; and toffee apples, candy floss and *donuts* demanded to be eaten.

Carnival fever was heightening the usual seaside euphoria, and even the senses of the most insensitive person would have been alerted; the smell of the sea mingling with sickly sweets and vinegar; the shrieks of children competing with thumping music, mechanical space invader jingles, and fun fair rides; and the fluorescent teenage beachwear jumping out from shopfronts.

Here are the British at their most uninhibited. Where else do grannies shed stockings, drink too much sherry and stay up late to play bingo? They certainly wouldn't in inland Bath or Birmingham. Where else can you pop into the shop in your bra and knickers, which is, after all, all that a bikini is? Where else can you eat rock, take donkey rides or have your palm read? And why is it that you can only buy dirty post-cards by the seaside? Perhaps because this is the only time that people really drop their guard.

Following suit, I dropped my inhibitions and entered Tess in the dog show.

The first competition was 'the dog most like its owner', which I secretly rather hoped to win. Tess had an excellent waistline, and per-sonally I consider her to be very handsome. I have no doubt that these were the thoughts going through the heads of my opponents, and we turned out to be no match for the black haired, black clothed lady ac-companied by her jet black setter, or the short squat man with his bull dog. Undaunted, we then entered the 'most obedient dog.'

I hauled Tess down the ring, repeating 'heel' in a fruitless manner, and told her to 'sit-a' — as copied from Barbara Woodhouse. But Tess wasn't listening to me. Instead she had her eyes glued to a small boy sitting on a trestle table and demolishing a bag of chips.

I suddenly realised what Tess had in mind next, and split seconds before she launched herself onto the trestle table anyway, I gave her the command; 'Jump on the table Tess!' And she did! The judge wasn't quite so impressed.

Unfortunately Tess continued to ignore everything I said outside the show ring. The next morning, as we walked through Clacton's camp-sites, she had soon stolen a frisbee from a group of energetic holiday-makers. By the time I caught up with her she was racing round the campsite sending all but the 'ah, isn't she a sweet doggy' lovers scurry-ing for cover.

Aware of the fact that I was being watched by dozens of pairs of eyes from behind net curtains, I started with the persuasive tactic, which became firm tactics, and then the swearing-and-puce-in-the-face tactics. Just as I was reaching the end of my fuse, I won the battle.

The prospect of the next ten months of chasing Tess around the coast filled me with desperation. I set off down the road yelling at her. 'I don't care what happens to you! I'll take you back to the home if there's any more nonsense!'

It was the start of a wake of destruction we left up the east coast of Britain; and the start of the most intensive dog training on the most extensive scale. It would range from South Shields shopping precinct, to the watchful eye of St Abbs Head; but now it continued up eight miles of windswept beach and passed eight miles of solid beach huts.

I became fascinated with the huts, each of which has a name; Fair-ways, The Chase, Seaview and even one called Tonga (I could definitely see the attraction of going to Tonga for the weekend). I saw one for sale for the princely sum of £1450, and nearing Frinton they are up to eight deep inland from the beach.

To avoid a large detour around the Rivers Stour and Orwell, we took an early morning commuter ferry from Harwich to Felixstowe, whose white beach and immaculate gardens were empty in the morning sun. The only other person enjoying the morning sun was a fisherman tending his crab pots. At last I had found someone who not only lives on this coast, but continues to make a living from the sea.

Felixstowe was also the first beach we had come across which tempted me for a swim, and I put this to the fisherman. The fisherman wrinkled up his nose and replied 'I wouldn't swim in there if I was you! The sea's really dirty just here. It all comes out from Harwich Harbour.' I made a mental note never to eat crab from Felixstowe.

(I later read in a MAFF Assessment Report that; 'the large majority of shellfish production [in this region of the North Sea] is subject to post-harvesting processing to reduce microbial contaminants derived from sewage pollution of growing waters.')

But the morning was made for walking, and we set off into Suffolk, passing the first of many Martello Towers. These squat, round towers were built in 1803-8 to counter threat of invasion by Napoleon. They were never used but many still remain as museums, cafes and other such uses. Although they can also be found on the Sussex coast, I saw fewer there. To me they became a symbol of Suffolk; as did picturesque estuary and coastal villages such as Orford, Dunwich and Southwold; expansive miles of beach; and terrific erosion.

In an attempt to avoid road walking, I decided to stick to the shingle beach once north of the River Deben. It was a terrible mistake and one I fruitlessly vowed never to make again. My boots disappeared beneath the small stones, and Tess' paws were splayed out at all angles. But while I accepted the fact that I had made a mistake and simply carried on, Tess voiced her complaining through her eyes. Dogs know no such thing as stiff upper lip.

Finally, at the aptly named hamlet of Shingle Street, we returned to firm ground and began a long detour inland to avoid the ten mile shingle spit which runs south from Aldeburgh. On the river banks we found ourselves on a well worn trail, banked with a late summer mat of grasses, docks and brambles which had gone to seed. Accompanying us were twitchers who peered expectantly between branches, and ducked through the undergrowth as if on safari.

A nature trail sign declared that avocets could be found in this area. I had never heard of an avocet, nor did they really much interest me; besides, I thought, I would never be able to identify one from any other long legged black and white bird. Little did I know the genuine excitement I would feel at seeing one nine months later. We walked on heading for Aldeburgh, via Snape.

Aldeburgh has become recognised as a centre of musical activity since the production of Benjamin Britten's opera *Peter Grimes* in 1945, based on the work of a local poet. Many of Britten's subsequent works were composed for local performance, and Aldeburgh now hosts its own music festival every June. This takes place at the Opera House at Snape, about six miles inland from Aldeburgh, which is housed in the old red brick granary buildings of this once busy inland port.

Snape was the scene of my second live radio interview, which could only be better than my first one from Southend. It had been early in the morning and my mind had been clouded with apprehension and sleep. When the interviewer had asked where we were going to next I had blurted out the first name that came to my head — Hull. This was some three hundred and sixty miles and three weeks later.

Being interviewed makes me feel like an animal stunned by headlights. I was going to have to get used to this over the next few months, but I was little prepared for it at the beginning as I walked northwards in a daze.

The village of Aldeburgh was seemingly oblivious to its fame. There was no music *drifting* from open doorways, no sincere quasi-musicians, and there were certainly not hordes of people. There were just fishing boats winched up onto the steeply shelving beach. The beach stretched away to the north for miles, repeatedly re-shaped by the grey North Sea which sucks and blows at the pebbles, and in the distance loomed the gigantic and dazzlingly white Sizewell nuclear power station, described in the guide book as 'a fine group of buildings.'

The building works of the new Sizewell B reactor meant that we were squashed right up against the sea, while the buildings, pipes and coolers towered over and above us and hissed 'keep away, keep away,' drowning out even the sound of the sea as it puffed out its chest and demonstrated its strength on the pebbles. I ran past feeling as though I was in the path of some enormous bulldozer which hadn't seen me. The sound of the pebbles became dominant again, and the wind battered and blew us five miles north to Dunwich.

Once a busy port, Dunwich boasted eight parish churches and two hospitals; and sent two members to parliament. But one stormy winter the bulk of this port slipped into the sea, including the famous church whose bells reputedly clang when the sea is rough, and which can be seen at low tide. The story of the drowned church of Dunwich precedes any visit to this one-shop village, but I neither saw nor heard anything.

The erosion of this coastline is there for all to see: Suffolk beach huts tilt at precarious angles, and lie in pieces on the beaches below. Much of this coast is actually below sea level, and if it wasn't for man's interference, acres of farmland and entire villages would disappear. Near Sea Palling I watched an experimental man made reef being built just off-shore — using enormous boulders imported from Russia and Holland! And the cost of this? £1.3 million, just to erect a temporary protective wall while the reef is under construction.

In heavily frequented areas the dunes are being fenced off, marram grass is being replanted, and on numerous occasions I saw rows of old Christmas trees being *planted* in the sand as temporary stabilisers. But the most common sea defences are groynes and sea walls, (either concrete ones, which double as promenades, or grassy sea walls). In East Anglia, 60% or more of the coast is protected in some way; and some 80% of Norfolk alone is protected. There must be side effects.

Left to nature, eroded sediment will be carried along the coast to form natural sea defences elsewhere. Without this, other parts of the coastline will therefore erode faster. Intermittent stretches of protection, such as groynes, exacerbate the situation, as the unprotected ends will be starved of sediment leading to aggravated erosion. Eventually, either the problem is pushed into someone else's territory, or we end up with a concrete coastline.

With the added problem of a rising sea level, the scene is similar to trying to save a fast sinking boat. But who am I to offer solutions? My livelihood doesn't depend on the land currently being saved. Yet, as the stories of Dunwich and other such ports illustrate, the sea will always be the ultimate master. I am inclined to think that Russian boulders might bring about a situation more disastrous then if we had never interfered. Time will tell.

Meanwhile, similar to a centrifugal force, a large proportion of Britain's population were being flung to the stretch of coast between Lowestoft and Winterton-on-Sea. I hoped they wouldn't prove too heavy for the sinking coastline; and I hoped that the sea wouldn't pick 12th August 1993 to take its revenge. We were to sample our first taste of life in a Haven Holiday Camp, at Gunton Hall, Lowestoft. (This was thanks to The Rank Organisation who were sponsoring us accommodation in Butlins and Haven holiday parks.)

I was the new girl at Gunton Hall. At 7pm everyone was running around as though they knew exactly where they were going, and had been going there for years. We made our way wearily to our chalet, where Tess gave Charles a welcoming but very fishy lick. She had been stealing fishermens' bait all day. I gave Tess her supper and climbed into a hot bath which relaxed the tight feeling in my hips, while Charles prepared the collecting boxes and balloons. We were determined to make the most of these centres for fundraising.

In the entertainments hall the Kiddies Talent Show was well under way, and a small knock kneed boy stood on stage wringing his hands. 'Where is Felixstowe?' A suitable pause. 'On the end of his foot!' The audience laughed and more lollypop jokes followed.

Mr Fizzer's Party was next. He was a large bear-like figure beneath which must have been a very hot Red Coat. He grinned his permanent grin, and partied clumsily around the stage to shrieks of delight from the children. Around the edge of the hall parents lined up the empty glasses and became quietly pissed, safe in the knowledge that their children were having as good a time as they were; and scattered throughout the hall the stars of the future slept in their prams.

Between Mr Fizzer's Party and the Disco Dancing Competition we were announced on the stage; 'Ladies and gentlemen, boys and girls, we have with us a special guest tonight. Tess, and her dog Spud, are walking . . .'

So, for the first of many Butlins/Haven evenings, I became Tess, while Spud snored in bed. We set off around the crowded hall with our Shelter tins, and the cheery holidaymakers dug deep into their pockets, and asked the inevitable question; 'How's Spud? Tired already?' I answered in the affirmative.

The sun shone and families frazzled behind windbreaks. The promenades were dense with people, as we walked through Great Yarmouth and began the long haul northwards towards California. But, while the hard sand should have made easy walking, my legs felt like lead weights. It felt progressively as though each foot was being pulled out of a tub of glue. I tried to concentrate on the way I was walking, and the words of my Alexander Technique teacher, Dave, came back to me.

'Feel your spine grow tall; tip your chin into your neck and look straight ahead, not up. Find your central balance. Stick your bottom out more. Bring your knees up as if you are kneeing someone in the balls!' The words of Dave helped a little, but I was feeling irritable, hot and bothered, and was suffering from period pains.

I stumbled on past Newport, laughing at the average person's ability to walk a maximum of 200 yards from their car before plonking themselves and their paraphernalia down cheek by jowl with a neighbour. I can only hope that they also had a good old laugh at me, as I blundered around the beach in ridiculously sturdy footwear, sweat pouring from every part of my body.

I was also mile and map watching, which was a sure way of making the miles infinitely slower. To take my mind off my pedometer, which was set to my stride and clipped on to the top of my shorts, I sung a ditty which I had been taught long ago by a very favourite spinster aunt. It had been her way of spurring on reluctant children during interminable walks. I repeated it in time to my stride, starting with the right foot:

'It serves you jolly well right . . right . . right, to leave the jolly good job that you left . . left . . left. It serves you jolly well jolly well, right . . right . . right . . .'

Suddenly I couldn't see Tess anywhere, and scanning the beach behind I saw her racing towards me with a piece of driftwood planking in her mouth. In her wake lay the ruins of an abandoned sandcastle which had once sported a drawbridge. I had a giggle and felt better.

Eventually the holidaymakers behind looked like ants crawling about the beach, with only one set of footprints and one set of pawprints joining us and them. We were entirely alone, as the virgin sand and sweeping coast took us to Mundesley, and then under the slumping clay cliffs of Trimmingham, (the first cliffs we had seen), to Cromer.

Initial preparations. Charles, Tess and I sort two hundred O/S maps, donated by the army.

CHAPTER TWO

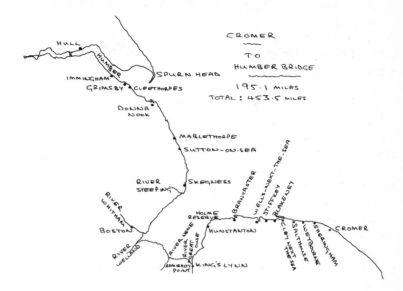

Until now the flat coast had meant that we had stumbled blindly into such towns as Walton, Harwich, Felixstowe etc., feeling our way through the streets and along the coast to the other side, unaware of what lay beyond the buildings to our left and right. It was as if those towns had been superficially imposed onto the flat landscape. Now the humble Norfolk hills gave Cromer more depth.

From a grassy mound near the lighthouse to the south, Cromer could been seen gaily bedecked with bunting. It was also carnival time here. People filled the narrow maze-like streets surrounding the sturdy church which, at a grand 160 feet, is the tallest in Norfolk; and the esplanade was alive. The small blue and red fishing boats sat temporarily neglected on the beach. The survival of the fishing industry (namely crabs), means that Cromer feels less temporary than so many east coast towns.

We dropped down and were swallowed up by Cromer. As we sped through the people I heard mutterings about the new explanatory sign which Charles had sewn onto my rucksack; and a green grocer adamantly refused payment for a bunch of bananas. Such incidences became daily events.

Charles had now left us and I wondered how we would possibly get on without her. She had spent hours sorting out the various Spudtruck quirks and generally looking after us, and I was sure that I couldn't expect the next 27 drivers to do the same. Tom was my guinea pig.

I had met Tom twice previously and now found him waiting by the Spudtruck in Cromer. It soon became clear that the enthusiasm each new driver brought was one of the benefits of having so many. Tom gave me a broad grin, while his eyes sparkled merrily through his glasses as he told me about his train journey.

I began to explain the different aspects of our life which needed handling: 'This is the clipboard with all the fundraising literature. Never be without it! The mobile phone should be switched on all the time, and plugs into the cigarette lighter. We try not to use it for outward calls since we have to pay for them.' This was only the beginning.

'The water tank leaks — so needs filling every day. There's an auxiliary battery for power. You have to remember to flick this switch every time you stop and start . . . !'

When I thought Tom had been bombarded with enough, I shouldered my rucksack, followed Tess to the door, and set off once more through Cromer. In my head I repeated 'out of sight, out of mind; out of sight, out of mind,' in time to my step, and tried not to think of what was happening to my home in the highways and byways of inland Britain. But I worried in equivalent time.

Ahead and to the left Beacon Hill rose out of the flat landscape — at 329 feet this is the highest hill in Norfolk. Relative to its flat landscape it looks like Everest, and my spirits soared with it. The sun was dipping in the west and I looked forward to the week ahead which, judging by the maps, was going to be very different. Above all my body was starting to adjust.

The coast now became a complex combination of shingle banks, sand dunes, salt marshes and mud flats. We took to a section of the Peddars Way and Norfolk Coast Path, using the ample churches as landmarks.

The churches rise out of the flat land like time honoured rocks in the midst of an eroding landscape, evidence of Norfolk's once booming wool trade. They came and went in our path — Weybourne, Salthouse and Blakeney — indicating villages which were once thriving ports serving Norwich during its hey day, but which are now well inland thanks to extensive drainage projects over the centuries.

It is hard to visualise this coast busy with trading vessels and ports. In Cley (or Cly if you want to be in with the locals), Blakeney, Wells and the rest, customs houses have been replaced by art galleries and delicatessens; trading and fishing vessels have been largely replaced by pleasure craft; ship building has been replaced by crafty enterprises; and the breadwinners are no longer sailors, but the birds.

As I write, August 1993, these bird-rich marshes are being declared a National Nature Reserve — an area covering 2,700 acres between Blakeney and Stiffkey. This new status is a formal recognition of the area as being not only of national importance for wildlife, but also of European importance under an E.C. habitats directive — meaning that ministers have a legal obligation to ensure the protection of this area.

East of Wells-next-the-Sea, the coast path took us through cool woodland, beyond which massive dunes rose and fell like waves in the sunshine. Tess revelled in the relative cool of the trees and raced in manic circles through the shadows, despite not knowing what exactly it was she was chasing. The bunnies knew they were safe. They lined up on the dunes to our right, paws up to their mouths, and had a good old laugh. It would take her 1,100 miles of frantic and circular bunny hunts before she was rewarded in a forest on the edge of the Moray Firth.

We were soon back out on sea walls and paths beneath a huge blue sky. I missed the real sea, but the salt water channels meandering inland reassured me that it was still there out beyond the expansive mauve-tinted marshes of sea lavender.

I could feel the loss of liquid sapping my strength, and when we reached Brancaster I bought food as if I hadn't seen any for days — three cans of isotonic drink, a loaf of bread and several packets of crisps. Sitting under a large tree I tore off chunks of bread to make rough crisp sandwiches, hoping this would immediately remedy the aching hips and severe energy depletion. Tess pleaded to the same ailments and ate the other half of the loaf.

She was also suffering from the heat. She licked her lips as soon as she saw the plastic container which I now carried for her to drink from, and I noticed that her nose was reaching the same vermilion as mine. Hers wasn't peeling though.

We followed plank walkways through the dunes of Holme Reserve. The tide was out, and the beach was so gradually shelving that its meticulous smoothness stretched far, far away from us, before reaching the blue strip of the distant sea which seemed to have been added as an afterthought.

We walked our twenty-sixth mile of the day on the still glorious sweep of beach and arrived below the cliffs of Hunstanton, famous as the east coast resort that faces west! It was good to have the sea close by again, but I was disappointed to see its colour here at the mouth of the Wash. It looked grey and very unappealing.

The grey sea cast a grey blanket over the town making sounds muffled and people unseeing, while the once grand buildings looked forlornly down on the kiosks and neon façades. Even the children lining the beach and promenade looked grubby. Was this due to my hot and fatigued senses? I wasn't sure.

Two American girls came up to us. 'Do you know where the chapel is please?' they asked. We had just walked past a rubble of stones in a vague square, which was the chapel. I pointed back to it. 'That's it?!' they laughed. At least Hunstanton is safe in the knowledge that it will always be the east coast resort which faces west.

At the base of the Wash, the town of King's Lynn jumped out from a geography exercise book. Along with Spalding and Wisbech it was depicted by a childishly drawn cabbage, and neat squares of green dots. These three market gardening towns on the fertile Wash must have featured in school text books throughout England.

Situated on the River Great Ouse, King's Lynn has thrived as a port since the fourteenth century. The diversity of old buildings which remain are testament to its wealth over the centuries; merchant's houses, warehouses, the Custom's House and other residential buildings flank the riverside in a mixture of flint, stone and red brick used over the years.

Also surviving the years is the small ferry across the Great Ouse, which has run for over 1200 years, despite the fact that the main road only crosses one mile upstream now.

We joined the sea wall the other side and set off downstream, watching the mudflats rapidly disappearing beneath the rising tide. It felt as though we were walking against the tide, and by the time we reached the Spudtruck at the isolated Admiralty Point I felt sure that nothing in the world would have persuaded me to walk further that day.

Tom was busy effusing about the birdlife. 'Did you see the greenshank on the flats?' he asked.

'I saw birds. But I don't know one from the next,' I admitted.

'But you should!'

Tom stood up and took the two paces possible in the Spudtruck before sitting down again. He bowed his head to emphasise a point, and waved his arms around like a scientist who has just made an important discovery. 'The marshes are so primeval. They're untouched by man and sustain such life.'

I couldn't feel Tom's affinity for the muddy and dirty estuaries, but his wealth of information about the plant and birdlife illustrated my ignorance.

Our conversation was ended by a cloud of clamorous ankle-biting mosquitoes, and I took refuge in the shower, where I noticed I had lost my St Christopher. I hated losing such things. It was a bad omen.

Five minutes later, as the water ran out just as I was covered in soap, Tom made another discovery. 'Tess!' I heard him wail. 'She's piddled on the seat!'

Sure enough, there was a large wet patch on the seat where she was fast asleep, and since there was no water anyway, it could only be piddle. The wet cushion would shortly be Tom's bed and he was looking at it with disgust. It crossed my mind that Tess (whom Tom treated as one might a cat with fleas) couldn't have picked a worse two weeks to develop an incontinence problem — or perhaps Tess was having a chuckle?

The next day I took Tess to the vet. Although he prescribed her antibiotics in case of infection, he thought it likely that it was a behavioural problem; while my own diagnosis was the dehydrating, shadeless miles of Norfolk's sea walls in the British heat wave. Either way, her problem did clear up — once Tom had gone.

With Tom's help I now began to put names to the birds. The colourful red, green and white ducks which flew in pairs over the marshes became shelduck; and they joined the brilliant oystercatchers which flew in unison, their red bills bright in the sun. The red legged and red billed waders became redshank; and the ducks which bobbed out on the waves became eider duck — (and I thought ducks only swam on ponds!) Out on the Wash, these birds and more became our companions.

The Wash is one of the biggest estuary areas in Britain. It is comprised of the estuaries of the Rivers Ouse, Nene, Welland and Witham which are gradually silting up the sweeping shallow Wash. This has allowed successive land claims, the first of which was recorded in Roman times, and the last in the 1970s, since when a cessation has been imposed.

At each successive drainage, an earth sea wall has been constructed. New saltmarsh then forms, so allowing further reclamation. Because the sea level is rising, each new wall has had to be higher than the last, so that much of the claimed land is now several metres below sea level. This has disastrous implications if the rise in sea level continues.

As far as the eye can see are marshes interlaced with rivulets, through which the speedy tide snakes its way inland or is literally sucked back out. Inland, there isn't a hill or tree in sight. The whole vista makes the sky tremendous, as it sweeps in an uninterrupted arc above. I could see that the world is round. It is an ideal landscape for a claustrophobic person; but a nightmare come true for an agrophobe.

Pacing each other, and occasionally punctuating the silence with a whistle or a snuffle, we detoured the River Nene and arrived back at its mouth. Suddenly, and without warning, a succession of jets roared deafeningly low directly over our heads and out to sea, where they swept up and out of sight, leaving only a thin trail of steam across the blue sky as evidence of their presence.

It seemed as though they were using us to line up their targets, and this disturbance continued intermittently until a prolonged silence lulled us into a false sense of security. I began to sing any doggy song I could think of. 'How much is that doggy in the window' and 'Nothing but a hound dog' were booed off by two as yet un-named birds, and I confessed to Tess that I had been turned down by all three choirs of all three schools I attended.

Another loud bang then interrupted our one-sided conversation and I looked round to see a flock of birds fly up in a start, except for a group left flailing around. Within minutes twenty people emerged from the sparse undergrowth and smothered the remaining birds with sacks. I thought that I was witnessing some sort of bird massacre or pest control.

But a rather portly and be-spectacled twitcher put me right. He was looking through a high powered telescope which sat on a tripod and was focused over a marshy field further on. He told me that they were routinely ringing the birds, and I was pleased that I hadn't raced off to report a bird massacre! Before long I was looking through the twitcher's telescope.

Wow! It was amazing. Suddenly the black dots took on forms with feathers of every colour, darting eyes, and a colourful array of legs and bills. It was like snorkelling in the sea — spying on a whole new life.

'What are the lovely brown speckled ones with long downward curving bills?' I asked, sold on the birds which could handle their incredible bills with such poise. 'Curlews.'

I like the name 'curlew'. It rolls off the tongue in a way which matches the form of the bird itself; perfectly proportioned, graceful, distinguished and individually aristocratic. I adopted them as my new friends.

Thus inspired, I found my walkman and set off listening to *The Lark Ascending*. The classical music made me feel good and at peace with myself and the walk. We were out of range of the jets, and the ground underfoot was hard but smooth and made easy walking. But such joyous moments were destined to be short-lived.

The walking deteriorated along an old sea wall running to Boston. It was overgrown with brambles, nettles and elder, and I stumbled furiously through the tangle of vegetation. Finally defeated, we took to the neighbouring fields, but even here our route was barred by bramble *hedges* which I hauled Tess over, and which scratched and stung my crampy, end-of-day legs.

On the banks of the River Whitham different obstacles lay in our path. This time we fought our way through the usual rubbish dumps, sewage works and piles of scrap metal which compete for estuarine positions. There wasn't a person in sight. It was as if a child had made a terrible mess of its playthings, and then left them for someone else to deal with — only there was no one dealing with this.

Away in the distance Boston's church tower, known as the Stump, competed for the skyline with electricity pylons, silos and cranes in a jumble of silhouetted forms. I longed to be stretched out horizontally on a hard floor and to feel my muscles relax; and dreamt of banana milkshakes and bread and honey.

So long as my legs never stopped, we would reach our destination. It was that simple. *The legs must never stop*, I thought.

The Saturday market was closing up in Boston square, leaving the usual debris of cabbage leaves, squashed tomatoes, and burger wrappers. The market stall holders laughed and joked to each other across the square, and their now empty stalls looked skeletal.

In the centre of town we found the spireless parish church of St Botolph, crowned by the Stump, and lay down on the beautifully mown lawn to wait for Tom. I looked up through the branches of the shady trees, shut my eyes, and felt the muscles relax.

We were woken by Tom, who was well into his role of organiser, housekeeper, chauffeur, financier and tourist guide. I no longer worried about my home, and also knew that he was making the most of every opportunity — whether befriending farmers to procure water, visiting places of interest along the way, or securing a church car park for the night as he had done in Boston.

That night we made our beds in the usual way. The drivers slept at the back of the truck, where the table dropped between the two seats and became a bed, while I slept above the cab. I had also decided that, since not every driver was going to be as fond of my dog as I was, Tess was going to have to sleep with me. But the narrow rungs of my portable ladder meant there was no option but to hoist her up, and so it was for the remaining nine months, one week, and three days — much to her obvious pleasure.

I was woken at seven the next morning for two reasons. The first was an extremely slug-like nose touching my nose, and I opened my eyes to find that Tess and I were sharing the pillow. I briefly wondered whether I would grow whiskers and find amusement in sticks by the end of the walk. The second thing which had woken me was the sound of voices outside the Spudtruck.

I parted the flimsy curtain which was drawn across the narrow window by my head and saw the congregation gathered outside the church. They were walking across the very patch of grass where Tess had left her mark the previous night, and I could have sworn I saw Tess smiling as her gaze followed mine through the window. We were like two naughty children lying belly down and sharing a secret.

The sun had disappeared, and the marshes looked ominous under the grey sky. For fourteen miles of sea walls we were joined only by cows and calves, chewing their cuds and watching our progress through indifferent eyes, while to our left were fields of cabbages, sugar beet and wheat, neatly arranged in grid formation by the presence of parallel dykes and banks.

The sea wall continued to the River Steeping, which I had been told we could cross via a sluice. But when we arrived here the gate was padlocked. I was determined to avoid the five mile detour inland, and knew I could negotiate the spikey pailings somehow. But first I had to make Tess think small and fit through a square hole at the base of the gate, about the size of a cat flap. But folding Tess up enough was a little like trying to thread a needle with baler twine, and I sat back with a defeated air, wishing for the first time that I had a miniature Chihuahua as company.

As I began to accept our position a man came out of the only house on the other side of the river. He had the air of one who had seen a good few people in the same predicament.

'The key's held by the NRA,' he told me.

'I was told it was open!'

'It is for one day of the year! For the annual run from Boston to Skegness!'

We were then joined by the man's wife, who was a homely figure wearing an apron. 'I've just been cooking a chicken, perhaps if I get a piece we could persuade her through?' she suggested.

That was all that was needed. Tess took one sniff of the woman's hand and popped through the hole, where she was duly rewarded. I scrambled over the spikes and we set off happily along the dunes to Skegness, pleased to have left behind the mud and marshes and dreaming of roast chicken.

The sandy beach runs northwards all the way to Cleethorpes, a distance of some forty miles. The beach excelled all my expectations of Britain's coast. If our weather was more reliable this coast would be crowded with resorts drawing Baywatch Babes, but as it is the miles of sand are largely undeveloped. Billy Butlin realised the potential of this coast and opened Skegness Butlins (or Funcoast World as it is now called) in 1936. Before this the only holiday camps existing were tented and often for men only!

By 1948 one in twenty holidaymakers went to Butlins; and Funcoast World now accommodates 12,000 people per night through the summer. All this started with five pounds and a hoopla stall.

That night we joined the statistics. Around us, toddlers, grannies, mothers, fathers, lovers and wheelchair bound holidaymakers danced and drank. It was like one huge party, with 12,000 of your most favourite friends. There was no threat of antagonism; no threat to the children; and, with 10,000 pints to drink, no threat of the beer running out! Just as I was beginning to wilt, more people were appearing and heading off to the various nightspots. I left Tom happily dancing with Funcoast World and joined Spud in the mobile home.

We left Skegness on a 'Skegness is so bracing' day, as the wind blew southwards down the wide beach, teasing out whispy clouds. It was a British Seaside day; a day for windbreaks and kite flying.

The tide was out and we walked on the hard sand near the water's edge. I liked watching my boots as they squeezed the water out of the patch of sand I stepped on. I remembered once hearing that there are more stars in the sky then there are grains of sand on the beaches of Britain. I had certainly never realised the incredible mileage of beach on England's east coast, and wondered who had ever counted the grains of sand.

Bent into the wind at Sutton-on-Sea, I noticed a familiar looking brindle dog haring towards a string of donkeys. When Tess arrived at the donkeys she circled them and crouched down, inviting them to play. The donkeys were oblivious. They continued to look melancholy and follow each other, nose to tail, in the footsteps of their minder who was absently trailing a stick.

The donkey minder had short spikey hair and was wearing an old sweatshirt and jeans. As he talked he lent casually on the neck of one donkey. 'Not the right weather for you today!' I resorted to the trusty introduction. 'Hasn't been the right season for us either.'

'Haven't you had the glorious weather?'

'Mm. But there haven't been the people.'

The donkeys agreed with this, and flicked their tails in unison. Tess was nose to nose with the front donkey who was only now looking vaguely interested in life. I wondered whether they were communicating.

There was certainly a surplus of donkeys to customers on this beach, especially on such a grey day. 'Are these all yours?' I asked.

'Mm,' he grinned wryly. He charged sixty pence for a ride, and with forty donkeys to feed, and four other minders to pay, I wondered how he could possibly survive.

Having declined the offer of a donkey on which to continue round the coast, we left them to it. It was the first day of a new week and I was in a good mood which nothing was going to ruin. I threw scarce shells and pebbles for Tess, who no longer barked at the sea as though it was some threatening monster, but still wouldn't even dip her big toe in it.

We skirted Donna Nook MOD range through the dunes. Far out to our right I saw some large boats heading out of the Humber, and beyond them was Spurn Head. It was a satisfying sight. As far as I was concerned we had arrived in the north of England — or at least the Midlands. It certainly felt as though we had travelled far enough to have reached another country.

In Cleethorpes we stayed with Beryl and Curley. On Tom's suggestion I had written to the Social Responsibility Officer in each of the coastal dioceses which we would walk through. Beryl and Curley had invited us to stay as a result of the Hull Social Responsibility Officer, and welcomed us two strangers into their house with unconditional hospitality.

Beryl opened the door and was followed out by Stanley the Staffordshire Bullterrier, who resembled a trunk on legs. Beryl was in her fifties and quietly spoken. 'You must be exhausted! Come in. Oh Stanley is pleased to have a friend!'

Beryl let out a school girl giggle, and Stanley was already puffing with the exertion of answering the door. Once inside the terraced house, our progress and conversation was dominated by Stanley's immediate adulation of Tess. Risking life and limb he followed Tess around with his nose never more than a few inches from her bottom, until his square sides heaved and I thought he should collapse with a coronary.

Beryl's actions were quick and her glasses, which were normally so shiny that you couldn't see her eyes, became completely misted over with the condensation in the shambolic kitchen. Meanwhile she told us that Curley worked on Grimsby docks, but that he was out playing darts, and went on to tell us about her two sons: 'One's in the merchant navy and away in Bosnia. The other lives here. He's a trained joiner but's been out of work for over a year. The decline of Grimsby Docks had tremendous knock-on effects.'

Beryl talked about her son with maternal worry. At one stage he had reached such a stage of unemployed frustration that, in a moment of despair, had thrown his entire tool set away. Luckily Beryl had rescued them. She talked of the sense of helplessness and the pessimism which a skilled craftsman, so long out of work, is bound to feel.

As I climbed gratefully into a gorgeous deep, double bed, surrounded by pink — pink towels, flannel and bath hat, pink duvet and fluffy cushions, pink slippers and tissues — it slowly dawned on me that this was a well lived in room, but they had no daughters! The room had every sign of female living (even the KY jelly) and with a great surge of guilt I realised that it must be Beryl and Curley's room.

I lay in bed squirming with guilt. If I got up to protest this would only cause embarrassment all round so, realising that there was nothing I could do, I fell into a pink, guilty but nevertheless deep sleep.

Grimsby Tower and its surrounding deserted dockland grew smaller behind us, and the other side of the Humber came closer. The water of the Humber looked brown and evil in the chilly wind. We passed oil refineries, Immingham Docks, and endless other works; and the smoke from the various chimneys merged with the low grey clouds so that it seemed as though years of smog had built up over the region. Yet with signs of civilisation at every turn, we didn't see a soul.

The sight of the Humber Bridge spurred us on, and the next morning we strode above the Humber feeling on top of the world. We had reached another red pin. I stopped in the middle to roll myself a cigarette, and Tess and I sat contemplating our achievement so far. Behind us, the traffic droned incessantly on.

Tess handled the interviews better than me.

CHAPTER THREE

I threw my cigarette over the side of the bridge and watched it until it was a mere speck. The water below held my attention, and I was overcome with the strange magnetic desire to throw myself over the edge! I wondered whether Tess would follow me if I jumped, or what else she would do. Secretly I hoped that such strength of loyalty would one day exist; but for now she just shivered by my side.

Once off the Humber Bridge, the dual carriageway squeezed us up against the estuary shoreline, until a cracked concrete wall ran parallel to the foundations of long forgotten riverside buildings. The thistles and dandelions grew through the concrete as though thriving on rich peat; our only companions were small groups of staring fishermen.

This wall brought us to the scene of the old docks, where the deterioration is so complete that it is hard to imagine the skeletal jetties were ever safe to use. The ruins cling tentatively to the shore as if reluctant to sever the final connection with their past, and a series of wooden supports rise out of the river in a final stance of pride, each one crowned by a gull.

Yet Hull felt as though it was shaking itself off in the way that a dog shakes off water. Sporadic new developments were appearing around the docks, and Hull still supports an important cargo port. Near the town centre was a smart new marina, and, although we saw a lot of derelict housing, there was a good deal of new housing.

To avoid the main roads, we set off along the seaward side of the working docklands, crossing the tiny River Hull via the closed lock gates, and following a path which the O/S map said would lead us back to the main road. A massive coal heap began to grow behind an imposing wire fence on our left.

After a while the tangled vegetation on our right squeezed us right up against the fence, and I hung onto the wire with each stride like a monkey swinging from branch to branch. The fence turned abruptly left, and we had no option but to accompany it.

Tess leapt the brambles and sneaked under the gorse. The fence ended at a point where it had obviously been decided that no one would be silly enough to try and reach, but they had underestimated Spud and Tess. We were now in amongst the coal, and Tess' white paws were instantly black, as we clambered over piles of it until reaching an old railway line which led to the gate.

I tried to look innocent as we approached the gate, but felt distinctly silly. Two men came out of their hut. 'What're you doing here?' they asked. I explained, but they didn't look amused. 'Well there's no path through here. If you follow this road you'll join the main road. And don't come walking through here again!'

Leaving a trail of black footprints and pawprints, we skirted the enormous hissing pipes and coolers of the BP works, where it seemed that a mad professor was conducting an over-size and potentially catastrophic experiment, and arrived at the tiny village of Paull. We fell into the Humber Tavern.

A pint of Tetleys heralded our arrival in Yorkshire. 'Walked far?' the barman asked in an off-hand way. Again I felt shy about telling people. It sounded completely unbelievable when I replied, 'from London!' I told Syd about the walk and he had soon signed his name on a yellow sponsor form. Such easy support and generosity was coming so freely from people.

Paull was once a thriving shrimping village, until the pollution became too bad, but even now it boasts three pubs along its tiny street. That night we felt it our duty to sample the Tetleys in each, as part of our liquid supper, but I soon realised that Tom had labelled The Victoria his favourite. Judging by Tom's subsequent glue-like gaze on the barlady there was a chance we would have company for the night. I felt that a little romance would have completed the syllabus for the drivers, so left Tom to it and joined Tess in the Spudtruck.

Perhaps the Spudtruck wasn't the best courting venue, and Tom was alone when I woke the next morning. This was our third day of negotiating the Humber but on the north shore there is no industry. Instead we set sail for Spurn Head along seldom used sea walls.

Fields of corn of various qualities bordered the path on our left, and to our right the wide marshes were occupied by feeding birds and estuary debris. I made the most of the silence and began a talking book. It was Somerset Maughan's *The Moon and Sixpence* and conjured up images of artist frequented cafes in Paris.

I could taste Paris. Baguettes, dripping bries, mind blowing goats cheese, coarse pates, and tangy salamis, were washed down with glasses of rough red wine, and the Parisian world drifted past. My stomach asked to be fed and after twelve miles I found a patch of shade behind a low wall. Thanks to imagination, when I closed my eyes the flaccid white bread sandwiches tasted of Paris.

At the northern mouth of the Humber, and at the end of one of the largest estuaries in Britain, is Spurn Head — a three and a half mile long spit which is just wide enough to permit a single track road serving the RNLI station at the end. Marshes have accumulated on the estuary side, while on the seaward side the beach faces the wrath of North Sea storms.

Spurn Head is a subject of contention locally as the whole spit, if left to mother nature, is likely to be swallowed by the sea. Spits are one of nature's most volatile features and move as a result of the various sea drifts and deposits. Parts of the road had already been washed away the previous winter, and people we spoke to thought that the same was going to happen last winter — (as I write it is still there). As usual the argument is over who pays — the RNLI or the ornithologists.

The tip of Spurn Head is a twitcher's haven. Small agile birds which, to a naive eye, fell into the category of gulls, turned out to be common terns. They darted up and down the shoreline looking for food, occasionally terrorised by villainous great skuas. Often the baddie won, but always their acrobatic agility at avoiding the skuas was fantastic to watch.

But it was tiny dunlins which entranced me, as they gracefully flew up to catch a breeze, then scurried about very close to the waves, the tiniest of which threatened to knock them off their skinny legs. But they judged the waves with meticulous precision — as if respect for the sea had been instilled in them at an early age. The dunlins joined the curlews as my firm favourites. From now on they accompanied us when there was no other bird in sight, and were seemingly never daunted by strong winds, rain or crashing waves.

It soon became clear that it is not just Spurn Head which is in danger of being washed away. The sandy coast north of here also catches the full force of the North Sea, and in places is disappearing at the phenomenal rate of 7.5 feet per year, making it one of the fastest eroding coastlines in the world.

In many places the erosion is aggravated by intensive farming. The land is cultivated right up to the cliff edge, and I often saw large sections of land which had slipped half way down the cliff, but on which that season's wheat was still ripening. This indicates the speed of erosion. The sea remains an unrelenting landlord demanding an annual payment.

The ground along the cliff tops was cracked and brittle, as were the slips below. I talked to Tess about the erosion. So far it seemed that the east coast would be in danger of disappearing if left to mother nature. What would our country look like thousands of years from now? Perhaps, if it was being continually eroded on the east coast and built up on the west coast, we would eventually bump into Ireland? I looked forward to finding out on the west coast, but pushed the thought of the west coast from my mind.

We were disturbed by a woman's voice coming from below. 'Excuse me .. Hello!' Tess' ears pricked up at the sound of another voice and we turned round to see a fraught lady and a young boy perched on a slip. 'Oh thank goodness someone's come along. We're stuck! My boy can't get up the cliff. We were caught by the tide.'

I scrambled down the cliff. It wasn't particularly hard going, but the boy was only six and I think they had panicked. The lady pushed her son from behind and I pulled from the top.

'The problem is my son's diabetic. He's due for insulin,' she explained. 'I don't know what we would have done if you hadn't turned up. We haven't seen any one since we left Withernsea.'

I steered them towards a solitary farmhouse, and in return the lady gave a donation. Tess and I had both done our good deeds for the week. She had found a lady's wallet in a roadside ditch near Boston. We had handed it into the police, and it was duly returned to its owner.

We found Tom in Withernsea and I collapsed with a cup of tea. Tom began to tell me about the churches that he had seen that day, the people he had met, the history of the East and West Ridings, the resulting social consequences, and no doubt other fascinating information. I couldn't concentrate my mind. I tried to focus on what he was saying, but couldn't. 'Hang on Tom. Slow down!'

'Hm?'

'You know, I've been finding it hard to concentrate on what you're saying in the evenings.'

Although I was primarily physically active during the day, my mind was as exhausted as my body at the end of each day, but I had been fighting the mental exhaustion in an effort not to appear thick to Tom! The result had been conversations which followed no particular train of thought, and incomprehensible slurs.

Although I recovered after a couple of hours each evening, I was never going to be able to sustain erudite conversations on the state of the world; yet while walking my mind was constantly active and full. What I really needed at the end of each day was an hour of peace, a period of recuperation at the time when I felt most edgy. I accepted this side effect on Tom's last night.

Tom is one of the lucky people who saw the light and escaped a high pressure job in London. He was returning to college to study agriculture. Although not even knowing where Tom had been to school, we had learnt a great deal about each other. I had learnt that he likes to shower in the morning; that he is not overly fond of dogs; that he has boundless enthusiasm for an enormous range of pastimes; that he prefers white bread and gin to brown bread and whisky; that he likes classical music; that his home would always be immaculate; that he is a closet train spotter; has a magnificent appreciation of the countryside; that he sleep talks; and has one favourite word which is 'curious'.

I would miss Tom, and he also seemed sad to be going. He drove us into Hull with an uncharacteristically and perhaps nostalgic respect of the Spudtruck; but I was to leave Hull with my right foot desperately searching for the brake again. Dee also had rally driving aspirations. 'Not too fast Dee, everything slides about,' I said nervously, as the first packet of pasta fell and landed on Tess' head.

I had met Dee briefly on several occasions, but all I knew about her was that she had her own floral design business. She was now straight into the fundraising, due partly to the fact that she had had Pops on the phone the previous night. 'He said something about never being anywhere without the clipboard?' she said. I laughed. The dreaded clipboard made you feel like a market researcher and was guaranteed to make anyone run a mile, but it had all the sponsor forms and literature on it. From now on it attached itself to Dee as though it was an extra limb.

Before the Spudtruck had been stationary in the Withernsea campsite for more than a few minutes, Dee was knocking up a delicious vegetarian delight of pasta complimented with various birdseeds. We then set out to explore Withernsea, which the tourist guide boasted had 'pubs and clubs for all tastes.'

We found ourselves in a small local pub where the locals sat round playing dominoes, and listening to the Coronation Street theme music. We were bought a drink by the elderly one-toothed appendage to the bar. 'Aye, Withernsea's very popular in the summer you know,' he told us.

He sat on a stool and his right elbow never left the bar, while his left arm dealt with his pint. His one tooth made him slurp a little. 'There's three night-clubs here you know — and then there's the headstand piano player,' he said with just a hint of pride.

Dee hid her smile in her drink. 'Aye, the headstand piano player is just down the road. He's in the Guinness Book of Records for playing the piano upside down for two hours!' Every town must have its claim to fame.

I slept soundly that night. My lower back and hips no longer ached and I was really beginning to feel as though my body had adjusted. Scrambling down a baked mud slide onto the deserted beach, we took to the water's edge where the sand was hard. The waves breaking onto the beach filled the air with their meditative whoosh . . . pause, whoosh . . . pause, and my feet fell in time. The sea was our friend, and seemed incapable of the terrific erosion and occasional fallen beach hut on our left. The flat sand stretched on and on. We were two tiny specks leaving one set of footprints and one set of paw prints on the otherwise flawless beach.

I decided that we could reach Cowden before the tide forced us off the beach. Once I had made this decision we had to stick to it, as the land above was another MOD bombing range. But I had underestimated the tide's speed.

The cliffs on our left began to look less friendly, as though they might collapse at any moment, and the waves seemed to be reaching out for us; whoosh . . . pause, whoosh . . . pause 'we're coming to get you' they were saying now.

The first waves began to break on the base of the cliffs, but still retreated some way back. Eventually it caught us and we scrambled up the cliffs, and sat down to watch the energy accumulated in every wave. Slowly, bit by bit, they were eating away at Britain. I remembered a recurring nightmare I had as a child of standing on a cliff which was disappearing from under my feet, and I had been unable to move back fast enough. Eventually I fell towards rocks below but woke at the last moment. I suspect this is a common dream for children but now here we were; here on the cliffs which had not long ago been friendly.

Like so many other MOD ranges, the one we found ourselves on is now based out to sea, but the range is still closed to the public. For this reason we received an icy reception from the control tower, and we were unceremoniously bundled into a Land Rover and taken to the gate. But nothing was going to dampen my spirits.

The straight stretch of coast had taken us across almost a whole map in a day, and I folded the map for the last time that day with a feeling of satisfaction. Now we were getting somewhere. The sun still shone, and backed up on our deserted clifftop in Hornsea that evening the massive blue and cloudless sky reached down and delved beyond the surface of the earth, as if wrapping us inside a peaceful world which consisted of only what we could see. A full moon took over, casting a bright path across the sea.

Ten miles of beach would take us to Bridlington. While I enjoyed these times of complete isolation, Tess found the beaches lacking in diversions. I threw a pebble for her and she looked skywards to where a gull was flying overhead. Tess thought this was the pebble. She looked confused when it never came down, and hurt when I laughed.

Our only interruption that morning was a figure ahead of us, walking slowly in the same direction. As we came closer I realised he was taking an uninhibited and stark naked stroll. Just because he wasn't wearing a stitch, my usual British pleasantry would somehow be awkward, but I didn't know what other line I could take. Laugh? Make a joke? Advise him on the strength of the sun he was walking straight into?

Before I had a chance to say anything he turned to me and said, 'Are you coming to join us?' It crossed my mind that a naked coastal walker might cause a stir, but I declined anyway.

The second naked figure seated himself in such a position that we would have to walk between him and the sea, and as we came closer he began to play with himself in full view. On his face was a disgusting lecherous smirk.

I could have quite easily ignored him if it hadn't been for Tess who, for some reason, acted completely out of character. Under normal circumstances any person caught sitting down, and therefore on her level, is considered 'fair game' and is wrestled to the floor. If this had been the case I would have had a good old laugh as she is exceptionally strong and has long and potentially lethal toenails! But now she went up, stood behind him and watched me, while completely ignoring my exasperated commands. The exhibitionist definitely had the last laugh, but I did wonder whether Tess was paying me back for a brutal swimming lesson (or, more correctly, dumping in the sea!)

Nearing Bridlington the holidaymakers were crammed together, and we weaved our way up onto the promenade where Tess began her resort ritual — nose glued to the pavement, she hoovered up squidgy chips, broken ice cream cones, trodden in chocolate and chewing gum. Bingo and candy floss hogged the sea front, while ahead the enticing green-topped chalk cliffs of Flamborough Head reached out to sea.

My pace quickened as we set off up the first hills of the walk. Here was real coastline; the pounding surf below, and the salty spray reaching up; the white ridged waves; and the crying gulls.

At four hundred feet, solid Bempton Cliffs made the waves look like mere ripples in a puddle, and way below us they were hitting the cliffs without causing the disruption we had seen on the beaches and cliffs further south. Also below us were hundreds of sea birds, spiralling on the various updraughts.

The RSPB own and manage about 3 miles of cliff here; cliffs which support the largest seabird colony in England, with as many as 200,000 seabirds breeding at Bempton alone — kittiwakes, razorbills, puffins and guillemots. The largest mainland gannetry is also here, and it was these that I watched as they hurled themselves towards the sea, disappearing from sight over the sheer edge of the cliffs. The gannets inspired me, and despite huffing and puffing we set off again at a good pace, each hill adding momentum to the walk.

The advantage of the flat land had been that I was never daunted by the miles ahead, because they hadn't been visible; but from Filey, with its spotless crescent beach and Georgian gentility, the day's walking stretched ahead, on and on, round that headland and the next. No sooner had we left Filey than Scarborough came into view. It was easy to see the destination and simply want to reach it, but if we walked the coast in this way we would never see anything. I had Tess as an example. She never knew the day's destination and took delight in what the moment had to offer.

Scarborough became a tourist destination in the eighteenth century, when Spa towns became fashionable for healthy holiday retreats. Since then it has survived as a popular holiday spot as well as maintaining its fishing industry. Daily fish auctions are still held on the harbour, which is sheltered by two quays cosily protecting the vessels. Along the steep streets behind the quay, old and new lie side by side. Scarborough's charm has not been lost.

We found the Spudtruck parked outside the Grand Butlins Hotel, and at that moment Dee came out. 'I've met the manager, who seems to be quite a character,' she said, smiling. 'And I think the average age of the guests must be about seventy!'

In the grand entrance hall, the high ceilings, pillars and sweeping staircase were painted in various shades of pastel pink and blue, and beneath this splendour the elderly guests sat in tea drinking groups. The odd set of dentures could be heard or seen being unsurrepticiously removed, and the high ceilings efficiently absorbed the inevitable high decibels emanating from the hard of hearing.

Michael, the manager, was certainly a character. He was also an actor, and his greatest performance of all was the monologue. 'I'll buy you a drink at the bar, but first we must raise you some money. Bring your collecting boxes and follow me,' he declared in a manner which would have made many a statesman envious. Dee and I trotted after him like faithful dogs.

With the tin shaking over, Michael steered us back to the bar. 'Do you like champagne? I thought we'd drink shampoo as a celebration!' He laughed a short but loud guffaw. 'I love shampoo, don't you?' He didn't wait for an answer.

A petit and heavily made up lady had joined us. 'This is my fiancée, Helen.' Helen perched herself on a bar stool and sipped daintily at the champagne. 'So when are you getting married?' Dee managed. 'Oh, it's not planned yet,' Michael took the stage again. 'There's no hurry. Actually I've been engaged four times already, but this is it!'

He put his arm round Helen. 'We met when Helen was staying here on holiday. One night our cabaret was an hypnotist. Helen was picked to be the victim and I was invited on stage to witness her hypnosis. Needless to say Helen doesn't remember the first time we met!' I found that almost impossible to believe.

The array of rings on Michael's fingers flashed brilliantly every time he raised his hand and declared 'More shampoo!' He then told us about his impressive array of clarets, and moved on to Butlins.

'You wouldn't recognise this place. We've done a lot to it in the last few years and it now runs at ninety per cent capacity all year round. We accommodate five hundred people, and they come on week long breaks. Many of them have been coming to Scarborough for years; they belong to a club and get discounts when they've been coming to Butlins for a certain length of time —'

Michael lifted his little finger into the air as he lifted his glass again. 'Our only rules are no children and no animals, but we'll make an exception tonight and you can bring your dog in,' he said with a great display of generosity.

The champagne was beginning to go to my head, and I tried to make my exit. 'Nonsense!' Michael exclaimed, ordering another bottle. I then remembered one of my life long ambitions — to have a champagne bath!

In between the monologue I voiced this ambition, my voice croaky with lack of use.

Michael took the floor again. 'Wow. I wonder how many bottles it would take to fill a bath? I reckon . . . er, let me think. To have a really deep bath you'd need a lot, but about thirty would be adequate!'

'Mm. It would have to be —'

'I know what,' Michael interrupted. 'I'll make you a deal. I'll personally pledge a bottle of Butlins champagne for every £1,000 you raise over the £60,000 you expect to raise from the walk, to go towards your bath!'

Michael had been determined we would raise more than our realistic £60,000, and now he was putting his money where his mouth was. He was already putting the deal in writing. 'You could have the bath on your return to London,' Michael's imagination was going now. 'It could be a PR stunt. We could invite the press along!'

Things were getting a little out of hand, but I put the signed card away safely. (Unfortunately, or perhaps fortunately, we never reached £60,000!)

We were now on the Cleveland Way which runs from Filey to Saltburn. The section from Scarborough to Redcar became one of my favourite stretches. It is an untamed coast of bleak headlands and sheltered bays harbouring villages steeped in a history of fishing and smuggling.

Far from slowing us down, the hills sped us on, and after six miles we dropped down a hill and into an oak and sycamore woodland. The majority of the coast had so far been tree-less, and here in Hayburn Wyke the trees were fighting a continual battle with the elements. They were sculpted into weird and wizened shapes by the incessant on-shore wind; and their branches and leaves, tinged brown with wind burn, were combed landwards as though trying to cover a bald patch.

Thanks to the railway line which ran along here, Hayburn Wyke was popular with Victorian ladies in search of clean air; while places such as Ravenscar thrived during the nineteenth century thanks to the excavation of alum. Alum is a crystal found in shale, which, after processing, was used for fixing dyes in textiles and for tanning leather. It was shipped from here all over Europe.

There is no beach or natural bay here, and to load up the alum must have involved a good deal of blood, sweat and ingenuity. In the hamlet of Port Mulgrave, the problem was solved by a mile long tunnel along which the alum was transported. There is still no road to Port Mulgrave.

But I decided that there can be few more romantic villages on the English coastline than Robin Hood's Bay. Tucked behind the headland of North Cheek, the jumble of russet coloured houses cling on to the hillside which drops steeply down to the water's edge. Winding up through these delightful buildings are cobbled and occasionally stepped alleys which just fit one woman and her dog, and therefore offer no vehicular access. It has been said that the houses are so close together because the women wished for company when the men were away at sea, but the real reason must surely have been to aid the swift dispersal of smuggled goods!

During the eighteenth century, when smuggling was at its peak, so many of the houses in Robin Hood's Bay had connecting passages that it was possible to smuggle a bale of silk from the shore to the top of the village without it ever coming above ground.

I loved the exciting and romantic image of the hardy vagabonds and their nocturnal lives, and the coastline which has been sculpted from the lives of the people that lived here — the smugglers, the fishermen and the alum miners. There are no frills or extravagances on the Yorkshire coastline. It is a coast which reflects the resilient and pragmatic men who worked it, as it reflects their adventurous and often unpredictable behaviour, upon which their livelihoods depended.

Realising we were late, I stopped to talk to Dee who I knew was superstitious that I had lost my St Christopher. The line was crackly, but Dee was there. 'We're fine,' I assured her. 'Fantastic. It's gorgeous out here. I feel high from the hills and the scenery — literally stoned!'

The endorphins produced by the increased exercise of the hills was surging through my body, leaving me high. This was 'our' coastline and we were into our stride. But endorphins or no endorphins we needed all the help we could get, and Dee presented me with a replacement St Christopher that evening.

The skeletal arches and gables of ruined Whitby Abbey took on an eerie twilight form when we reached its hilltop position at 6.45 that evening. The situation of the Abbey (founded by St Hilda in 657) ensured the appropriate solitude and discomfort which were regarded by some as necessary steps towards a state of goodness and grace.

We spent the next thirty-six hours in Whitby, staying at the Royal Hotel (a member of the Thistle group, who were also sponsoring us accommodation), and being superbly looked after by Fred the manager. His office was soon snowed under with Shelter paraphernalia.

Helping with the fundraising was a committee of twenty people, through whom we had written to some five hundred companies. We continued to dispatch letters throughout the walk, and the pledges came in slowly. The paperwork seemed monumental, but all fitted into secret corners of the Spudtruck. We even had an old typewriter in there. But it was people like Fred who made things much easier. It was also a consolation that the majority of our fundraising was in pubs, thus enabling us to mix business with pleasure!

The lights of the cosy Duke of York across the River Esk from the hotel were too much for us to resist. On Saturday night the pub was full of fishermen and young people, and we were greeted like locals by the barman. 'Hello girls! Two pints of cider? Oh, and a drink for Tess!' Tess wagged her tail in agreement, and soon had people digging in their pockets for Shelter.

Throughout the bar are references to Whitby's biggest hero — Captain Cook — who learnt his navigational skills here and completed his first voyage round the world in a Whitby built boat. Whitby is also famous as the home of Dracula whose author, Bram Stoker, lived here. I have no doubt that he was inspired by the ghostly ruins of Whitby Abbey which shone out as we retraced our tracks through the harbour; past the now closed kipper and whelk kiosks, and past the stacked pots, quiet boats and sleeping gulls.

On top of the delightful harbour and pubs which make up Whitby, there is also a magnificent stretch of beach round the headland to the north. Yet Whitby has remained remarkably unspoilt. There is a warmly rugged feeling in Whitby, and it is best experienced by walking there. This gives you the feeling that the rest of the world could be many miles away, as inaccessible as once it was.

Twelve miles north of Whitby is Boulby Cliff: at 213 metres the highest cliff in England. Sheep grazed our path, and to our right a series of past slips are grassed over to produce an unpredictable descent to the sea. I kept my head turned to the right, to ignore the chimneys of Middlesbrough which puffed smoke as desperately as I once did behind the bicycle shed. But from the top of Warsett Hill, with its array of eight foot metal sculptures comprised of starfish and anchors, they were impossible to ignore.

We sat down to mourn the imminent end of the Yorkshire coast, and my spirits sagged to think of the forthcoming urban walking. I tried to tell myself that it was all part of the walk; that, in its own way, it would be interesting. But three long days of the industrial north clouded any good intentions. Even Tess sensed my depletion in mood, and wistfully sniffed the air beside me. I suppose we were due to be brought down to earth.

CHAPTER FOUR

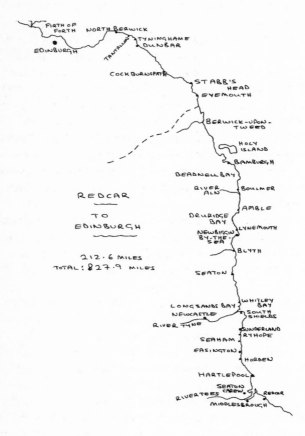

We negotiated the various roundabout exits at a run and started down the verge of the busy A1085 dual carriageway to Middlesbrough. The road stretched ahead of us in a dead straight line; the cars transporting themselves from one end of the road to the other without even noticing they had done so. It was several miles long and there was not a hill or bend to break its monotony.

My map swung round my neck and it was impossible not to check every landmark — an electricity line, a smaller road, or a patch of green. This made the miles longer; as did pedometer watching.

Tess, meanwhile, was pleading ignorance of the novel lead. The faster I walked, the faster she wanted to go and the more she strained. I pulled her back and commanded her to 'heel', but she was displaying selective understanding.

I got angry with her, and yanked her back; then felt bad because, after all, this was not her choice to be walking down the A1085. I apologised for my shortness of temper brought about by the circumstances, and she wagged her tail.

Again she strained, and again I commanded her back to heel. Again she forgot, and again I lost my temper, yanked her back, felt bad and apologised. She wagged her tail and the process would be repeated.

Finally, cursing each other, apologising and map watching we branched off this main road and found ourselves in a nameless Middlesbrough suburb — it was not an experience I shall easily forget.

We were, quite literally, flanked by one boarded up house after another. If the windows were not boarded up then their glass was smashed and the piles of broken glass were visible amongst the faded, broken and abandoned children's toys, through which the jungle of a long time neglected garden grew.

Similar to a programmed robot, I continued step by insignificant step along this desolation as though watching a bad film in slow motion. Why were the houses empty? Why did the few people I saw seem to emanate utter despair? Where was the vigour, the lifeblood of this neglected community?

It struck a nerve to think of the bureaucracy and incompetence which often causes this ironic situation, and leads to the most aesthetically uninspiring community for its other members. Is it hardly surprising that those who live amongst such shambolic disrepair may stray from the course of basic human values, not least struggle to retain their outward pride?

It was as if a grey blanket of suffocation and despondency had been thrown over the area, trapping and stagnating everything and everyone beneath it. If we stopped, we too would be trapped. But my legs had taken control, and led us safely to the edge of the blanket. They carried me involuntarily, but my body stayed with that street. It had been physically wrenched from its Yorkshire idyll.

We reached the Transporter Bridge over the River Tees, which is an incongruous construction. It consists of one tower each side of the river, which support the pulley mechanism (160 feet up) for the transporting platform below. It was built like this so that the ships which once served Stockton could pass beneath it. It was built in 1911 and is the largest working bridge of this type in the world. The only other one of its type is found in Newport, South Wales — too many miles away to think about.

I was determined to reach Seaton Carew that evening, which meant six miles through the largest industrial chemical area in Britain. We had walked twenty miles that morning, and would now be on a main and verge-less road. Tess was in the Spudtruck. I felt incomplete without her; a niggling awareness that I had forgotten something! I also missed the happy tinkling of her disk.

I walked into the oncoming traffic, and was occasionally forced onto the grimy bank. It felt as though the bitumen on these main roads was harder than the bitumen on the small roads, and I could feel my toes and heels complaining.

An interruption from the Tyne Tees TV crew only succeeded in delaying me further, and when they left me it was getting dark on that hostile road with its stream of unseeing cars. For the first time I felt really vulnerable. I willed Will (my brother-in-law, who was now driving) to come back, and dug out my radio in the hope that he might have turned his on, but there was a definite silence on the other end. At 8pm I reached Seaton Carew.

The car park on the sea front of Seaton Carew is not the place to take a holiday in a campervan at the beginning of September. I awoke the next morning and briefly wondered how we had come to be on a boat. The howling downpour was hitting the roof two feet above my head and for the first time I asked myself what I was doing. I peered over the covers to Tess, who was pretending to be asleep in the hope that the day would be forgotten.

I got out of bed with the same resignation as one faces a day's work on a farm in mid winter, or perhaps a long dreaded executive meeting. It was simply something we had to do.

We had only taken a few strides when Tess stopped and looked back at the cosy Spudtruck. Shivering miserably, she turned to give me a look of complete disbelief. 'Come on Tess!' I encouraged her with a stick. Her ears pricked up for a minute, but she glanced back at the Spudtruck. 'It'll get better. I promise. You'll warm up once you're going.'

She couldn't spot the white lie, and bounded over, jumped up to take the stick from my hand, and set off through Hartlepool.

To reach the sea again we found a footpath running between a factory, hidden by a tall and barbed wire topped fence, and the railway line. The fence which separated us from the railway line was four strands of wire, three of which had broken and lay saggy and useless across our path at intervals. The path itself was black and cinder, and took us through a golf course and on to deserted caravans looking sadly onto an angry black sea.

For the past month I had been appalled by the appearance and smell of the North Sea. Although it is naturally turbid due to the churning effect of its shallowness and strong tides, the on-shore nauseous smell of dirty oil in water can only be put down to pollution; and there is no doubt that the coalfields contribute to the sea's blackness. Between Hartlepool and Lynemouth I passed colliery after colliery; and between Redcar and Lynemouth I saw the worst abuse of the sea, the estuaries and surrounding land.

But coal mining has shaped the face of this area; has seen it grow, prosper and flourish — and now start to slip sadly into decline, leaving men redundant, and a landscape floundering.

Perhaps the miners are pleased to be free from their dirty and punishingly hard life underground? I know I would be. But the sense of despair here is evident by walking, watching people and chatting to passers-by.

Finding the appointed church where Will and I had arranged to meet in Horden, I took shelter from the rain in the draughty doorway of a small butchers shop. After a few minutes the butcher came out and insisted we took refuge inside. He gave me a cup of coffee as he was clearing away his meat. 'Is it half day today?' I asked.

'No love. We always close at midday,' he said, producing a bone for Tess. 'It's not worth opening for more than that around here. There's just not the custom. There's so little money. You'll find that all the shops here shut at midday.'

I thought of all the huge supermarkets which stay open virtually 24 hours per day, seven days per week — and always seem to be full. But, like all butchers, this one was a jovial guy and as he came round the counter he handed me two pasties. 'Here, for your lunch.'

Will appeared and the butcher shut his shop. He had asked me nothing about myself, and didn't notice the Spudtruck. I was grateful to him for just accepting my presence.

In the retailing part of the town each shop window displayed its trade, neither standing on each other's toes. The ironmonger, the fishmonger, the cobbler, the newsagent — no pedestrian precincts, Spar, 8-till-Late or other jack-of-all-trades. Tradesmanship was alive — but, sure enough, most of them were closed.

We left Horden via the residential section, through tunnels of identical red brick terraced houses with identical backyards, and came level with a lady making her way slowly up the street with several bags of shopping. I said hello. 'Oh, hello love,' she said, giving a great sigh which made me turn to her again. 'Oh you won't believe it,' she began. 'They say there's nothing they can do about it, but our power is off just now. I ask you, it's four o'clock in the afternoon and three children coming home from school —'

The lady was in her late thirties and had two severely protruding front teeth. She was wearing a grey trousers and a navy sweater, over which was a short plastic mac. 'They say it'll be on and off for the next three weeks —' She gave another sigh and a shake of her head.

'I hope you've got plenty of candles!'

'Uh? Oh yes dear.'

The lady began to complain of electricity bills in general, and I listened. I was a fellow being again. I was there as an ear. Above all I was pleased not to be asked about my presence. I may have been watched suspiciously, but common humanity can never finally be denied.

We reached her house. 'Where are you heading?' she asked, looking at me for the first time. 'Sunderland.'

'You can catch a bus from the station. Top of the road, turn right and it's down there.' I thanked her and continued, wondering whether she often saw people with walking boots, rucksack and an O/S map walking through Horden.

Back on the coast to Seaham, Easington Colliery obliterated the horizon, its lights lit like a runway in the gloom. Running parallel to the coast was the biggest mound of coal you have ever seen.

Every visible thing was black. The railway line, shuttling never ending trains of coal filled carriages, was sprinkled with many years of coal dust. The soil we walked on was black. The sky was black. The beach was black. The vegetation was black.

By far the most black was the sea, sand and coastline. Long conveyor belts run from the various collieries to the sea, transporting coal waste to be dumped in the shallows. It is sometimes possible to see black mountains rising above the surface of the sea.

The black path squeezed us between the black railway line and the black sea; and on the black cliff top we came across a fisherman. 'Caught anything?' I asked.

'Only this.' He held up an insignificant fish. 'What's that?'

'A coalie.'

'A what?!'

'A coal fish.'

He had to be joking. This was evolution at its most impressive! (I later discovered that this is another name for a saithe.) 'Can you eat it?'

'They're not very nice. I'll give this to the cat —' No doubt a black cat called Sooty.

Apart from the fisherman, there was little life above ground. For Sale signs were plentiful in deserted Seaham; and more coal heaps joined us to Ryhope.

My morale was lowered, but stone-mason Will was a familiar figure; he was also sensitive and saw that to attempt to fundraise here would be to rob the very people who might soon be needing the money. Instead he was spending money and shopping with a vengeance. Will is a compulsive shopper.

Each day there was a new purchase — psychedelic yo-yo's, a tea pot, tapes, and a seemingly toy-like but apparently collectible motorbike complete with rider. This acquisition was held in Will's highest esteem and was reverently shuttled around the Spudtruck, along with Will's array of hats and coats, whenever the Spudtruck was transformed from kitchen to bedroom to vehicle. Woe betide anyone who mocked the bike!

Will also enjoyed shopping for food. His catering included plenty of meat and cholesterol, and treats of steaks and wine were not uncommon. 'I thought you needed cheering up!' Will would say. How right he was. Food was definitely a comfort.

My legs felt crampy when I climbed the ladder to bed that night, and I was vaguely aware of another pain in my left shin. I read one page of my book and fell asleep.

The next day the pain in my left shin couldn't be ignored. I was soon wincing each time my left foot hit the unforgiving pavement. I resorted to walking with a wooden left ankle, and, feeling woefully sorry for myself, willed whatever it was to disappear.

I was disturbed by an old man with a grin from ear to ear, a rubbery face and thick northern accent who simply declared 'You look great. Absolutely great!' (I presume that he was referring to my bright colours!)

What simple actions and words can pick you up! I had felt largely alienated over the last few urban days, enveloped in the cloud of distrust which ignored my own 'hello's'. I felt like an intruder; a vulnerable fish out of water. I shall remember the old man with the rubbery face and broad grin as an ally. His cheery face stayed with me that day — as did the shin.

Before the walk I had never done any long distance walking. I had chased sheep up and down hills all day, but I had never purposefully walked twenty miles on several consecutive days. To say I wasn't prepared would be an understatement. I didn't have any idea about physical problems — shin splints, warming up, stretching etc.

Twenty miles per day had sounded like a nice round figure, and one morning, during the early preparatory stages, I had walked twenty miles along a flat, straight Roman road. It had been a beautiful morning. *What a nice way of spending ten months* I had naively thought!   Now here we were hobbling after just 500 miles. Perhaps it served me right; but I was not going to let any of the Berghaus crew know when we shuffled up to their Tyne and Wear factory that afternoon. 'How are you feeling?' they asked as we had sandwiches in the office.

'A little sore but fine really,' I lied. I could have sworn that Tess looked up to me and said 'liar!'

I put my shin down to all the road walking, but I had no idea how I would feel in the morning. Would the pain persist? If it did, and I carried on walking, could I do permanent damage? What would I be like after another four thousand miles?

The next morning I got up and set off walking. It never occurred to me to do anything else. It was hard to pin point exactly what it was, but there was something out of my control which was driving me on — whatever. The strength in my mind was more important than the strength in my body — or so it seemed.

On Long Sands Beach a diversion took my mind off the shin. In our path was a fully grown cormorant covered from bill to toe in oil. Immobilised, it stood shivering and terrified on the sand, not far from the incoming tide which would certainly drown it.

On the same beach a tractor was religiously raking up *messy* seaweed, and dogs are banned. Yet here was a wild animal covered in a much worse pollutant than seaweed or dog shit. Furthermore, I discovered that it was a Blue Flag beach. What a farce! How on earth have our priorities become so mixed up?

When I later looked into the pollution of the North Sea, I discovered that such pollution more than likely comes from the deliberate dumping of ship's waste. Eight times the amount of oil lost from the Tanker Braer (Shetlands, 1993), is deliberately dumped by ships in the North Sea every year. This kind of pollution is unreported and therefore difficult to assess accurately, but with 400,000 ships using the North Sea every year, (making this one of the busiest waterways in the world), many of them transporting oil, toxic waste or other hazardous products, it is inevitable that a percentage must end up in the sea.

I can still picture that cormorant; its white chest barely noticeable below the slick, brown, globular substance; its heavy and suddenly comparatively useless wings; its look of incomprehension at its own state; and its terror but wild pride when I tried to approach it. There it sat, a black oily blot on a sickeningly *clean* beach; a symbol for all the other hundreds of birds and other marine life which must be affected.

We called the RSPB and hobbled on to Whitley Bay, where the seaweed was again being raked up on the empty beach. As expected, the beach warden appeared to command Tess off the beach:

'I've just found a cormorant covered in oil back there, and you're telling me to take my dog off an empty beach!' I began. 'What's a bit of dog shit compared to oil. Oil on the beaches — I mean it was dying from oil. That's what you should be cleaning up — not seaweed and dog shit. I mean, it's disgusting! It's crazy! It's all cosmetic! You should never have been given a flag. I mean who's in charge of this farce?! Anyway, this beach is empty and my dog never craps at this time of day —' etc. etc! I ranted on.

The warden looked shell-shocked. 'I'm sorry but that's the law,' was all he managed. I don't believe he would have been surprised if I had stripped off, padlocked myself and Tess to the blue flag, and stayed there for two weeks refusing food or water!

I hobbled on, along more *clean* beaches which returned, all too soon, to main roads, collieries, power stations, docks and more rain. We crossed the River Blyth and reached the final blot on this poor coastline, Lynemouth — the largest undersea coal seam in Europe. It stretches 7 miles out under the sea, and is worked 24 hours per day, still using pit ponies.

Up ahead, the grey conveyor belts appeared to have been laid down like a child's set of lego, and once upon them they criss-crossed like pick-up-sticks all around us. As we passed under the final stick, a lone jogger stopped on the other side of the quiet road. He looked at us in a quizzical way and, trying to catch his breath, asked where we had walked from. 'London,' I replied. 'Via the coast.'

'I don't suppose you remember someone running up to you outside Cromer, and giving a donation?' I did remember. He had made such an effort to catch up with us. 'Well that was me. I was on holiday there. Well done, you've come a long way.'

Over the last four days we had walked nearly ninety miles along the edge of one of the most populated and industrialised areas in Britain. It felt as though we ourselves had been processed through some vast factory machine, and had finally been regurgitated at the other end.

We were regurgitated on 10th September, stepping out onto the six miles of uninterrupted sand of Druridge Bay, while the sun shone overhead. Even my shin made a dramatic recovery.

Over the next few days of the Northumberland coast we were either passing landmark castles, or making inland river detours to avoid quicksands. But on nearing the River Aln I fell into step with a girl whose guide book stated you could wade across the Aln for one and a half hours around low tide. It was now nearing, or as good as, low tide.

Luckily it was a warm day as I stripped down to my t-shirt and knickers and launched myself into the waist deep river. Tess raced frantically up and down the bank looking for an alternative crossing. Realising she had no option she took a few tentative steps, before the bottom disappeared from under her and she was doing a grand doggy paddle. When we reached the other side a cheer went up from the group of weekenders gathered.

I continued up the beach in my t-shirt and knickers until privacy allowed me to put on long-johns. I tied my wet knickers onto the back of my rucksack — but of course forgot about them for the rest of the day. It was not until we had promenaded through the villagers of Boulmer, who were out enjoying the sunshine, that I remembered them.

We were now on a beautiful stretch of National Trust owned coast-line, comprised of more strategically positioned castles commanding the horizon from one place to the next, rocky headlands, and sweeping bays of really golden sand backed by large dunes. Out to sea the sun was catching the waves, producing dazzling water resembling whisked egg whites which raced towards us over the sand. The sea looked bluer and cleaner then it had so far, and my feet demanded to be released.

My feet were startlingly white in contrast to my tanned legs, and positively phosphorescent in the water. I had still not had any blisters, but after 700 miles my feet were anything but tough. Every pebble and shell made me wince.

Tess' swimming lesson in the River Aln had not cured her water phobia, but I now gave her no option and gave her a ducking. Tess was testing the ancient animal method of disguise, in the firm belief that once she smelt like a sheep she would be mistaken for one. Unfortunately her reason was also to do with ancient survival — she was still chasing sheep.

Each time I optimistically dropped my guard, she would take just a sneaky run at a breakaway mob. It would never be malicious, but more a display of the (often warped) Bullterrier sense of humour. Nevertheless, knowing that the farmers wouldn't see the funny side, I would scold her in no uncertain manner. There would then follow a period of subdued silence, before one of us would make peace. Sometimes Tess brought me a peace offering, and on more than one occasion this was a piece of sheep shit! Coincidence? Perhaps.

With Tess smelling more like a dog again, we continued round the bays and over the rocky headlands. It was great to be on grassland after the dusty harvest and dead looking soil cracked into deep fissures. The ground here was also dry, but the green was kinder then the yellows and browns of ripe wheat, straw and stubble; and the smell of manure more vital than the smell of dusty corn.

Bamburgh, with its Norman castle indestructibly situated on a basalt crag, indicated the end of the week — and another red pin. We decided to go to Holy Island for my day off.

From the first time I visited Holy Island (or Lindisfarne) as a child, I have always loved its island charm. It is reached via a mile long causeway, when the tide allows, and was one of the earliest strongholds of Christianity thanks to St Aidan, who arrived here from Iona in 635 and became the first Bishop of Lindisfarne.

Weathered sandstone ruins remain of the eleventh century priory (which replaced the earliest one), and close by are the ruins of the castle, beneath which we parked for the night.

The next morning I sat writing letters, while the rain beat down from every angle. Through the smeared back window the sea was being flattened, and the mainland appeared and disappeared at intervals. The oystercatchers, dressed like smart men going out to dinner, looked unconcerned by the rain. How familiar the scene looked to me; the sea, the birdlife, the Spudtruck and Tess were my companions. Together we had walked seven hundred miles, and there seemed no reason why, in theory, we could not achieve the next three thousand eight hundred!

Tess stirred from her beanbag, but refused to set foot in the downpour unless really necessary. She has inherited the Bullterrier coat designed for lounging in tropical paradise, and certainly wasn't prepared for eight hours of walking in Scottish rain with a damp and draughty Spudtruck to return to.

When we had visited Berghaus someone had suggested a coat for Tess, but I had laughed it off. I couldn't possibly have a dog wearing a coat! Perhaps it was time to swallow my pride, and force Tess to swallow hers. I wrote to Berghaus giving Tess' exact measurements.

Will left from Bamburgh, and we were joined by Pops who had nobly stood in at the last minute. I was very proud of my sixty-four year old father for committing himself to a week of glorified camping. Unfortunately a rainy Tuesday morning set the scene for the rest of the week.

I climbed down, got dressed quickly, and went outside for a piddle while Pops got dressed. Tess still lay snoring on my bed and we piled Pops' (damp) bedding up around her while she had a lie in. The centre of the bed came up and formed the table. 'Where am I going to shave?' Pops asked waving his wash bag around.

'I'll put the kettle on. There's a plastic basin which pops out in the bathroom —' at least it sounded very grand. Pops opened the bathroom/cupboard door. 'I need a mirror!'

'The wing mirror?'

When the kettle had boiled Pops dashed from the cupboard to the wing mirror covered in shaving foam, while I boiled water for his mandatory egg, and went outside to clean my teeth. Everything took much longer in the Spudtruck.

The sea now bore no resemblance to the friendly blue shallows I had paddled in two days previously. It was flung onto the shore in a disorderly fashion and when it hit the beach the waves turned to spume, which skidded up the beach towards us, hotly pursued by Tess. The sea was making a mockery of the coast.

The gap between the sea and the dunes narrowed and we took shelter in the dunes, from where the odd startled curlew flew up, buoyed by the wind and calling its shrill 'curl-i'. The marram grass whispered in reply, and the cocooned passage of grazed dunes led us to Berwick-upon-Tweed.

Setting off for the final stretch of England's east coast I tried to comprehend our achievement so far; but the whole walk was racing by. I desperately wanted to stop time and take in the situation. I was thinking so much about the border that I barely spoke to Tess. When I did speak my voice sounded oddly small in the soaked world. 'This is it Tess. From now on it could be like this every day.' In reply she blinked at me through the raindrops.

Perhaps Tess wasn't fully aware of the achievement so far; but only she had walked the 720 miles with me, and only she knew the moments of misery offset by the moments of elation, companionship and happiness. I felt enormous affection for Tess that day.

We reached the hair-raisingly busy A1, and ran across it to the waiting Spudtruck. No sooner had we appeared than the first true bottle of Scotch whisky was opened — and how fine it tasted in that damp elation!

Between 6.30 and 7.30pm that blustery mid September night a party took place within the confines of a campervan pulled into a lay-by on the A1 Trunk road. At its peak there were eleven well wishers and, although there was barely enough space to lift the plastic cup to your mouth, everyone succeeded in this somehow.

Tess' moment of triumph came with the eventual arrival of the piper. As if deciding to check out the validity of her first true Scotsman, she greeted him by shoving her long snout firmly up his kilt. This only made him turn bluer, as finally, after umpteen rehearsals of crossing the border, we were ceremoniously piped into Scotland. The sound of the piper and the whoops of encouragement could not be diminished by the weather, which was, after all, further assurance that we were in Scotland.

When the party dispersed, we drove inland to a friend, Mike's, house. Here the whisky kept us going till 3am when I retired to bed without a passing thought of what the next day would bring.

The next day brought agonising effects of Scottish hospitality; and an inaccessible coastline. The footpaths stopped abruptly, and within three miles an impassable bank stood in our way. I cursed the whisky and the border; swore never to walk with a thumping head again; and promised to have revenge on Mike.

I made myself walk a few miles past Eyemouth harbour before giving myself the reward of resting my leaden legs. This was one way of making myself complete the miles. Sometimes when I reached the appointed rest spot (the carrot) I would tell myself that it was the next headland I had meant. It was as though there were two people completing the walk; one was walking (and complaining); and the other one was bossing. On a clifftop north of Eyemouth the *boss* let me rest. Below us, a mass of gannets were onto a large shoal of fish.

Gannets are fantastic to watch as they can dive from heights of up to 120 feet, reaching speeds of 60 mph when they hit the water; neatly tucking their wings back at the split second before impact.

Away from this group I watched one lone shag who dived down with far less fuss, and reappeared triumphant after three minutes. I liked the shags. They resemble sleek black shadows as they fly close to the sea's surface. I often watched to see if their wing tips ever touched the water, but never saw such carelessness.

The gloatingly tee-total Tess came up and roused me into action. It was still, clear and calm. Out to sea there wasn't a fleck of white water, and the sea sat as an immense blue and calming mass, ruffled only where it hit the base of the cliffs. We were walking towards the headland of St Abbs and, although I wished for once that I was on the flat lands of East Anglia, there was no way I could fail to enjoy these giant, green, roller coasting hills of St Abbs Head. But it was one thing to enjoy them, and quite another to walk them.

On a normal day the cliffs would have inspired me; but now they were there to test my stamina and to show me just how hard Scotland was going to be. The cliffs said 'beware, don't be fooled'; but the sea and the birds said 'we're your friends, stay calm'.

St Abbs was named after Aebbe — daughter of King Edilfred of Northumbria — who was shipwrecked on this headland in the seventh century, and subsequently started a monastic settlement here. The thought of Aebbes' stamina made me, the self-abused, intrepid modern day walker, feel positively exhausted. In fact the perseverance of all the historical characters — from monks to smugglers to pilgrims — was really brought alive to me as I reached places by the same method that they had done.

The magnificent greenness of St Abbs Head swallowed us up and, briefly wondering whether Aebbe ever suffered hangovers, we turned north again. The obstacles came thick and fast in our path.

If we weren't bulldozing through scratchy hedges, then I was hoisting Tess over fences, scrambling down valleys, and losing the coast behind hills before suddenly coming face to face with a sheer drop. Often we had to backtrack and find alternative routes, and I cursed and swore and always I expected an angry farmer to manhandle me off his land, but not a soul greeted us that afternoon.

Somehow I got through the hardest day so far. I went to bed worrying that things would be the same for the next three months; but north of Cockburnspath the empty cliffs gave way to more populated landscape where there were paths, farm tracks and beaches.

The sun returned when Pops boarded the train south. The next driver wasn't due until a day later and I was to have the first night on my own since we had left Tower Bridge. Many people had asked me if I didn't get lonely, and often the words of Shelter's director went through my head. She had known a guy who had done something similar, 'but' she said, 'he just got lonely.' These were just the words I needed with seven days till departure.

Perhaps she had said this to spur me on? Doubters certainly strengthened my resolve, and even the person who shows no competitiveness hides a certain level. But so far I hadn't felt lonely anyway. The eight hours of walking were easily filled, and then I had the antics of the drivers. Instead of feeling lonely I craved personal space

Although I knew that I could never complete the walk without the invaluable support of the drivers, our living conditions required mutual tolerance. We were, after all, living in a space seven foot by fourteen foot, which offered perhaps a maximum of fifteen square foot of floor space.

With only the two of us it felt palatial in the quiet campsite in Dunbar. I felt houseproud, and fussed around like a broody hen, shaking out carpets and bedding to dry in the evening sun, while Tess chewed her Dunbar bone. When I sat down with a plate of pasta and a beer, I felt that I had just turned eighteen and was experiencing my first taste of independence.

Tess ensured that we were up at 7am. The Spudtruck looked so clean and orderly and was a far cry from my usually disorderly lifestyle. But by having my home in disciplined order, the walking discipline was easier to maintain. If one crashed, then the other would too.

Another quicksand bay forced us inland, along farm tracks and into Tyninghame Estate with its trees showing the first signs of autumn; sycamores, chestnuts, maple and rowans. A row of magnificent beeches ran in a mile long avenue to the beach, their smooth white trunks dappled by the shadows of their leaves above, which were just beginning to turn at the edges. At the end of the avenue we popped out on a secret beach.

My feet fell into their beach rhythm; it was an easy rhythm to maintain on the hard and regular surface of the sand. I listened to Salsa music which conjured up images of grass skirts and cha-cha-cha on a Caribbean island. I swayed my hips, and was lost in a world of coconut cocktails, frangipani and palm trees; until a large, dour pile of a castle sat in our path and ruined my daydream.

Of all the castles I passed, Tantallon Castle is the most spectacularly and precariously situated. Built in 1350, it is flanked by sheer cliffs dropping to the sea on one side, and a deep, natural cleft forming a moat on the other side. Thus it is inaccessible from any point other than the drawbridge entrance. It is perfectly sited to guard the Firth of Forth.

We found a bench in the castle courtyard and had our sandwiches looking out over the firth. In front of us Bass Rock was surrounded by a white cloud of birds. It is home to the world's oldest known gannetry, the first sightings being in the sixteenth century. As I ate my cheese sandwiches, I read in a leaflet that during this time gannets were eaten. They were barbarically caught by fastening bait onto pieces of wood which were suspended just below the surface of the water. When the gannet dived for the bait, its beak would get stuck in the wood!

I could hardly believe we were on the Firth of Forth, and whistled and sang the afternoon away without the help of my walkman. The scenery changed regularly from castles to woodland to beaches and finally to golf courses. No sooner had we sneaked around one golf course then there was another one; each one was full. Luckily Tess' eyesight wasn't good enough to see the whizzing balls, but I picked up several and juggled them as I walked.

North Berwick came and went, and with Aidan as our new driver we completed the final foot slogging miles of road into Edinburgh on 19th September. I didn't care that it was raining — again. We had walked to Edinburgh.

CHAPTER FIVE

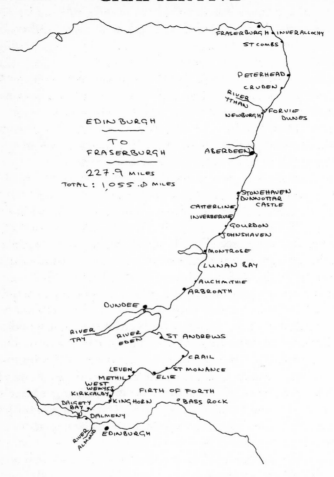

Jimmy was wearing jeans, braces, t-shirt and peaked cap, and was sitting on his denim bag outside one of Prince's Street's department stores selling the Big Issue. I bought a magazine from him and then crouched down next to him. From that angle all you could see were legs and bottoms passing in the street.

As way of introduction I mentioned the walk. 'It's just that my dog and I are walking . . .'

Jimmy's hand went straight to his pocket and he tried to give me some money. 'No, no! I'm not asking for money —' Oh dear, I had got this all wrong. 'I just wanted to sit and chat.'

He put his money away, and asked me a little about the walk, while doing a roaring trade. He knew many of his customers and was never pushy, but had a heart warming and ageless smile for them all, or a cheeky compliment for the ladies.

'Where do you sleep?' I asked. 'Do you find hostels and things?' I shivered just to think of sleeping out in this weather, and it was only September. 'No. Usually I sleep out in various places,' Jimmy said. 'There's an underground walkway not far from here, although it's sometimes too much down there. So long as you've got a good sleeping bag it's alright,' he said patting the bag he was sitting on. 'A sleeping bag's the most important thing. I never lose sight of mine.

'How did you become homeless?' I asked.

'Just circumstances —' and he didn't expand.

He took a cigarette and we sat there, smoking and watching the parade of legs. The words of Steve, a Big Issue vendor in London, came back to me: 'If it wasn't for charities such as Shelter the homeless problem would be a great deal worse than it is now.' These words were etched on my brain, and now Jimmy's completely selfless act would also remain with me. I decided that there were a good many people who could have learnt a lesson from him.

We left Edinburgh on a frosty Monday morning, accompanied by a new walking companion, Rupert, who had procured sponsors to walk with us for a week. I had met Rupert once, and the only thing I knew was that he was a model. I had contemplated fastening a mirror to the end of a stick to wave in front of him as he walked, in place of the proverbial carrot; and wondered how he would cope with the total lack of mirrors in our life. Privately I also had mixed feelings about a walking companion.

But from day one Rupert fitted into our routine. Whether or not he found our pace fast, I heard not a squeak from him that day. Tess, meanwhile, was delighted to have another companion, and had soon badgered Rupert into a dog's favourite game — sticks.

We crossed the River Almond into Dalmeny Estate, where the leaves fell noiselessly from the old trees, and we kicked our way through their already fallen counterparts. At the edge of the woodland, the two Forth bridges came into view; the clumsy but magnificent red girders of the rail bridge, and the simple span of the suspension road bridge which we walked across.

The water of the Firth of Forth was flat calm. The sun was out and seals sunned themselves on the rocks. In Dalgety Bay we stopped at a ruined church and looked out over the small shingle beach, and, without realising it, I started pointing out various birds. I felt possessive about the birds, and I am not sure whether Rupert was listening or not, but he said 'Oh' in the same vaguely interested fashion that I would have replied to 'greenshank' two months previously.

The north shore of the Firth of Forth is a working coastline, sustaining a variety of industries. Oil terminals compete with sewage works, collieries, castle remains, and fishing harbours; but each of these appeared to be on their last legs. The sea looked filthy and also on its last legs.

I wondered how much abuse the sea could take, and a fisherman in Kinghorn shed a little light: 'There aren't many fish left in the Forth. There are a few crabs, but that's about all.' Judging by the look of the water I reckoned that they would have to go through the same treatment as Felixstowe crabs.

Next came the path blackened by coal deposits; and mine shafts, conveyor belts and engine houses abandoned to weeds and brambles. Arriving in West Wemyss was like walking onto an hastily abandoned film set. The silence was foreboding.

The only person we came across was a lone builder. 'Where is everyone?' I asked, intrigued. 'Why's it so empty here?'

'Well, it's West Wemyss,' he replied, and carried on with his work as if the rest was obvious. *Perhaps this is what the north east of England will be like in twenty years time?* I thought, and wondered where the miners had gone, and what they were doing now. I may have complained about the coal and the pollution, but I'd rather see thriving communities than these deserted villages.

Rupert, meanwhile, had his head down and was relying on me to tell him how we were getting on. 'Where are we sleeping tonight?'

'Leven. There's a camping site the other side.'

'Are we nearly there?'

He didn't seem very interested in seeing the map, but then I didn't think I could trust anyone else anyway. 'About another two miles.'

We were on the outskirts of Methil, and the miles were always longer on the outskirts of towns. This was the time I would speed up, to shorten the period of pain. But companions always slowed down at the end of the day. We passed an open pub, and Rupert persuaded me to go in, 'just for a quick sit down.'

The only other people in the bar were two men pacing each other in the drinking stakes. In front of them was a copy of The Herald, in which was a picture of Tess and I experiencing the foot numbing consequences of small scale fame — paddling in the Firth of Forth. In return for signing the photo we were offered a trip around the largest spirit bottling plant in Europe the following morning.

That night I sweated out the cold I had been nurturing since Edinburgh, and perpetually woke up either hot or cold. Tess was like a massive hot water bottle, but never seemed to be there when I was cold. Meanwhile, Aidan slept on the floor in a howling draught. His feet were tucked under the table, which was now Rupert's bed, and his head was where my ladder should have been. Luckily neither Tess nor I wanted to go out in the night.

The mornings now required time and motion in the Spudtruck. It was like three people trying to get organised in a British Rail sleeper cabin, with the added obstacles of a dog, dirty washing, boots, bedding and two hundred maps. There was no room for modesty, though I was very pleased with a new pair of pyjamas which meant no more undignified ascents to bed while trying to control an unruly t-shirt.

But Rupert the dude was in a quandary over his wardrobe, again. Very soon he would learn that this was no place for vanity. You got up, you put on clothes, and you walked. I had certainly deposited any excess social baggage some time ago, and for now felt about as cool as a vindaloo with my nose as red as a beetroot and my eyes scratchy and puffy.

Rupert decided on his tracksuit bums, again, and secured his rather more cool bandana and shades. His footwear was certainly not cool when we turned up at the entrance to United Distillers at eight o'clock that morning — he was wearing slippers.

Our bleary eyed host kept to his word, and we were shown the entire process from the recycling of the storage barrels, to whisky blending, bottling and labelling. Respectable gentlewomen might have once managed a wee dram for breakfast, but I couldn't bring myself to follow suit. It is not even necessary to drink Scotch to suffer its effects. Because whisky breathes while maturing, a good deal evaporates — as much as 4 million gallons each year! A distillery is the best place to go for consumption through inhalation.

We reached the end of the Firth of Forth at Elie, with its sheds of drying haddock, where Bass rock finally disappeared from sight. We fell into St Monance for lunch and Aidan looked as though he had had enough. 'It took two f . . . hours to mend the miserable indicator!'

We pulled out the bread and cheese for our sandwiches. At least we had plenty of food while Aidan was with us; we were trying to get all our food donated, and Aidan's Irish charm was working wonders with the female supermarket managers. 'Relax Aids!' I tried, knowing only too well the frustration of the Spudtruck ailments.

In Edinburgh we had had to dip into the lump sum of money (donated for petrol and running costs), to replace the Spudtruck's worn out clutch. This had been successful; but yet another attempt at solving the riddle of the electrics hadn't worked. The tangle of multi-coloured wires which apparently made this campervan 'different from any other' remained an enigma, and cold showers and candlelight were more reliable. It wasn't until Fraserburgh that they would eventually be fixed.

That night we found a hot bath when the Golf Hotel in Crail offered us a room. This was to be one advantage of walking through Scotland's winter desertion. Admittedly the twin room was about the same size as the Spudtruck, but it was warm. We pushed the two beds together and I climbed into bed first. I had a good night's sleep sandwiched between the boys, who snuffled and snored in unison, while Tess lay like a heavy paperweight with whom we had to wrestle for precious corners of duvet.

From Crail we followed the Fife Coast Path along low grassy cliffs where gorse and bunnies thrived, while low tide exposed a wide shelf of rock. The rock strata running away from the coast accommodated hundreds of rock pools — and the usual array of plastic debris.

Every beached plastic bottle I investigated was some sort of cleaner — normally the products of various countries. I read in a MAFF report that 75% of litter found in the sea comes from fishermen, so I could only conclude that fishermen take a great interest in personal hygiene — a conclusion repeatedly dashed when one finds oneself in the company of freshly landed fishermen.

It was early afternoon when we reached St Andrews, which is far smaller than its reputation had led me to believe. In my eyes the size of a town depended on the miles of stoloniferous suburbs, and St Andrews had none. We reached the centre painlessly.

In the centre are the ruins of the sixteenth century cathedral. The end walls remain, standing precariously tall and supported by nothing, but otherwise there are only vague outlines of old stone walls and an immaculately mown graveyard. The original cathedral built on this site in the twelfth century took 200 years to build, and burnt down 60 years later!

We parked up in the High Street and I wrote letters. I wrote to everyone we had stayed with; people who had recently given money; people who might give money (for example the Royal and Ancient Golf Club); and occasionally to the committee. I enjoyed writing the address: The Spudtruck, St Andrews, Fife. September 28th 1993. In the last fifty nine days we had had fifty nine addresses.

In between letters I gazed out of the back window, feeling much like a disinterested goldfish. St Andrews is definitely a student town, and between Scotland's oldest university and golf the reputation of St Andrews revolves.

I was amused by one (possibly apocryphal?!) story of the origin of golf: a bored shepherd was one day swinging at stones with his crook, and when one landed in a rabbit hole he repeated the action to see if he could do it again! Whatever the real origins of golf, its origins in St Andrews date back from 1350 — how basic it would have been then compared to the lightweight clubs and motorised buggies of today.

We followed a track through the Royal and Ancient golf course, passing greens as smooth and green as a billiard table, without a speck of dirt or stray leaf in sight. Tess was on the lead to prevent her from retrieving a Royal and Ancient golf ball, or chasing a Royal and Ancient bunny. She began to shiver pathetically, and when the threatening clouds finally dropped their load I dug out her smart new coat. It slipped over her head and was tied under her belly. Emblazoned along the side the word 'Berghaus' gave her the air of a real expedition dog.

She flicked her body nose to tail like a worm out of soil, desperately trying to remove the thing. She then rubbed herself along every bush and wall, before resorting to violent rolling on the ground. By this time it hung off her at a rakish angle, and when she set off chasing dune bunnies I didn't expect it would last long. But it stood up to such treatment very well.

For twelve miles we skirted a softwood forest north of the River Eden. Under the dark sky the pine trees looked jet black, and under the deluge the normally carefree sand was heavy and sodden. Only the occasional group of autumnal birch trees provided splashes of yellow. In such weather there was little point in hanging around. I cranked up my wet weather pace, and Rupert kept up. The three of us were bonded by the conditions and the resulting tiredness which made itself known when our minds were no longer otherwise occupied. We walked in silence.

At last the bridge over the River Tay brought us down into Dundee, where we were given the wrong directions by a man with a dead pan face. Flanking us on each side were a jumble of architecturally shambolic buildings. I later read that since the eleventh century Dundee has managed repeatedly to pick the wrong side in all of Scotland's conflicts, and an eighteenth century historian wrote: 'Perhaps no town in Scotland has been oftener sacked, pillaged and destroyed than Dundee.' It looked as though it was still being pillaged.

Aidan and Rupert were in a partying mood, and Aidan's Irish eyes lit up when he discovered that there was a Guinness promotion night in the Thistle Hotel bar. Pints were £1. Sadly I didn't share their Saturday night fever. Instead, I wrote my diary in the company of dear Tess, and spread the soggy maps out to dry in the hotel heat. I felt inexplicably depressed, and alienated from Rupert and Aidan.

In two days time they would both be leaving. Aidan would be returning to his chickens, (six weeks previously he had started a job as a trainee farm manager, and now he had already taken two weeks of his three weeks annual holiday — it was, quite definitely, a noble gesture). Rupert would be returning to a London life of modelling — a life so many millions of miles away.

For both of them this had been a novel two weeks break, which would quickly fade into memories. It must have been hard for them to comprehend that this, for now, was my life; and that I would be doing the same thing for the next eight months.

I tried a brief sojourn in the throbbing bar, but I felt sober, dull, and disinclined to watch the human courtship ritual at its most bizarre. I gave up and went to bed.

At some unearthly hour of the night the boys lurched into my room. 'Herewe'vebrought-youshupper!' they announced, as though announcing royalty. They swayed a little in unison, as did the pizza, before joining Tess in a dishevelled heap on the bed. I'm not sure about cake, but Dundee clearly serves a mean Guinness.

The following morning Rupert joined Aidan in the Spudtruck. He had a persistent pain in his Achilles heel, which might have been aggravated by Guinness and the Chelsea v West Ham footy match. But he had already completed his 120 miles, and I felt proud of him for doing so.

Once Rupert had gone I felt another surge of strength, and with each stride the depression of the previous night became more distant. Walking has always enabled me to work out problems or emotions, clearing my mind so that mountains become molehills once more: 'Solvitur ambulando' — (It is solved by walking) — even after 930 miles. I hoped I wouldn't be taking this to the extreme over the next eight months.

A south-westerly wind was making the sea choppy, and whatever was being deposited into the Tay estuary between Perth and Dundee was passing us, as it tried to make its escape to the open sea. The beach was narrow and backed with debris of every type; broken up buoys, old fishing lines, beer cans faded by salt, pieces of polystyrene and a large boot. As we walked through all this, a St Bernard called Charlie came into view.

It was hard to tell the difference between Charlie and his owner, who was as rotund as Charlie and had shaggy hair and large jowels. He also had the ruddy complexion of a fisherman, and he told me that the excessive beach debris was due to a violent storm ten days previously. I had already heard of this from two other fishermen further south. One had only lost his outboard, while the other had lost a handful of kreel. Charlie's owner told me, with a cheerful resignation, that he had *only* lost 100 kreel. 'There are a lot worse off than me,' he concluded.

Charlie's owner was typical of the people we were meeting. It is an east coast resilience brought about by the unpredictable nature of the sea. When I experienced my share of the cruel east coast weather I began to understand that to make a life and a living here requires the dogged determination of the hardiest of Scots.

Charlie was standing patiently and was panting despite the cold wind. 'Where're you walking to?'

'Arbroath — to find a smokie!' Charlie's owner chuckled a weather beaten chuckle.

'Oh aye, you'll find plenty of them there! Enjoy your walk then.'

Past Arbroath, with its rusty, weathered, but still colourful boats we followed a network of lanes and tracks which serve scattered farms, while separating us from the sea were eroded red cliffs. These cliffs took us to the tiny village of Auchmithie which was the initial home of the smokie, and on to the crescent expanse of sand at Lunan Bay. That night Aidan and Rupert left and we were joined by Jo.

Jo climbed into the Spudtruck and took stock of things. 'So this is it? This is our home for the next week?' She opened the top of the sink and then the cooker. 'And this is my kitchen? Right.'

I went to put the kettle on. 'No, get out! It's my kitchen now. You're banished,' she said, laughing. Suitably chastised I sat back down, while Jo unpacked.

'The honey goes up there,' I explained.

'No that's no good there,' she said, and opened another cupboard from where several packets of Shreddies fell out. 'So those'll have to go somewhere else,' and she removed them.

'Everything has to be tightly wedged, Jo. It's like a ship . . .'

'Never you mind!' Jo laughed and waved her arms at me to shut me up. I wondered whether Jo walked into everyone's home and rearranged their kitchens!

At the end of five mile Montrose Beach we climbed back up the cliffs to cross the fields to Johnshaven — the first of a string of tiny fishing villages sculpted into the rocky coastline. We found the Spudtruck in Gourdon, a delightful harbour with houses which jostle close to each other like penguins huddled together for warmth.

As we slurped soup, which had miraculously spent the morning acting as spirit level on top of the Spudtruck's cooker, there was a knock on the door and Jo's new friend, Willy, stood there.

Willy was a small sixty year old with wispy dark hair and a grey beard. He wore sea spray spattered glasses pushed firmly up his nose, and had a permanent hand rolled cigarette (rollie) on the go. His face had the healthy complexion of fishermen, but not to the red veined extent of some. He had also lost kreel in the storm. Behind his glasses his eyes were bright and he smiled easily, although shyness was a trait implied by the fact that at least one hand was always shoved into a pocket.

'I've brought you some fresh fish,' Willy said, one hand in pocket. 'I was also wondering, are you going to Inverbervie? I thought I might try to raise you some money there. I live there you see. It won't be much.'

'Ahhh Willy. You are sweet,' Jo's face said it all.

She went up and put her arms round him, smothering him in her rather saucy but natural warmth of character. Willy flushed with pleasurable embarrassment. He was caught in her grip! 'I'll come with you Willy,' she concluded, and Willy blushed again.

Jo and Willy made an irresistible pair in Inverbervie, where I measured the afternoon's miles with my thumb. From the tip to the first joint was exactly an inch, and I found this the most accurate method of planning the days.

I made my destination Dunottar Castle, and showed Jo on the map. There was no path and I knew it would be hard going. Willy added his advice; 'It shelves steeply down to the sea and it's rough going through bracken and stuff. I should go on the road.'

I had been through this several times. I believed I knew my capabilities by now, whereas locals didn't. 'There's a lot of people who've been lost along this coast,' Willy continued. 'Only a couple of weeks ago someone broke their leg out there.'

But my belief in myself was stronger. I gave Willy a big hug, briefly arranged a rendezvous with Jo in Catterline, and set off.

The coast was indeed tough, across well-fenced farmland grazed by sheep (which Tess had for now decided were boring), and through numerous gorse hedgerows; and all the time there were steep and jumbled cliffs dropping straight to the sea.

We were just nearing Catterline when I saw a red figure standing on a hill up ahead. I knew it must be Jo and I waved. She didn't wave back but I was convinced that she had heard my frantic yells for Tess, who had disappeared after her first deer.

But the figure vanished and when we reached Catterline there was no sign of the Spudtruck. We sat to wait on a grassy bank. I repeatedly tried the two way radio, but it made all the wrong noises; while the phone hated such rural areas. It was getting late and began to get cold. When the cold got the better of us I decided to walk on to Dunnottar, hoping that Jo would head there. She might even be waiting there.

We had walked over twenty hard miles already and were both exhausted as we set out for the four miles to Dunnottar. When we reached Dunnottar it was completely dark and there was no sign of Jo. The wary lady from the gatehouse hadn't seen her either.

Back out in the darkness, the black outline of the ruins of Dunnottar Castle looked really sinister. At one time covenantors were left to rot in the dungeons of this massive castle, sitting on its rock 160 feet above the sea. But I was more interested in trying to get warm. I dug out all the clothing I could find, and Tess' coat, and we sheltered below the Castle entrance wall. Tess climbed onto my lap, where she tried to fold herself up as small as possible. I knew the feeling. Have you ever been so cold that you want to shrink as small as possible to squeeze into tiny sheltered spots?

So we sat behind the wall, trying to shrink and exchanging body heat. Although Tess said she was cold her coat felt wonderfully warm to me and I wrapped my hands round her and rubbed my cold nose in her coat. The main road was about two hundred yards up the small road, and a continual stream of lights whizzed past. With each one that turned onto our small road I said confidently to Tess, 'Here's Jo,' but it never was.

I thought of a huge, crackling, open fire, tea and crumpets dripping with melted butter, and roast lamb; then the realisation dawned that we were going to have to hitch back to Catterline.

If ever anyone trudged, we did, back to the main road. I stuck my thumb out, and was surprised when the third car stopped.

The landlady of the Catterline pub greeted us. 'Ahh. There you are! There'll be a few people pleased to see you!' She sounded relieved but looked indifferent. I asked if she knew where Jo was. 'Not exactly. But the police'll know. I'll call them to let them know you're OK.'

'The POLICE!'

We then learnt that the coastguards had been alerted, and by the time the policeman turned up I was in desperate need of the brandy he had soon bought me. He was shortly followed by Jo, who threw her arms around me and yelled 'You BITCH!' The nice policeman bought her a brandy too.

Poor Jo had been regaled with coastal horror stories all afternoon, and was convinced I was at the bottom of a cliff. I had forgotten it was her first day.

That day I had covered twenty-five miles, but I believe that Tess, with her deer hunt plus all the rabbit activity, could easily have covered forty. After her supper she went to the front of the Spudtruck and asked to go to bed, where she fell into a sleep from which there could be no rousing her. The following day she stayed in the Spudtruck, while I raced through Stonehaven in fear of the knicker thief who, according to the local paper, was 'still at large!'

The downpour of the previous night, which had resulted in sodden walls and healthy leaks in the Spudtruck, was evident everywhere. On Stonehaven's closed golf course the bunkers looked like ponds enclosed by a narrow rim of sand; and rakes lay by the bunkers like children's hurriedly abandoned beach toys. I negotiated brambles on the edge of the cliff, and picked a way through small fields. I couldn't have been sticking closer to the coast if I'd tried, but the going was tough with bottomless mud in places. I thought of food.

After eight miles I came across a village shop and bought myself two snickers bars, which I ate one after another. I put the wrappers in my pocket which was full of other soggy wrappers, a golf ball and various pebbles which had once looked so nice and shiny. Plugging myself into 'The Police' I stumbled on to Aberdeen, dreaming of the Thistle Hotel; and wondering if I should put a message in a bottle as the song suggested, or whether this was hypocritical after my disgust at the pollution.

The granite city of Aberdeen must be one of the most isolated cities in Britain — and probably the most exposed. It lies between two rivers, the Don and the Dee, and is the third largest fishing port in Britain. But Aberdeen means one thing — Oil.

The benefits of being the gateway to East Scotland's forty-nine oil-fields are obvious in the busy streets and totally outrageously large granite buildings, topped with spires and turrets. The Thistle Hotel was equally grand.

The sponsorship by the Thistle group was ideal because, not only were they in cities, where parking places for the Spudtruck were difficult, but they also appeared when a spoiling experience was in order.

The deep piled carpet felt like very fine and warm sand; and the bar was modern with bamboo chairs and glass topped tables. We sat at the tall bar drinking cocktails from slender glasses and munching complimentary peanuts. I felt like one of 007's eternally elegant and beautiful challenges. Relativity is a wonderful thing.

Before breakfast the next morning we took Tess out into the cold grey day. We walked passed some suited businessmen outside our hotel, and in the adjacent pristine garden an old man was staggering towards a bench. His clothes declared 'homeless'. He sat down, produced a bottle of cider from under his overcoat, and wrestled with the top. He took several desperate slurps.

'Morning,' we said, our English accents snobby. 'Not much of a day is it? Looks like it's going to rain.'

He took another slurp and replied, 'Aye, but what's it to me?'

On the front page of the local paper that day the Aberdeen homeless problem was being commented on by the Lord Provost. Once again the main cause of the homelessness was being reiterated — the sale of the council houses and lack of replacements. In October 1993 the council house waiting list in Aberdeen alone was 5,000 — what a daunting prospect to be told you were number 5,001.

Shelter had organised a photocall at the Aberdeen football stadium, and waiting for us there were a couple of newspaper reporters and Grampian TV. The secretary of the football club took charge of us. 'We've got Duncan Shearer and Stewart McKimmie for your photocall.' For all I knew they were fictitious characters.

We had also been joined by Fiona from Shelter and she smiled at the mention of these two footballers. 'My daughter will be furious! She's an avid football fan.' I took Fiona aside for any information. 'Well the most important thing is that they're in the first division,' she told me. That was enough. At least I could say something.

'Congratulations for being in the first division!' I blurted during one of our re-runs of leaving the stadium, and immediately wished that the pitch would swallow me up. The local heroes were unconcerned.

During our ordeal at the football stadium the rain was becoming more incessant, and the Spudtruck almost waterlogged. Leaving Jo and Fiona setting off in search of a roofer, Tess and I set off into a violent headwind for twelve and a half miles of rain-lashed beach. The white breakers were the only distinction between a grey sea and grey sky. I got some respite under my dripping hood and soggy earphones with a talking book — Vita Sackville-West's *All Passion Spent*. Somewhere in the midst of this we crossed our one thousandth mile.

We were walking miles of this bleak coastline, exposed to elements which threatened to pick us up and hurl us contemptuously to the ground. River estuaries were sanctuaries; gentle areas of refuge. During a brief patch of sunshine the next morning Jo and I crossed the River Ythan towards Forvie Dunes, and in that area of refuge I put my early birth-day present to the test — a pair of binoculars.

Since receiving them, the birdlife had become three dimensional. I had marvelled at the dunlins so well camouflaged on shingle, and had nosily followed the hierarchal behaviour of gulls. I had seen the black eyes of the curlew, and the real frailty of the redshank's legs.

Forvie Dunes form one of the largest dune areas in Britain — at their longest they are about four miles long and one mile wide, and some of the dunes reach 200 feet high. They were smothered in flowering heather and rose and fell around us in a subtle purple swell, until they shelve away to the beach at the point where Forvie village once stood. It was drowned by the shifting dunes, so that all that remains are the shoulder height ruins of the tiny thirteenth century church.

When the dunes ended we took to the quiet roads. Making the most of the calm weather I began to make a tape to another sister, Poopa, who lives in Laos. Tapes were an excellent way of making the miles disappear; one hours talking into my walkman/dictaphone meant four miles had passed.

I talked about the countryside around us, related recent news, gave sound effects of streams or eating blackberries, and got Tess' disc to tinkle on the tape as her way of saying hello. Whether or not they were listened to they helped me enormously. The only conditions were a calm day (wind over the microphone obliterated my voice entirely), and flat, even ground. Even in these conditions I sounded like David Attenborough on the verge of an evolutionary discovery.

Back on the beach at Cruden it was low tide and the firm sand made the walking easier. Tess was on a dune bunny quest and she returned with muddy paws — or was it mud? I called her over, and realised it was oil.

Over the last few days I had noticed signs saying 'beware of seaborne oil pollution'. It seemed to me that the only reason such blatant pollution not only exists, but appears to be taken for granted here, is because these beaches are rarely visited by bucket and spade holidaymakers; the sea and the wind making sitting on the beach an exceptionally chilly experience.

I then went to pick up a stone for Tess, and realised that the whole beach was covered in tar. We sped on to escape the filth — though there really seemed to be no escaping it. The continuing filthiness of the North Sea, and its pervading smell, had paled into a daily occurrence.

My goal was to reach John O' Groats by November 1st and at the moment we were still on schedule. But it was a battle. During the last week this area had had 600% more rain than the seasonal norm, while the relentless wind had blown every feature off the earth's surface so that only the bare basics were left — the skeleton of the landscape.

In Peterhead the granite buildings were harshly squared off, and the streets strangely clean from the persistent sweeping of the wind. Those people who weren't hibernating were hurrying from one place to another, and even their faces were harsh and sculpted as if the elements had been at work here too, leaving all but the necessary features on these gaunt and angular characters. This wasn't my favourite stretch of coast, but there is something admirable about it. Above all it is a coast to respect.

To reach its culmination we faced a further 15 miles of solitary beach walking to Fraserburgh. At between three and four miles per hour this meant five hours of Tess, the sand, the drizzle, the sea, the dunlins and my own company — or so I thought.

The sand is a lovely orange colour, not too fine, and the tide was out. I threw hard to find pebbles for Tess, and walked in time to mundane thoughts, pacing them apart. I was suddenly surprised to see a policewoman ahead.

The policewoman had to be on the wrong film set; it simply wasn't possible to find a policewoman four miles up the beach from Peterhead, and six miles from the nearest road access the other way. Of all the people to find on this hostile coast I could think of none more bizarre. My imagination started to race.

I came up level with her, and she looked frozen in her policewomen's skirt. 'Sorry love you can't go any further,' she declared.

'Why not?'

'A ship full of drugs was wrecked just off here and the debris is coming ashore here. Don't you read the papers?'

'Umm . . Not really. When I try to read the papers I fall asleep because we've walked over 1,000 miles now —'

She looked at me sympathetically. Hadn't she seen the news? After all we'd been on the news two days ago!

The beach was scattered with £13 million worth of drugs. The mind boggled, and I subconsciously scanned the beach around us. 'You'll have to head inland. You can't return to the beach for three miles,' the policewoman concluded.

We left the almost redundant policewoman for the next coastal walker and clambered up the dunes for three miles of ankle deep dune walking. Feeling like a bedouin who has lost his camel, we reached the top of a crest and came across a police encampment. I hauled Tess over the temporary wire fence and walked straight into the middle of the wreckage strewn encampment. A policeman's hand landed on my shoulder. 'You shouldn't be here,' he reprimanded. They were to be the only words he offered. We were frogmarched off in silence, while Tess showed no inclination towards a career as a sniffer dog.

For the rest of the afternoon I kept my eyes peeled for any suspicious packages, until at last the beach came to an end at Inverallochy. The rain continued to lash down — both inside and outside the Spudtruck. There was no escaping the water.

Jo climbed into the driver's seat. She turned the key, but nothing happened. We looked at each other in despair — then Jo said tentatively; 'You've got to laugh — haven't you?'

'I suppose,' I said, feeling soggy, weary and hungry.

A passing car gave us a wet jump start, and we drove to St Combs where we sheltered outside the Tufted Duck hotel. As supper cooked, Jo produced a bottle of red wine. Jo and red wine had a great affinity for each other. I piled on the layers and forgot about the leaks, battery and the rain — until the lights started dimming. I turned around and saw the familiar but ominous red light. We were then plunged into darkness again.

There was a pause. 'Well you've really got to laugh, haven't you?!' said Jo, suddenly trying to stem uncontrollable giggles in case of my reaction. She was right. It was impossible not to see the funny side, and I was enveloped in a wave of gratitude for Jo's company. We stayed up well into the night, pulling the world apart and putting it back together by candlelight.

CHAPTER SIX

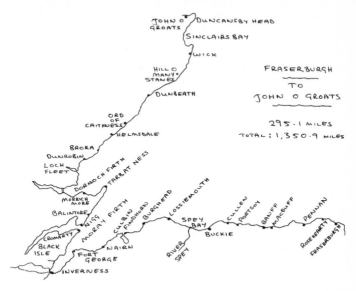

By Sunday lunchtime we found ourselves in the small bar of The Mason's Arms, Rosehearty, where the locals talked among themselves as if they were at an informal party in someone's house. Occasionally one person took the floor to relate a local incident, and one guy was most prominent in this aspect. The one thing they all had in common was that they were getting slowly pissed.

When I had finished monopolising the phone, I joined Jo and the prominent figure. 'Chas is trying to teach me the local lingo,' Jo introduced us.

'Fit like quine?'

'You what?'

'It means 'how are you?' to a girl,' Jo said, knowledgeably.

'Yer a pair a bonnie quines!' Chas was persistent. He said something else and I looked helplessly at Jo and then at Chas. 'What did you say?'

'I said 'you're friend told me you've walked a long way'. You must be f . . . . mad. Where's your dog?'

'Sleeping probably.'

'Sounds like that's what you should be doing. It's f . . . nasty weather to walk, but good on you. It's a f . . . disgrace there're so many homeless people.' His words came out in a jumble of harsh dialect punctuated by swearwords. Throughout the nineteenth century the people in this area spoke Doric, and it seemed they were still speaking it.

Chas was in his thirties. He had short black hair once swept back off his face, a gaunt face so typical of the people in this area, and obviously lived on a liquid diet. But even in his inebriated state he managed to dart about the pub with a certain amount of agility as he forced people to put money into a pint glass for us.

We were then joined by a guy I shall call Steve who, thanks to an obviously abused body, looked prematurely middle aged. His face was round and puffy, and his short brown hair greasy. Despite drinking pints as fast as the others, he retained an air of sobriety. He turned the conversation back to the walk. 'Where do you stay?'

'We've got a rather wet campervan! It's leaking like a sieve.'

'Yeah, you're better off getting wet on the inside! Ah, you're a pair a bonnie quines!' Chas offered, dipping and swaying in and out of the conversation.

Steve offered to try and fix the Spudtruck's leaks then and there, and the afternoon progressed in a relay of Steve's attempts at roofer, Chas' whisky beer chasers, and finally a game of golf. Well, it could only just be called golf.

In Jo's words, the clubs we used 'weren't at all Royal, but very Ancient.' These were swung with gay abandon, but rarely came into contact with the right balls. Chas had about the same chance of getting the ball into the hole as the shepherd had had with his crook and the stone.

When we got back to the Spudtruck the door was unlocked. Inside were the discarded remains of our wallets and bags — all our cash, cheque books, credit cards and cameras had gone; while it seemed that Tess had welcomed the burglar with a wag of her tail. How could they? This was my home; my security; my base. It was my life?

The Mason's Arms fell silent and the collective finger pointed at one person, now absent from the scene. Chas went red in the face: 'That bloody Steve. I'll f... kill him. I'll get him... What'll you quines think of this place now?' All his drunkenness changed to anger, and I felt briefly sorry for the person at whom his wrath was aimed.

PC Paul came for tea in the Spudtruck. He had a kind face and was quick to smile his self conscious smile. He sidled into the grubby seat and had his ears cleaned by Tess, who was getting used to policemen. 'Haven't you got a drink for me? What's this tea — yuk! Where's the whisky?' Chas said, sitting squeezed between PC Paul and Tess.

Another Roseheartian then stuck his head through the window, clinging on to the back of the Spudtruck as though he was on a ship in a ferocious sea. 'Hello Oshifer,' he said waving his car keys in the hand which wasn't stabilising him. 'I wash going to shdrive home but shince you're here I thought I'd ashk you firsht.'

A fresh waft of alcohol fumes entered the Spudtruck. PC Paul raised his eyebrows in mock despair, and gave a wry smile. That was all that was needed and the face disappeared.

Unfortunately PC Paul was unable to locate our belongings, but over the next twenty four hours news of the burglary spread fast. Even the verbose traffic warden in Fraserburgh declared — 'och, aye, that'll be Steve!' And the mechanic who finally deciphered the Spudtruck's electrics had once caught him red-handedly trying to steal his car!

The only person who didn't know Steve's tendencies was his new wife, who, along with the rest of the fishwives which comprised his family, almost, but not quite, discovered our whereabouts that night. For once the Spudtruck rose to the occasion, started first time and left the hair pulling females shaking their fists at the Spudtruck's exhaust fumes.

Peregrine was already waiting at Fraserburgh bus station the next morning. He had stepped in to drive at the last minute, and I had never met him before. Before long he was being buttered up by Tess. 'I think Tess likes me,' he said in the cheerful manner Tess elicits from everyone. I didn't tell Peregrine that Tess even liked burglars.

Fraserburgh, perched out on its lonely point, was now unrecognisable to the sleepy town I had walked through on Sunday morning when all the fishermen had been sleeping off Saturday night. Now the harbour was virtually empty of boats.

The butcher we found was as cheery and generous as butchers are. He produced some mince which was compacted into triangles, and then said confidently, and also in Doric, 'I suppose some white pudding to go with it?'

'Well, err, no!' I mumbled once we had had the translation.

'What? But you can't have mince without white pudding!' he said incredulously, further astounded by our intentions of spaghetti Bolognaise.

'You've never heard of white pudding? What a terrible shame!' he said, running to the back of the shop declaring that the English were a funny race.

He reappeared holding two steaming flaccid sausages oozing out of their skins and held at their ends by kitchen roll. My stomach gave a lurch, but soon decided that it was actually quite tasty; while Peregrine dealt with his as if it might eat him.

'Now that's what you eat with mince. Mince, white pudding, neeps and tatties,' the butcher said, putting some of each in a bag. 'You Eng-

lish! Spaghetti Bolognaise!' he tutted. Our friend refused money, and we
parted as firm friends and converts.

The supermarket manager presented us with a large and heavy box.
Whether supermarkets donated food or not depended on the individual
manager — or else on dramatic mis-ordering. We rummaged through
the lucky dip of tins, and discovered fourteen tins of macaroni cheese
and one of spaghetti and meatballs. 'I know you need plenty of pasta as
carbohydrate,' the manager had said knowingly. Peregrine's nose
twitched as he summed up the weeks' menu: flaccid white pudding,
mountains of neeps and tatties, triangles of mince, and outdated, tinned
macaroni cheese. (By general taste consensus the tins remained as
Spudtruck ballast until Inverness, where they were passed on again.)

It was then time to tackle the Spudtruck's loo. A crowd of people
waited for a bus in the shelter next door to the coach station public loo,
near which we parked the Spudtruck on a double yellow line. We had
just negotiated the stinking compartment through the side door when a
traffic warden appeared. 'Ohh . . . Are you that girl who's walking
around the world? Ffyona someone?' she said excitedly. Tess clearly
confused her with a piper and did her nose-up-the-skirt routine. The
traffic warden appeared not to notice. 'Ffyona Campbell?'

'Yes, that's it — is that you?'

'Not unless she's made a massive detour from Africa.'

But the warden was truly interested anyway. She had a cold and was
oblivious to stinking compartment at our feet. Several people waiting
for the bus moved further away. 'We'll just —' I began.

'Aye, and a friend of my brother's cycled from Land's End to John
O' Groats . . .' I bent down to pick up the loo again. 'So where do you
go from here?' I put the loo down again and we repeated this scene
several times, before making a dash for it and leaving Tess guarding the
warden, guarding the illegally parked Spudtruck. She did a grand job at
not doing her job.

We tipped and sloshed and swilled. If the drivers survived this on
day one, they could survive anything. Considering white pudding on an
empty stomach, Peregrine survived particularly well.

The coast was now tremendously hilly, along high cliffs which dropped
away in folds like pleated green material tucked into the sea; and occasionally we descended to negotiate once tiny burns which had now burst
their banks. Always the ground was bottomless, as it also tried to cope
with the huge rainfall, and sodden wheat and oil seed rape crops had
been regularly abandoned. It wasn't worth harvesting them.

We stopped at Pennan Head. Below us, pushed onto the shore by the cliffs, like a fairground game with its cliff edge of copper pennies which never quite topple, was precipitous Pennan village. Beyond its rooves the view along the Moray Firth was spectacular, and in a momentary patch of blue sky we could see for miles. But it was Pennan Farm which had stopped me.

The old farm house was square and practical, but windowless and deserted. My dream of owning my own farm had arrived, and I pictured myself up on this spacious and wild hilltop, accompanied by my small holding of animals, and untouched by anything man made.

The walk would either cure me of a permanent restlessness, or strengthen it. So far it was curing it and I was already thinking of such a dream place to settle. The thought of not constantly moving was appealing and for the rest of the day I dreamt my dreams of Pennan Farm.

We found Peregrine at the end of a no-through road on the edge of Macduff. The Spudtruck was parked so close to the wild sea that from inside you couldn't see the intervening shingle beach; it felt as though we were on a boat, and were certainly rocking in a similar fashion.

Peregrine appeared happy. I had complete confidence in him already and had been delighted to discover that he was a carpenter. There were always plenty of repairs in the Spudtruck.

Before my body stiffened up completely, I decided to test the newly fixed auxiliary battery before it had a chance to run out, and began to empty the shower cupboard. Out came my dripping waterproofs; out came a pile of dirty clothes; out came Tess' new bag of dog food; and up came the floor.

I had now known Peregrine a little over twenty four hours, and was stripping off in front of him in our luggage filled BR cabin, and entering that area of personal space normally only permitted to a select few. I found some sort of privacy in the cupboard.

I turned the gas on and opened the window to let the fumes out. The rain dripped off the open window in a never ending waterfall, and I could see the seaweed brought up by the high tides. The cold draught of air cooled me almost as fast as the hot water warmed me; but the effort of drying myself in the cupboard always succeeded in warming me up more then the rest of the procedure.

The rain buffeted us all night, and seeped and spread down the Spudtruck walls. In the morning the weather was confused as to what element to try next. Rain squalls, sunspots and subsequent rainbows competed for the sky. After a couple of miles I had warmed up and stopped to take off a layer, but two miles further on I realised I'd left the map behind.

Tess looked confused when I turned around, and the sea looked peculiar on my left — like a right handed person writing with their left hand. I was forced to retrace my steps in this way on numerous occasions, and it always occurred to me that if someone said 'right, turn round and walk back to London now,' I wouldn't have been physically able to. It felt fitting to be walking in a circle of sorts; what goes around comes around.

The cliffs decreased in height, broken up by the fishing ports of Buckie, Banff, Macduff, Burghead, and Portsoy, which all grew up and thrived on the herring industry. It certainly boasted one of the biggest concentrations of fishing boats on Britain's coast.

The small village of Cullen is dwarfed by a magnificent but redundant railway viaduct spanning a tiny burn. I was discovering the staggering number of railway lines which once weaved their way to corners of Britain. They are clearly marked on O/S maps and the old bridges were useful for crossing rivers.

The banks of the Spey were flanked with birch and maple trees shedding their yellow, orange and brown leaves. It was ten days since we had walked through any woodland, on a river detour on Montrose Bay. I remembered it for its novelty!

A slight wind blew the remaining leaves earthwards, and I caught a falling leaf for good luck and put it in my map case. It was so quiet without the roar of the sea, and as we came further inland so we were shielded more and more from the wind until the leaves stopped falling and not even a bird could be heard. The woodland was a world of peacefulness; even Tess was uncharacteristically calm. The only thing which moved was the peaty water of the Spey as it hurried over the pebbles to a new life at sea. Above us a weak winter sun appeared and a feeling of intense contentment and well being ran through every cell. I was glad to be walking; glad to be alone.

Yet I couldn't help thinking that we should never have let these railways close. As fast as they close we build more land-stealing roads. Why? As I stood on that quiet bridge, reviving all these redundant lines seemed such an obvious solution to our traffic problem.

Tess got bored first and I felt her front paws on my side. She stretched in this position and yawned a large yawn, saying 'let's keep going and see what's in store.' Her red and swollen toenails had recovered now that we were off sandy beaches, but she was suffering from teenage acne on her chest — but with none of the self consciousness. Other dogs didn't tease and shout 'pizza chest.' Nevertheless, a trip to Lossiemouth vet ensued.

We arrived at the designated Lossiemouth car park at the same time as the Spudtruck ground to a halt. 'Nearly made it this time!' Peregrine grinned.

'Not bad!' Peregrine's tardiness was a standing joke between us, and luckily Scotland's liberal licensing laws meant I could match meeting points with PH's.

The Spudtruck was littered with carpenter's debris, and when I opened the cutlery compartment it no longer came away in my hand. 'I've put magnetic fasteners on all the compartments. The pasta won't fall on Tess' head now,' Peregrine said. 'Also I've nailed down the carpet.'

'No luck with the roof or the front heater?' I asked.

'No . . . Oh, I bought something. Look in the cupboard.'

I opened the cupboard. 'Great, a loo roll holder! Just what we need!' We had water pouring through the roof, a heater which blew out arctic air and left the carpet like a saturated sponge (which sometimes froze) — but at least the loo roll would be secure.

The coast west of Lossiemouth is rocky and dotted with caves which are cut off at high tide, and the peaty path was bordered with flowering heather. We walked in silence, breathing great clouds of condensation, until disturbing a beautiful curlew which flew off with unhurried ease. I called my mandatory greeting to it, and to the shags which stood out on the rocks drying their cloak-like wings and chatting to each other like a group of ladies in the launderette.

The curlew flew off and the black silhouettes of shags on the rocks came and went. I returned to the idyllic desert island of William Golding's *Lord of the Flies*, which was becoming less and less idyllic by the minute. Seven miles of beach took us to Findhorn.

The Spudtruck now resembled a mobile freezer rather than a mobile home, and we tried to warm up with tea and whisky. When Peregrine started cooking, he had to open the skylight to let out the fumes. But we had decided it was better to be full and cold rather than hungry and warm. We huddled in front of the oven.

The newspaper headlines the next day read: 'Coldest October for more than forty years.' 'Temperatures drop to -9°c.' Aberdeen had two inches of snow, and there was thick snow inland from us and across the Moray Firth. I packed away my leggings and shorts till next summer, and likewise the Shreddies. From now on it was red woolly trousers and porridge.

Findhorn village is built out on a promontory of unstable sand dunes, and is widely known for the Findhorn Foundation — an international alternative lifestyle community. We entered the gates of the Foundation and wandered around a little, but didn't see a soul. It was too cold for sandals and sarongs, and there was probably some sort of communal hibernation going on.

The click of my pedometer was audible as we notched up the miles in the novel silence of the Findhorn estuary, but this peace was nothing compared to the eerie silence which enveloped us in fifteen miles of Culbin Forest.

The trees which marched away from the path in endless processions threw our voices back with disdain, and the impenetrable layer of pine needles allows only weird and colourful fungi to grow below in a world of pixies. We followed the forestry tracks marked on the map, but had no way of knowing whether these were up to date, or whether we were on the right one; every track looked the same. We could have been walking in circles.

It was like walking in a totally blind state; one false turn, or one path outdated, and we could still be there now. It felt more dangerous than even the sheerest cliffs, most perilous footpaths or strongest winds — or so I thought at the time.

The absence of wildlife added to the oppressiveness of this deathly world, until, after two hours of seeing nothing, a lone deer stood in a patch of sunlight ahead of us like a momentary apparition. After another six miles a bird resembling a lost turkey was difficult to miss, as it crashed through the branches in clumsy flight. It was a male capercaillie. Throughout the fifteen miles to Nairn these were the only two pieces of wildlife we saw.

The Moray Firth claims to have the largest share of sunshine in Scotland and, unlike the fishing ports we had recently passed through, Nairn capitalises on this and its proximity to surrounding castles and battlefields. One local attraction is Fort George situated on a promontory jutting out into the Moray Firth.

From here the sheer faced cliffs of the Black Isle rise out from the sea less than a mile across the Moray Firth; while stretching northwards the snow covered hills filled me with apprehension. Would we be walking in the snow? Would we be able to walk along the base of the cliffs? Would it be accessible for the Spudtruck? It was impossible to believe we were actually hoping to walk those cliffs.

I told myself that that would be another day, and another week, and tried to push it from my mind. But the folly of walking Scotland in the winter often came back to me.

I first had the idea to walk Britain's coast in January, which was the time of year we should have left — so minimising the winter months.

But I was reluctant to postpone the project for a whole year. Instead, it had taken six months of planning and we left in mid summer.

Nowhere was going to be particularly warm in the winter! If we reached Glasgow by Christmas we would have covered the most isolated coastline before the very severe weather set in, and benefited from the supposed Gulf Stream. We would then be heading south to more populated areas in spring and then summer, so enabling more fundraising.

We now had no driver and had no choice but to take a week off in Inverness, where we stayed with friends of Pops', Ant and Lindy Loo. Throughout the week if Ant wasn't under, in or on top of the Spudtruck, then he was in the workshop playing with Spudtruck parts as though they were lego. I frequently wondered whether we would be leaving Inverness carrying the Spudtruck in pieces, rather than vice versa. Meanwhile Lindy Loo made thermal curtains and fruit cakes, and I wrote my latest newsletter.

I wrote these every six weeks, and sent them to sponsors; but now all I wanted to do was to have one complete day off the walk. The only phone calls I made concerned drivers or fundraising, and after that I had no inclination for social calls. People rarely called me (either they couldn't get through or they presumed that they would be roped into something). I felt that I was losing friends as fast as I was making them. My life had been taken over. As long as I was awake I was an ambassador for Shelter and, of course, people always wanted to hear about the walk.

I found solace in Ant and Lindy Loo, who knew me for who I was; and I found solace in Tess, who asked no questions and expected no answers. When Tess saw the Spudtruck being reloaded, she was the first one inside, and on Sunday 25th October, accompanied by a friend from agricultural college, Jo, and her whippet, Freckle, we set off down Inverness High Street — hobbling. My body ached from my waist down. Weeks off were definitely not a good thing.

On the other side of Kessock Bridge there was no path. The steep hills were thick with the tangle of autumnal bracken, which made walking similar to wading through a plate of spaghetti; I tripped constantly, my hips ached, and our progress was slow. We came face to face with an eight foot deer fence.

I felt depressed by everything. Depressed by the pain in my hips and legs; depressed by the inaccessible country and our slow progress; and depressed by Tess, who had just done her well rehearsed disappearing act, which had led to my equally well rehearsed 'I couldn't care less if you run off and never come back' routine. Arguing with Tess was like arguing with your best friend. I sat on a log and felt sorry for myself.

The still guilty Tess came over and put her head on my lap. Her tail began to wag slowly, and as I smiled it increased in speed and confidence. 'You're a hopeless dog!' She put her paws on my lap and gave me a big lick.

I tried to calm myself. There was no point letting little things get us down, and we were going to have to get used to deer fencing and inaccessible country. But while my mind battled with despondency, my body battled with soreness.

By the end of the day, as we clambered over brambles and were forced up hill by burns at the base of the Black Isle cliffs, which had looked so imposing from across the now still Moray Firth, each step used as much energy as twenty. On the last hill Tess repeatedly stopped to wait for me, as though sensing my fatigue and despair; and when Jo walked to meet us I wanted to tell her that I was depressed and sore — but this wouldn't change much. There was nothing either of us could do.

I felt even worse the next morning, and concentrated on telling each leg to move until the lubrication in my joints returned, slightly. We walked northwards on the quiet road; it was like drifting across the surface of the land after the previous day's battle.

Cromarty is a name familiarised by the shipping forecasts, and the town, with its lovely Georgian architecture, came as a great surprise; juxtaposed with the oil platforms anchored beyond in the Cromarty Firth.

There were nine rigs sitting in the Firth, like large, mechanical, amphibious spiders from some science fiction film, poised for action on the calm water. They are anchored here for storage or to await repairs at the Nigg construction yard.

North of here there are few natural harbours, and geographically the Cromarty Firth is an ideal location for the rigs because it is sheltered and deep. This also makes it a safe anchorage for naval fleets, and it is thought to have sheltered Viking fleets.

Rising up on each side of the entrance, the two headlands of North and South Sutor stand higher than the surrounding hills, guarding the entrance to Cromarty Firth. From the top of Cromarty's South Sutor you can apparently see seven counties.

The name Sutor is Scots for shoemaker, and there is a local legend that the two headlands were named after two giant shoemakers who lived on their respective headlands, sharing their tools which they threw to one another across the Firth.

We crossed the Cromarty Firth to Nigg on the Kings Ferry, then cut across the headland of North Sutor, and rejoined the coast at Balintore. From here our final seven miles of the day were along a lovely grassy path where we were joined by numerous herons. They stood haughtily on the rocks, before laboriously taking off and flying in a lugubrious fashion. I loved to watch them. They are less graceful then the nimble waders, but they have a character of their own. I often saw them being remorselessly chased by seagulls, and they were so ungainly that they looked as though they might fall out of the sky during such skirmishes, which they always lost. I personified them as gangly hippies, but once wrote in my diary; 'the herons remind me of me, always on their own and in the middle of nowhere!'

The clocks had now gone back and it was disconcerting to find it still dark at 7am. Jo was putting the kettle on. After a reluctance to leave her bed on the first morning, she had bounded out of bed on the second morning declaring; 'I've decided that the last thing you need in the mornings is to be prising a reluctant slob from bed!' She was right.

I climbed gingerly down my ladder. When my feet hit the floor they experienced a strange sensation; it was as if I was permanently wearing shoes, yet the shoes had inadequate soles. A padded layer had attached itself to the soles.

We rounded Tarbat Ness, and on the south side of the Dornoch Firth, Morrich More MOD Range barred the coast. While the jets roared overhead, encompassing several months of our walking in a matter of seconds, the loyal and oblivious birds stayed with us. There is no danger of these pockets of noisy land ever being developed, and they are therefore safe havens for the birds. There are 220 SSSi's (Sites of Special Scientific Interest) on MOD land.

After the Dornoch Firth we had one more estuary to negotiate before the coast became a straight route to John O' Groats — Loch Fleet. We walked along the beach to the mouth of the loch, where the dunes give way to a quiet lane. After a little while we came across two men with their telescopes pointing out over the loch. I offered a twitcher-type greeting, and had soon discarded my matchbox toy binoculars and was peering through their machine. This time it was a mass of duck — red breasted mergansers, scoters, wigeon and eider. Then a whooper swan, an arctic visitor, caused great excitement. From time to time a seal surfaced, and blew raspberries at us.

While they were looking I noticed a monument on a hill to the north. This is a monument to the Duke of Sutherland — a name synonymous with the Highland Clearances because it was on his land that some of the most brutal clearances took place.

North of the Sutherland's turreted, Germanic home of Dunrobin Castle, we had no option but to join the main road running along the strip of flat land between the rugged hills and the sea. We met Jo at a deserted caravan park in Brora. 'Are we allowed to stay here?'

'Just. It took a little persuasion. Apparently they get the spectrum of John O' Groats to Land's End fundraisers here!'

This is definitely compassion fatigue. If it's not supermarket trolleys or monocycles, then it's pushing peas or crawling. We had arrived in the land of fundraising with a difference, and for the next few days we were regarded with indifference. Although people still stopped us to give donations on the road, it became a less common occurrence here. For us John O' Groats wouldn't even be one third of the way.

My body had readjusted, but I hated walking on the tarmac. The consolation was that I didn't have to worry about my feet, and looked lefthanded to the uninterrupted Highland colours of autumn oranges and russetts of bog grasses smothering the hills, harmonised by expanses of purple heather. Flecking white across the hills were splashes of cotton grass. Drying bracken clogged small gullies, broken up by still green gorse and large grey boulders.

This was Scotland, and in the clear calm day the magnificent hills beckoned. They filled me with renewed inspiration, and wooed me with their calm and serene beauty. But at the top of the Ord of Caithness they threw down their warning, and the mist enveloped the Spudtruck. It was not one of our best lunchtime views.

At Dunbeath the Highlands dissipate and a moonscape of low and lazy hills opens up. Isolated crofts dot the countryside, served by a network of straight tracks and lanes breaking up small fields holding a few stock. In other fields, the harvest was still underway; and three months after seeing the efficient Essex harvest I saw soggy oats being harvested by an antiquated Caithness combine.

That night we parked in a muddy gateway next door to the Hill O' Many Stanes — a fan shaped arrangement of 250 standing stones believed to have been here since 2000BC. A full moon threw out their shadows.

Tess raced off around a nearby field in vast concentric circles. Her unleashed energy matched her level of indignation at having been left in the Spudtruck for two days while I had been on the main road. She pointedly sat by Jo that evening, and then tried to jump out of our elevated letter-box bed to rejoin Jo. I certainly wasn't prepared to relinquish my hot water bottle, but she didn't prove very efficient as a sulky ball at my feet. The next day I had to take her if I wanted her ever to talk to me again.

Meanwhile, fragile Freckle stood behind the curtain with her front paws on the edge of the window, keeping watch for rabbits in the darkness. Her bones rattled audibly. Suddenly the lights from a vehicle fell on the back of the Spudtruck. 'What's that?'

Jo looked behind the curtain. 'It's a vehicle in the field, they're swinging round this way again.' There was a loud shot, followed by another one. 'Shit. They're shooting! Spotlighting!'

'What, spotlighting campervans?!'

A spray of shot hit the Spudtruck several times, as the vehicle disappeared and reappeared at intervals. Something about being found in pyjamas by an irate farmer wielding a shot gun deterred us from going to bed, and we resorted to a game of 'pass the pigs' until I could no longer keep my eyes open. In the light of morning we discovered several more holes in the Spudtruck.

With John O' Groats in sight, and the prospect of two nights in the Thistle Hotel in Wick, twenty miles passed easily along the varied coastline. We cut across gentle hills covered in flowering heather, walked along empty beaches, and passed six castles in one day. Inland the landscape became flat and featureless.

I felt secretly disappointed at the lack of birthday mail waiting for us at the Thistle Hotel, but when we entered our room a tuneful rendition of 'happy birthday' came from within the bathroom. Pops and his girl-friend, Gillie, appeared for the perfect surprise birthday.

As we were on our way out that evening, Tess was befriended in the corridor, and at the lady's request I hastily found a sponsor form. When we returned to the hotel in a hazy state that night I was handed an envelope containing a cheque. I registered £5 — but looked again. I almost dropped the cheque. It said £500! Tess was definitely the most successful fundraiser.

On 1st November, my 26th birthday, we rounded Britain's most north easterly point, Duncansby Head, with its needles of rock piercing through the sea's surface, and reached the small township of John O' Groats. We could go no further northwards. It was like standing on the edge of a void; a chasm of bottomless blueness. Somewhere up there beyond the uncommonly still Pentland Firth and the Orkneys was the Arctic Circle.

A sign by the harbour in John O' Groats pointed south and read 'Land's End 874', and the following day Tess and I set off to walk there via the longest route. I had no idea what mileage we would cover, and had no desire to know. We had so far covered 1,341.1 miles.

CHAPTER SEVEN

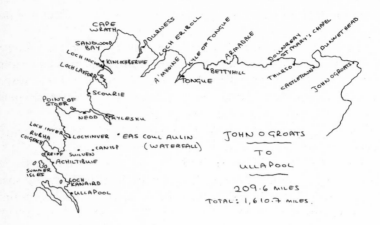

Throughout the nineteenth century, Caithness was the scene of a thriving flagstone industry. The flagstones were shipped all over the world — even the streets of Calcutta were paved with Caithness flagstone. Now the industry has declined, but the flagstones are still evident in 'Caithness hedges', when the stones of varying shapes have been dug into the ground providing solid sheep-proof barriers.

The disused pier that we parked on a mile from Castletown was also built from flagstones; and throughout that dark evening we were interrupted by a series of 'thuds' on the side of the Spudtruck. Caithness flagstones can also be used as ammunition.

It seemed as though everyone was determined to pepper our already leaking home with more holes — this was the funny side. But there was definitely a hint of apprehension in our giggles. 'OK. That's it. Next time!' I said several times with a bravery I didn't feel.

Finally I roused Tess from her slumbers, trying to encourage her to look fierce, and opened the door onto a night so black I thought my eyes were closed. 'Whoever's out there, if you don't stop now we're calling the police,' I said and slammed the door. 'Well, they don't know the phone's not working!'

The threat worked; and the battle weary Spudtruck lived on with only a few more dents to balance up the original ones. But one subsequent newspaper article blew this event out of proportion, and the ambiguous headline read 'Walker Stoned in Scotland.'

The flagstones were stacked upon each other along the low cliffs like piles of pancakes, or lay in dishevelled heaps at the base. Occasional solitary seals vacated rocks when they saw us. They would often join us, parallel to the shore, their beady eyes watching us like submarine periscopes.

Nearing Dounreay power station we came across several old cemeteries nestled in the peat, and solitary St Mary's chapel is overshadowed by an area of MOD land, surrounded by signs warning of radioactivity. Even here old and new stand side by side: and even on this far flung coast the reason for the walk surfaced.

That evening, enveloped in the warmth of our host, John's, house, we talked about the walk, and the conversation progressed as it so often did: 'What made you choose Shelter?'

I had my answer ready. 'Aye. But many of them choose to be on the streets. They don't help themselves,' John replied. How many times had I heard this argument!

'There're people who now know no other life; the old people mainly who've been on the streets for years. But it's the young people who're really up against the vicious circle. If they lose their home they can't get a job, and vice versa. There's no way out. If you're young and single you have no chance. There are an estimated 3 million homeless people, you never hear about most of them, and they certainly don't choose to be there.'

'But I've always worked hard and found a job. Why don't they?'

My mind was wavering with fatigue. No matter how much you believe in something, few arguments can be won when your brain isn't functioning properly. My words sounded slurred. 'People are victims of circumstances beyond their control,' I said, and told him about Steve, the Big Issue vendor in London.

'Steve was made redundant from his job in Glasgow. He travelled to London to look for work and on the train he had all his belongings stolen. He arrived in London with nothing, and no job prospects. That was hardly his fault.'

I battled on, and don't remember going to bed; but the next morning there was an envelope containing a donation from John.

We left behind flat Caithness, and were absorbed by increasingly dramatic hills. At intervals we rejoined the main road to cross rivers, before passing sparklingly clean beaches whose water was turquoise under the winter sun, and branching off to find our own route around headlands.

Tess followed me over the network of peat gullies in an uncertain fashion, and tip-toed over the heather as if expecting something to jump out and say *Boo!*

We were newcomers to the Highlands, and treated them with cautious respect. Like dipping a toe in water to test its temperature, we felt our way across the country.

We slept in Armadale, and set out with an old lady walking her sheep, Dolly, up the road. The air was clear and clean, and there wasn't a sound to be heard. 'Beautiful isn't it?'

The woman was wearing wellies, an old blue skirt, and plenty of woollies to fend off morning chill. Her accent was broad but gentle. 'Where're you off to?' she asked.

Dolly stopped to have a nibble of grass and Tess ignored her. She was, at last, cured. 'I want to follow this track to Poulou-Scaig. There're some ruins marked there.'

'Ach, aye. That's an old settlement. There's no one there now. I haven't been there for years myself. You've got a bonnie day for it!'

Poulou-Scaig consists of the remains of three old dwellings; solid thick dry stone walls which are testament to the skillful building of crofters long since gone. Surrounding these roofless shells are ruined walls which once held sheep, but now the sheep come and go as they please.

We sat alone in the doorway of one ruin, daydreaming in a way that we would frequently over the next month. I built up a picture of the crofters who once survived this harsh existence. In my dreams I acquired such a ruin, and reconstructed their life — the sheep, the lazy beds of tatties, the pack pony to get out, the chickens, perhaps even a still!

After twenty four hilly miles we skirted the still, reflective water of Tongue Bay, and up to our left distinctive Ben Tongue was turned a deep mauve colour by the last hints of daylight. In the morning it was wrapped up in low lying mist.

The mist swirled low over the glass-like surface of the Kyle of Tongue, and A'mhoine, the most rugged of the north coast peninsulas, was not even visible. The first seven miles took us down a dead end road through hamlets with wonderfully unpronounceable names such as Achinahuagh and Libinvulin, where bright red phone boxes add splashes of colour and sheep are the only traffic.

Piles of symmetrically cut peat were stacked between cottages, and peaty smoke rose from the cottages in billowy columns, until its smell dropped to reach us; the delicious smell of Scotland.

At the end of the road Jo joined us along a track to Loch na h-Uamhachd. The mist stayed stubbornly low, and ahead of us lay fifteen miles of rough terrain. Not a single track served the peninsula from the loch, and the contours showed how steep it was. The sea was nowhere in sight.

We bumped into the loch and stopped to discuss the scene. 'Have you got a compass?' Jo asked.

'Mm. But I've only used it once, and that wasn't very successful. This mist might clear though.'

'But then it might not!'

'If I stick to the contours I should be alright.'

'But you can't see the hills!'

'I'll stick to the low ground then!'

I felt invincible, and spurred on by the power beyond my control. This over-rode any rational thought and I decided to go on. I watched Jo and Freckle being swallowed up like apparitions in the mist, then got out my compass and tried to set it to another loch three miles away. But the compass was as confused as I was. The needle flicked around and I turned in circles trying to make head or tail of it. If we walked the way it said I felt sure we would end up in the sea. I put it away and trusted to instinct.

We were in a world where humans have no place, and the physical isolation bore down on me from all sides. Involuntarily I blinked and blinked again, trying to clear the hazy film from my eyes. I didn't let my legs stop; my pace increased, and all the time I watched every incline or decline that we came to, checking them as best I could. Tess stayed close by.

The appropriate black loch appeared, and at Whiten Head we turned south. The mist cleared, and the knowledge that we had just negotiated fifteen miles of mist blanketed hills increased my enjoyment, and the hills rose up through my body, filling me with their wilderness and well being. Herds of stags adorned every horizon, before smelling or sensing us and bounding away, making a mockery of our slow progress. The scale of everything held me in awe as I bounced from one springy sphagnum moss to another, enjoying the sensation of walking on thick foam.

We scrambled around the edge of the last hill and joined a track to take us to the road, where a worried Jo was waiting.

'I'm pleased to see you!'

'The radio's aren't much good among these hills. Have you had a good day?'

While I had walked twenty five miles, Jo had had all day to drive eight miles along an empty road. 'OK,' she sounded depressed. 'The isolation's pretty real. I've seen three cars all day —' Poor Jo. I was pleased that we had each other.

That night my diary read: 'Today has been a bloody hard day and I'm sure if I added up all the heights which I climbed up or down it would be a huge mountain . . . if you keep healthy you can do most things — as long as you are strong mentally and believe in yourself you can achieve your goal.'

We parked for the night in a lay-by on the edge of Loch Erriboll, and I wondered what everyone else was doing that Saturday night. There would be parties, discos, hectic pubs, night clubs, candlelit dinners, flirting, pub brawls, one night stands, cinemas, theatres and raves; but in the Spudtruck the new heater (successfully bartered for a donated industrial one in Inverness!) threw out sufficient heat to make it seem cosy, the poker dice rolled, and the whisky tasted fine.

Outside, the Highlands did their own thing; they slept or hunted in their dark world. The thought of pubs, nightclubs, parties and even candlelit dinners terrified me. I could never have coped with such pretensions. Security was the hills around us, which were including us in their world. I felt privileged to be part of it. No amount of money, fancy goods or wooing could have persuaded me to leave; even when it rained hard in the night and the leaks returned with a vengeance. Resignation set in.

I walked down the middle of the single track A838 to round Loch Erriboll, just to prove its emptiness, watched by a few sheep, some courting seals and the amphitheatre of hills. Nearing Durness the countryside flattens out a little, and the road turns south, leaving us to cross the Kyle of Durness and negotiate Cape Wrath.

Ominous sounding Cape Wrath is the most north westerly point of mainland Britain. It has no road access. In the summer it can be reached via a ferry, but in the winter no such service exists and Cape Wrath is left to the elements — and the army.

The drinkers of the only pub in Durness told us that the following day was safe to round Cape Wrath, and after that the army were bombing for two weeks. We contacted the summer time ferry man, John, and met him on the shore of the Kyle of Durness at first light the next morning.

On the other side we started up the track a little, before stopping to watch the boat becoming a mere speck. The tide was low, and stretching sand banks showed along the edge of the sea loch, as smooth as the flawless surface of the water which was only disturbed by the vague wake of the disappearing boat. How small and fragile I felt.

At the top of the first hill a yellow and black sentry box came into view, and a startled looking soldier emerged. 'You can't go any further,' he blurted. My heart sank at his words. 'They're bombing today, and for the next fortnight.'

'We were told we could. We have to walk Cape Wrath! It's important.'

Tess disappeared into the sentry box, and found an old sandwich wrapper to demolish. 'Well, you've got two options,' the soldier continued. 'Either you go back and try in two weeks — or,' he paused. 'I could run you across on the motorbike when there's a lull in firing.' There was only one option.

'How far does the range stretch?'

'About seven miles.' There wasn't a soldier or tank in sight; and no sound of firing. 'They fire from boats. It's a huge operation. Forces come from all over.'

'When's the next break?' He looked at his watch.

'About two hours.'

At that moment a lot of backfiring preceded a dilapidated bike enveloped in black smoke. 'That's the bike! I'm Wig by the way, and this is Dave.' Dave got off the bike as it stalled to a halt.

After a while the four of us dropped down the hill to Stan's solitary cottage. Professor-like Stan was in his fifties, and for five months of the year he rented this remote cottage, partly to escape his wife (his own words) but mainly to enjoy the seclusion and lifestyle enforced by such a location.

I hated having to wait when I knew that I still had sixteen miles to walk (on top of the seven miles on the back of a bike), and our companions didn't help. 'You're not wise to be completing Cape Wrath in the winter,' Stan said. 'It's a wild place, and very unpredictable. The winds can get up to 100mph with frightening speed.'

The sun was still shining, but I constantly expected to hear the wind rattling the window panes. 'We've seen it pretty wild,' Wig continued. 'Don't be fooled by that sunshine; it can disappear very quickly. When it rains, it rains!'

I was restless and nervous. The sweet tea and butterflies were making my stomach churn, and a quiet peat gully called. 'Perhaps I could just dodge the bombs!' I still couldn't hear anything.

'Actually, you could have insisted on walking if you wanted,' Wig said.

'You didn't tell me that earlier!'

'The entire exercise would have had to stop for you. It would have been a massive task, and cost the tax payer millions!' The thought of this amused me, but not enough to do.

'You're never going to make it before dark,' Stan was persistent in his pessimism.

'I walk four miles an hour. I shouldn't be much more than four hours.'

'The terrain's hard . . .'

The terrain didn't look as tough as it had been on A'mhoine, and I felt I knew my capabilities. This didn't stop me from listening though. 'The worst thing on Cape Wrath is definitely the wind . . .'

On and on they went with their warnings, and eleven o'clock came — and went. The lull in firing was postponed for another hour.

I sat down again, reluctantly. My feet tapped and I looked at my map and rummaged through my rucksack for the umpteenth time. Finally Wig saw my exasperation. 'OK. We'll make a dash for it.' Becoming moving targets was infinitely preferable to listening to horror stories.

At this point, experience of sheepdogs and exceedingly old farm bikes came into use. Wig climbed onto the front, and I hoisted Tess into my arms and climbed on behind him, sandwiching Tess between us. Mouthing a good bye to Dave and Stan, we were off with a back fire and a hiccup.

The track consists of two rutted concrete strips, with a boggy centre of heather; but Wig was undeterred. The bike groaned up hills and took off downhill, all the time emitting deafening back fires. I held tightly on to Tess who, in Wig's words, 'took to the bike like Evil Canevil.'

After seven miles of this bone shaking experience we reached safety, and I watched Wig set off, listening to the retreating bike with its stream of exhaust as it disappeared and reappeared over the hills like a speeded up cartoon film. Before peace had properly resumed I had found my peat gully.

From the cliffs the lighthouse came into view a mile to the north. I was angry to miss the left hand turn it signified, but the words of Wig, Stan and Dave were ringing in my ears. Instead, I took a purposeful left turning on the cliff. We were now heading south.

It felt immediately different because the sun, which was still with us, was hitting us face on. Although I expected to see the sky suddenly black and the wind screeching towards us, the sky remained a pale blue interrupted by harmless clouds. I slowly accepted that the wind wasn't going to live up to its reputation, and our world was once more the Highlands — the heather and bog grasses, the grouse, and the stags which crowned every horizon.

Shortly before reaching Sandwood Bay we passed a small bothy, and I remembered Stan's words; 'A hermit lives there whose criminal record is as long as one's arm. At the top of the list is manslaughter!' It was the first of numerous hermits residences we passed on this west Highland coast.

We didn't linger long, and in front of us, squeezed between two rocky headlands, appeared Sandwood Bay, the most beautiful beach I had so far seen. Beyond the moorland, the planed and strangely blue breakers were crowned with phosphorescence, before erupting in a cotton wool roll of white water, dazzling in the sunshine.

I was overawed and humbled by the power and size of nature here — the waves, the cliffs, the hills and the expanse of untamed wilderness. We were mere specks on the surface; disposable toys to the whims of nature and the elements. Alongside this was the infinite gratitude and satisfaction of reaching this important point. I felt stronger and fitter than I had for a long time. My surroundings filled me with a strength which only the natural world could do. To celebrate we jumped in the squeaky dunes.

The largest fish auction of the week was taking place in Kinlochbervie that night, in a warehouse the size of half a football pitch. The harbour was lit up like a metropolis as the fishermen, many of whom travel from Buckie to fish the west coast, unloaded their catch.

We parked for the night outside the Deep Sea Fisherman's Mission, where showers and washing machines were always available. The fishermen sat around formica topped tables in the cafe, watching Coronation Street with steaming mugs of tea and toasted burgers and chips. They then progressed to the one and only pub to consume their quota of beer before the sea called.

I now had no idea how we would tackle the mass of sea lochs and jagged peninsulas of the west coast, but on day one we spent the whole morning rounding Loch Inchard, which was less than a mile across the mouth.

The walking was hard around the track-less peninsula we then faced, not because of high hills (which would have been easier) but because of the moonscape of endless glacier smoothed rocks, and constantly flowing peat bogs and waterways which give this corner of Sutherland the name Flow Country. It was hard to stick right on the coast, due to the jumble of boulders, some of which are like smooth slides running into the sea, so we moved inland to the higher ground. But this wasn't constant, and we found ourselves in the bottom of peat bogs from where the country looked continually the same. I caught occasional glimpses of the sea, as one might catch brief sight of the horizon from the top of a storm ravaged wave.

The going was made even harder by the bogs which had long since reached winter levels, and as we squelched our way I felt sure that both of us would suffer from mouldy feet. I also wondered whether Harry the farmer had ever actually tried to walk his coastline which he had confidently said was 'nae problem' to follow!

I was exhausted, daunted, soggy and depressed by the end of the day. We had covered twenty miles, but had only rounded one sea loch and one peninsula.

I tried to hide my despondency as we demolished some Kinlochbervie haddock and celebrated 1,000 miles with a bottle of bubbly. Our new driver, HB, hadn't taken a holiday from his London business for a year, and it would not do for him to have to cope with a miserable walker. It was all my mad idea anyway to be parked on a deserted and sloping dead end road in the pouring rain of Scotland's winter.

We at least hoped that the slope would mean that the heavy rain would run off the roof, but this proved to be falsely optimistic. Instead I found myself waking up through the night and pulling myself back to my pillow from a crumpled and damp heap which I was sharing with Tess at the bottom of the bed.

During the day I had Van Morrison as company, but continued to be surprisingly social. Life was cosier here then the north coast; the people happier and very laid back; and their accents gentle compared to Doric!

Every fellow pedestrian stopped to chat. Men spending EC grants on widening stretches of single track road would push back their caps, and settle their legs in a chatting stance when they saw us approach. Some of them had seen us in the local papers, and pontificated slowly, gently, as though trying to comprehend all that walking. As I left them I would feel their eyes on my back, and know that they were still trying to make sense of the whole thing — something which even I had difficulty doing.

Farmers we came across on the small roads which seek out the hidden communities, always stopped their tractors and got out for a chat, barring the road both physically and verbally. Artists in search of Highland inspiration and seclusion joined us for stretches; cars regularly stopped, either to give donations, to offer lifts, or simply to say hello; and the same postman would pass us for several days in succession so that we greeted each other with familiarity until we moved onto the next one's territory.

During another stretch of one-car-an-hour main road a large army truck appeared at my side, and Wig's face peered down. It was with unconcealed pride that I told him how easily we had negotiated Cape

Wrath. I took his address in Poole and he trundled off on his mammoth drive.

On one dead end road a note stuck to the letterbox of a house hidden from view by the hills read 'Spud, come in for coffee if you're passing, Dominic,' and the name Spud had caught my eye in the same way as it does when overheard. I had followed the gravel track inland and come across Dominic the writer and watchmaker, whose existence on his wild spot had made me envious.

The shopkeeper in Scourie was equally chatty, and reiterated the assurance that they all gave, 'No. The snow won't reach us. It never reaches the coast.' Stupidly I believed them.

I walked around the novel shop, which sold everything from birth-day cards to tights to meatballs, nappy pins and desiccated coconut. But it kept its stock low and the shelves resembled a display of raffle prizes. A solitary packet of Jaffa cakes demanded a home and I shared them with the now rather skinny Tess.

With the added enthusiasm of HB, we swerved inland and upwards to visit Britain's highest waterfall — Eas a Chual Aluinn. A bottomless track runs 3 miles from the road to the top of the 670 feet waterfall. Having spent the majority of the last few months on trackless country, the boggy motor-way demonstrated the worst of erosion. Despite being a cold November day we came across the only two walkers we met in Scotland!

The tiny burn disappears over the edge, and you can not even see the waterfall. We sat as if on the edge of the world, looking at the miniscule and uninhabited land below — the absence of a single man made feature stealing any perspective. But the plummeting temperature prevented any enjoyment of the scene, and we raced back in a downpour of rain and sleety snow. I fled to the relative warmth of the coast.

The tiny burns now hit the road in a thunderous burst. The result was deafening, as though we were walking under the lip of Victoria Falls. I walked tunnelled by my hood until a tooting behind heralded the Spudtruck. HB was getting a run up at one of the double arrowed hills (gradient of 1 in 5 and steeper), which we normally tried to avoid (Jo had recently got stuck half way up one), but which now had no alternative. He inched his way up, and thankfully met no one coming the other way.

The other obstacle was petrol. The few garages or shops that we did pass were closed. Sometimes pubs double as fuel pumps, but often the Spudtruck was forced inland in search of fuel — so using more. It was a vicious circle.

I climbed into the Spudtruck at Nedd as though I had just stepped out of a bath with all my clothes on.

I shed my layers and stuffed my wet Scarpa boots with wet newspaper, and removed the wet paper from the others. They hadn't dried out properly, but were no longer squelchy and had still not given me a blister. Thank goodness for Berghaus.

At first I had turned my ignorant nose up at the array of synthetic clothing which Berghaus had recommended and which generated enough electricity to run the Spudtruck for the entire ten months. The t-shirts clung to my skin like cling film; but now they were imperative. They soaked up sweat, but dried quickly, and the thought of going without them now made me cold. I could never have survived the winter without Berghaus.

Contrary to most peoples expectations, I had not found socks a problem. The only ones which had been donated were two pairs of unwearoutable socks, which lived up to their name, but usually the cheapest pair sufficed.

John Merrill, who walked Britain's coast in 1978, wore out a staggering 33 pairs of socks! I was perpetually jealous of this statistic and regularly checked my socks in the hope that there would at least be one hole to show for the miles. But the only holes I had were one where my left toenail had become too long; and the other where a pair had fallen from their storage compartment (which they shared with mugs and glasses) and had landed in front of Tess!

At 7am it was pitch black. 'It must be the middle of the night' was the customary driver response. At 8am the first hint of daylight allowed us to get going.

Tess jumped straight into fifth gear, and had soon set off after two roe deer. Such unleashed energy in the morning was enviable, but then it would be no use letting breakfast escape while your muscles warmed up.

I stuck to the verge, passing randomly placed crofts looking out over the blissfully clean sea. The sea here isn't a sink for waste disposal, because there is little waste to dispose of. It does not serve power stations; nor in fact much tourism. The sea here is left to its own ebb and flow; it can be enjoyed, admired, respected and harvested on a personal and localised scale.

This sea is wilder and less tamed than the abused North Sea; the sea is ubiquitous here. It sneaks into small bays and probes deep into lochs; it scurries round headlands and beats against small islands. The sea was no longer just on our right, but appeared regularly in some form or other all round us. It has a character of its own; it is a free spirit.

We branched off the road and crossed a small sea loch via a narrow bridge. The next thing I knew a new arm of the sea was in front of us, and across Loch Inver the row of Scottish grey terraced houses which comprise Lochinver were majestically framed by the landscape. In the distance, the mountains of Suilven and Canisp rose up above the rest of the hills, topped with daubs of snow like iced buns.

I knew we were getting towards the end of the week because it felt as though I had half a ploughed field on my boots; but the icy ground of shaded woodland made this impossible in practice. There was no track to follow south of Lochinver, and Tess shifted from paw to paw as I looked at the map. She looked at me impatiently; 'Make up your mind then!'

'OK Tessie. We'll cut through this wood.' As soon as I took a step in one direction she was off.

Our route was soon obstructed by gorse, birch trees and boulders. Each haul over a branch was a supreme effort, and for the last leg of the woodland I followed Tess' example and resorted to hands and knees. In this way we popped out from the woodland to be faced by an irate woman waving a tea towel in a matronly way. If I had not felt so weighed down I would have laughed at our situation. 'That dog's not supposed to be here. Don't bring it next time!' she chided.

After one more scramble we rose to the top of a hill and the countryside ahead took on the more regal sweep of gradual hills culminating in escarpments and prominent peaks. Below to our right was the relatively flat and very wet peninsula of Rubha Coigeach.

It seems that each point (or peninsula) has to have two Gaelic names. They are nearly always called Rubha Mor (Big Point) and are frequently given second names. Although the speaking of Gaelic largely declined during the Clearances, there is still a deep rooted loyalty to the language. Every roadsign in the Highlands is written in Gaelic and English, and many primary schools teach solely in Gaelic.

The peninsula would take us six miles around to another dead end road, where I hoped to meet HB. I hardly knew myself on the flat land and in the weak sun, and I drifted into a Highland daydream. After two miles I was disturbed by Tess barking. She had disturbed an otter.

The otter snarled and arched its back at Tess, but sloped away appearing really quite unconcerned. Thoughts of the otter stayed with me for the rest of the afternoon, but I saw no more. As the light began to disappear we cut across the final point and made a beeline for our meeting point.

The Spudtruck was parked among the small cluster of cottages at Reiff. It was 5pm and dark, but there was no sign of life. I found my key and let Tess and myself in, chatting to Tess; 'We'll have a role reversal, and have tea ready for HB!'

The kettle boiled, and I drunk several cups of tea, but there was still no HB. I fed Tess, and did a mound of washing up which HB always wedged into the sink in the hope that it might wash itself as he went along.

After more than an hour had passed and I had run out of things to do, I reluctantly put my boots on and rummaged under the table to find the torch. It looked efficient, but offered a pathetic orange glimmer. I plunged out into the darkness, leaving a bewildered looking Tess.

I stumbled over boulders and through muddy gateways to the end of the track, where I stopped to call. Again there was no reply, and I thought it folly to carry on and get lost myself. I went back to the Spudtruck, imagining that by now HB must be washed off some rock.

I was just approaching the cottage for help when a figure appeared out of the darkness. 'HB?'

'Spuddle!'

'Where have you been?'

'I walked out to find you. I saw some otters!'

He appeared quite unconcerned that I had been worried, and I thought of all the drivers who had been worried when I had been late. The two Jo's, Dee, Charles and probably the rest at some point. We set off to Achiltibuie, where we were being lent a cottage.

My sense of humour, lost with fatigue and worry, started to reappear. 'I did the washing up while worrying about you. I bet that was all a ploy to avoid doing it!'

'You shouldn't have worried.'

'It's not something you can stop yourself doing, as I just found out. If it's you out there, and you know you're alright, then it's easy to presume the other person knows you're ok.'

The crofts in Achiltibuie run in strips from the communally grazed hills down through the individually rented land, usually small scale arable cultivations, to the sea. Crofter's earnings were once boosted by fishing, but this is no longer the case and their farming has become so uneconomic that they survive largely on subsidies.

I am firmly of the belief that this is right. Without crofting in the Highlands, depopulation of these areas would become complete, except for holiday cottages and tourists with their necessary services.

However, in many villages I was shocked at the state of some of the crofts. Fencing hangs in disrepair; rusting corrugated iron and barbed wire litters the land; plastic bags, tins, flaking paint and general rubbish lie scattered. These crofts lie between smartly painted but empty holiday cottages whose lawns are neatly mown and fencing intact to keep out wandering sheep. The juxtaposition is complete — the obscene, empty neatness, and the subsidised shambles!

Also here in Achiltibuie are the affects of the Gulf Stream. This was mid November but I saw shrubs in leaf, and sweet peas and roses in flower. I even found blackberries, and remembered Charles feeding Tess blackberries three months ago in Suffolk.

From Achiltibuie we took the appropriately named Rock Path, squeezed between the densely packed map contours. We were soon scrambling over recently fallen rocks, and being scratched by thick gorse and brambles. Tess' claws scratched the boulders like nails on a blackboard, and I put her on the lead so that if one of us went then we would both go. Rock climbing certainly made a change from walking.

We reached a wild and spacious hill top, and a river valley appeared below. Out in Loch Kanaird there were two toy looking fish farms and around the next small headland was Ullapool — another red pin.

To the south, the rugged arms of the west coast protruded into the sea in a never ending series. At that moment I didn't feel daunted. Each day was another step south, and a reason to be alive and healthy amidst such stunning scenery.

Snowy scenes to come. Tess, William and the Spudtruck.

CHAPTER EIGHT

The West Highland coast is not the place for the clock watching, itiner-ary-minded. Things get done — at their own speed. 'Och, you've got plenty of time. Someone'll take you,' I was assured by one of the drink-ers in the Ferry Boat Inn, Ullapool, while on the hunt for a lift across Loch Broom to Alt na h-Airbhe. I had no doubt that they would take us, but I wondered who. 'Ian'll do it,' they assured me.

'Where do I find him?'

'He'll be here soon — or he'll be here tomorrow.'

The following day, my day off, brought Ian to the pub as predicted; and on the Tuesday morning he took us across the loch. Likewise the tyre which we had been told would be 'ready when it's ready' was, in fact, ready on time.

The west coast idea of time is similar to the Spanish 'mañana' or the Ozzie/Kiwi 'she'll be right till tomorrow mate'. What a fuss they must think visitors make, demanding this and that by deadlines. Things would get done, and so what if they weren't done till tomorrow? But I was focused on my schedule — mañana, or no mañana.

Monday also saw the arrival of Gemma and Nonnie. Gemma, whom I had met twice, had been prised from the pavements of London. She was petit and fragile, had 'London' written all over her, and was very apprehensive. 'My friends in London have given me three days before they think I'll go home!' she laughingly admitted. (She was supposed to be with us for ten days.) Nonnie was a squat and deceptively tough looking Battersea Dogs Home *bitsa*.

A magical sunrise greeted us the next morning. Beneath the first hints of warm red and orange colours from the far off sun, the hills around took on jet black silhouettes, and the loch lay calm and secret. I turned on the Spudtruck lights and cooked up some porridge, while Gemma sat muffled up on the seat opposite looking positively sick.

But, like the fact that I had no option but to keep on walking, once we had left Gemma she had no option but to turn up at the village of Badluachrach, two peninsulas to the south and reached via a long detour inland. A short experiment with the gears had shown that she would be alright as long as she was going in a forward direction.

It was a sunny day and the silence of frost made walking the vehicle free peninsula which separates Loch Broom from Little Loch Broom a time of peace. For the inhabitants of the hamlets of Scoraig and Rhireavach this is the norm. Their inaccessibility makes them naturally self sufficient communities.

The community boat, laden with wood waiting to be unloaded and made into another boat, ran us across Little Loch Broom to Badluarach, from where we scaled another stag-crowned hill, passing endless ditches from where peat has been dug. I crumbled some peat in my hand. It is cold, and tangibly vegetative — the years of decomposed birch trees and heather. It has an infinitely satisfying texture.

I used a handful of yellow sphagnum to wipe the peat off my hands. Its shoots are surprisingly long, but the fibres are densely packed so that from the top it is impossible to know their depth. I was continually fascinated by sphagnum, which has been used for a remarkably wide range of things — from wound dressings during the War to a component of sanitary towels. I used them to clean Tess of her wildlife disguises, or like refreshing towels that they give you on an aeroplane.

The heather was almost over, but the dried flowers of the bell heather clung to their stems making the hills mauve tinted. Flecking white across the hills were individual cotton grasses. This host of life was Scotland — a magical ecosystem stretching for miles in every direction.

We dropped back onto a narrow road, which Tess criss-crossed in front of me, smelling one side and then the other, and using passing places to pass sheep. We passed Gruinard Island, and in the frosty peace I could hear the click of my pedometer as it notched up each precious stride and each precious mile. The repetitive 'click' kept me to my stride, and each stride produced a 'click' — we kept each other going. Ahead of us a buzzard balanced on a telegraph pole, before flying off, heavy yet graceful. We followed the flight of the buzzard onto boggy moorland.

Fourteen miles around Greenstone Point took us four hours; while Gemma drove four miles in a matter of minutes. Yet, like all the other drivers, she had found things to fill her day, and she looked happier when we found her in Aultbea.

My Sundays were now more lonely affairs, and in Midtown, on the shore of Loch Ewe, I witnessed the real religious significance still bestowed on the Sabbath by some remote Presbyterian communities. Entering the village there is a large board for all to see, on which are written several bible excerpts and sayings proclaiming that 'the Sabbath is a day of absolute rest — for men, women, servant and sheep'.

We tip-toed past the sign and the quiet cottages and sleeping sheep, hoping that we would not be found and condemned to a life of fire and brimstone, and turned onto the path which leads to Rubha Reidh through birch woodland and past small mirror-like lochs.

At the end of the headland we climbed higher and higher above the beautiful beach of Camas Mor. From the highest point we faced west towards Lewis, Harris and Uist, while Skye was just visible to the south west. 'Come on then, Tessie', I encouraged. 'Gemma should be down by the lighthouse.'

We scrambled down to the road and Gemma hobbled into view. 'The road was closed to vehicles. I thought I'd better walk down and meet you,' she said.

'Are you alright? Where's the Spudtruck?' Gemma wasn't looking very happy.

'I've got a blister coming, and a sore shin. It's about three miles back to the Spudtruck.'

My stomach was telling me that it was way past lunchtime, having already walked sixteen miles. 'Let's go —' I made a move, but Gemma hesitated, then grinned 'aren't there any taxis round here?' (Taxis, like McDonalds, Chinese takeaways and unfortunately even hot baths were now markedly missing from Gemma's life.) Gemma hobbled back to the Spudtruck — and hung up her walking boots.

In the small village of Badachro the sea was frozen several feet out from the shore, and ice covered the seaweed and rocks. My theory was confirmed — the Gulf Stream is a myth. (Of course, everyone declared that this weather was 'most uncommon'.)

We slithered along the icy road, then took to a path to Lower Diabaig. It had been frozen for a few days now and the sphagnums were solid. The rutted peat tripped me up, and sections of the path were sheet ice which always caught me just as I was gazing off into the distance. Similar to falling off a horse, I was perfecting a way of falling which ensured no pain, and I always had to pick myself up quickly or risk losing my hat to Tess.

North facing slopes and permanently shadowed villages such as Lower Diabaig were frozen to a standstill. The steep hill out of the village warmed me up. But my sweat quickly turned cold, and I shivered from tiredness induced bone numbing cold.

It was another twenty six mile day. Round each bend in the narrow road I expected to catch a glimpse of the Spudtruck. Tess trotted along quietly now, and also looked expectantly around each corner. 'Nearly home Tess —'

Home? Which home?

I frequently told her this at the end of a day, as if encouraging us both. To Tess the Spudtruck was definitely home since it was where she had spent the majority of her short life with me and, despite the apparently unsettling nature of our life, I didn't feel rootless, homeless. The Spudtruck and all it signified was definitely 'home.'

It appeared round the last corner at the top of Loch Torridon. The kettle billowed out steam, there was tea and fruit cake, the heater was on, and the curtains shut. 'Are you alright? You must be exhausted. Sit down,' Gemma mothered and pampered me.

'Poor Gemma. You must think I'm mad!'

'I'm certainly not taking any clothes off when I go to bed tonight!' she declared. By the looks of things she didn't have any more to put on.

We got supper going, and the whisky helped a little. I went outside for a piddle, and this soon froze to become a lethal obstacle for the next arctic foray, since straying too far from the Spudtruck was avoided.

We ate supper wearing hats and gloves, and went to bed. Nonnie was under Gemma's bedding with her two coats on; and Gemma wore the same as she wore before. Tess was under the sheepskin. We were just drifting off when Gemma's muffled voice piped up, 'Spud?'

'Yes Gemma?'

'Perhaps we should set the alarm for 3am.'

'Why?'

'So we can make sure we're still alive!'

I have to admit that I wrote in my diary that night: 'I only hope that we survive the night and are not found as corpses in the morning.'

We did survive, but the next morning the condensation on the wall several inches from my head was frozen. I scraped some off with my nail before warming my hands back up under the duvet. A mug of water on the sideboard was covered in a layer of ice, as was the dog's water. The water on the roof of the Spudtruck remained frozen all that day, and the sea on the edge of Loch Torridon was also frozen.

The air was crisp and clean like immaculately starched sheets. It was so cold to breathe in that it seemed to be tangible in my mouth, like drinking a satisfying but too cold glass of water.

We took to the road, and passed through Shieldaig. I spelt that — S . . h . . i . . e . . l . . d . . a . . i . . g, in time to my strides. I was becoming good at spelling the names of villages because more and more my mind switched to this strange pastime. Ahead of us was Ardheslaig — A . . r . . d . . h . . e . . s . . l . . a . . i . . g. which was a difficult one, but took us a little further.

Applecross peninsula is circumnavigated by a road which was only built in 1976, before which the small villages were only reached by boat. Consequently the quiet road is littered with many ruined houses which are now being slowly re-inhabited.

The graceful forms of countless stags looked down on us from the hills. They were always so incredibly close, and I wondered why stalkers spend so many cold wet hours on their bellies. While I was watching a group, one of the few passing cars stopped to see what I was looking at.

If they hadn't seen me watching the stags they wouldn't have noticed them; and probably hadn't seen any while racing around in the car. I felt closer to nature than ever before, and protective towards my world. I was being accepted by the hills, only if I proved myself against every element.

Tess was also integrating. She now leapt the peat gullies with an enviable ease; and raced flat out across the heather after grouse or deer, no longer afraid of what might say *Boo!*

After three disappointing nights of cold baths, we finally got our hot, if small, bath in Applecross. From here I hoped to walk a high path to Loch Kishorn, and then across country to the road. 'The path you want to take is pretty rough,' Wendy, our hostess, said. 'It'll take you all day from the start of it.' How many times had I heard this warning.

'It's about fourteen miles,' I said. 'We should make it in around four hours.'

'I think that's very optimistic. I know the track.' I knew my capabilities.

Meanwhile Gemma was wondering whether to face the highest road in Britain, or retrace her tracks and make a detour of sixty miles, risking running our of petrol. 'What's the road like?' she asked Wendy.

'Very steep, with hair pin bends. With the ice it will be lethal. At the top it reaches 2,053 feet. It's not recommended for caravans at the best of times.' I left the decision to Gemma, and the next morning she crossed the highest road in Britain on thick ice.

Tess and I covered the fourteen mile track to the shore of Loch Kishorn in our predicted four hours, and had plenty more daylight left. I expected to find Gemma swigging brandy in the Spudtruck, but she was comparatively calm. 'We made it!' she declared. 'It was pretty hair-raising. The road was still icy and we crawled around the hair pin bends.'

Here was the apparently least suited driver tackling the coldest and hardest week; yet it was obvious she was deriving intense, if masochistic, satisfaction from overcoming each worry. Furthermore I was sure the adventure would make a great story back in London!

We swapped stories, and then Tess and I set off through the tiny village of Andarroch. After a mile we approached a van parked on the roadside. Tess realised what it was before I did and bounded ahead to jump up at the counter of the travelling butcher's van. 'And what do you want cheeky!?' the butcher asked Tess, who was fluttering her eyelashes in her most appealing manner. 'Spare bones for a walking dog?'

'Depends how far she's walked!' I told him what we were doing. 'How far do you walk per day?'

'Between twenty and twenty five miles, sometimes more.'

'That's a marathon a day.' I had never thought of it like that.

Tess was getting used to the white vans which indicated either travelling butchers or, more common further south, travelling bakers. We always bought doughnuts from the latter, who sell the proper doughnuts rather than the cheapskate variety which have a hole instead of a puddle of jam. I never licked the sugar off my lips until the whole doughnut had been eaten, for good luck, but never quite managed to teach Tess this superstition.

With Tess' nose glued to the donated bone at the base of my rucksack, we negotiated the final miles through spooky pine forests and reached Lochcarron in the dark.

Lochcarron has the absurd title of being the longest village in Britain, but all we were concerned with was the Kyle Hotel — the first pub we had seen for several days. We were drawn to the bar like weary desert travellers, feeling the companionship of people who have come through an ordeal together. Gemma's week was almost at an end. Her boyfriend was coming up the next day, and was generously putting us up in a hotel in Kyle of Lochalsh.

While we were drinking I made my usual donations plea to the manager. She gave us an option; 'Either you can have dinner, bed and breakfast here; or £50 donation for Shelter.'

Gemma's eyes lit up, and she looked expectantly at me. I am afraid I disappointed her. In my view there as no choice, and we took the donation. 'Well, we've got a night of luxury tomorrow, and then you're going home anyway.'

We left the pub feeling lightheaded, and found an empty lay-by where we stayed up chatting until midnight. 'I'm pleased that we stayed in the Spudtruck tonight,' Gemma confessed during the evening. Despite leaks, ice, mould, and the various smells of dog, cooking, Tess' farts and bodies there was definitely something cosy about the Spudtruck.

In the morning, down at the fish farm on the shore of Loch Carron, I approached a likely looking guy, who said he would take us across Loch Carron. He handed me an oversized orange rubber jumpsuit. 'If you fall into the water you won't last long without one of these.' There was no sign of a similar doggy suit.

The orange and yellow suited men began loading up the small boats with sacks of vicious pink fish food. 'We feed them all by hand. That way we can control how much they're eating, and generally keep an eye on them,' my friend explained as we climbed into the boat as the daylight got stronger. 'Who owns this farm?'

'Marine Harvest. This is one of a number that they own in Scotland.'

'We've seen so many fish farms down the coast. Almost every loch seems to have one.'

My friend gave a wry smile as we motored slowly out onto the calm loch. 'It certainly employs a lot of people. But I don't know for how much longer. The trouble is Norway.' I had heard this before. 'We can't compete with them. They get subsidies, and we get nothing. It's the small farms which are really suffering.'

On a gorgeous morning the work looked pleasant, but it is not a job for those who suffer sea sickness. My friend went on; 'We get a lot of storms, and lose a good many salmon and cages. Would you like to have a look around the farm?' I jumped at the opportunity.

We steered towards one of the thirty cages where the salmon were leaping in a boiling mass of fish, a feeding frenzy. On the edge of the cage was a small platform just wide enough for human feet. One of the men was standing on this, balancing a bag of fish food and throwing scoopfuls of food out into the cauldron of fish. We tied our boat onto the platform.

I got to my unseaworthy legs and manoeuvred Tess and myself onto the slippery platform, beneath which the water lapped at the soles of my boots. I was now holding Tess up so that her front legs were on the top rail of the cage. Her ears pricked up at the seething life before her. One of us was surely going to end up in the water.

The pellets of food continued to hit the water like a downpour of hail. 'How many fish are there in here?'

'About thirteen thousand. There are about 400,000 in this loch.'

'How on earth do you deal with them?'

'We've got a large vacuum which sucks them up, enabling us to transfer them from cage to cage. Putting them through the vacuum helps remove the sea lice too.'

He showed me a fish which had sea lice. They pick them up from wild salmon, and normally they are removed with chemicals. Here was a token piece of organic salmon farming.

'We move the cages periodically to stop the seabed becoming stale,' our friend continued. 'We use the vacuum for that too. The biggest predators are seals, but there's not much you can do about them.'

(One salmon farmer found a solution. He produced a lifesize fibreglass killer whale which is suspended amongst the cages and is effectively keeping the seals away!)

The scale of fish farming in Scotland was more than I had ever imagined. Although I can't help thinking it is unnatural to keep these normally migratory fish in such conditions, similar to battery chickens or intensive pig rearing, without salmon farming the Highland economy would suffer even more than it has already. To many small communities fish farming has been a saving grace.

Tess launched herself back into the boat with a better knowledge of salmon farming, and we were dropped at Stromeferry, which was under permafrost. From here we followed a railway line which I had learnt was used by two trains per day. At Plockton we returned to small roads to Kyle of Lochalsh.

By mid afternoon Tess looked miserable. She trotted along dejectedly, disinterested in her surroundings and in sticks I offered her. I even offered her a precious glove, which were normally irresistible, but she looked at me with a certain amount of hatred. I stopped to give her a cuddle. 'I'm sorry Tess, but we have to walk along the road. There's no other way.' I knew she was hating the road, not because it hurt her pads, but because she had simply decided she would rather be elsewhere.

I tried to stay permanently cheerful to make things easier, and when I was down I hid it. Dogs do as they please — and Tess was depressed. She looked skinny, weak and fed-up, and nothing like the enthusiastic dog who had watched salmon that morning. I was determined to make it up to her.

In Kyle of Lochalsh I tied the resigned Tess up outside a shop and bought her a roast chicken. But when she smelt the chicken she looked at me saying 'I know that's for you, so don't tease me!'

I cooked her rice and chicken which made my stomach rumble, and she wolfed it down with more enthusiasm then she had recently had for food. 'You'd better not think you're going to get this every night!'

But Tess' mood had got to me. I felt intensely lonely and homesick in a way I felt when I first went to boarding school. Everything was a million miles away; I craved familiarity. I wanted to go to a party; to talk about normal things; to put on clean smelling clothes; to stop lugging bags and dog's bedding in and out of people's homes and hotels. My mood was highlighted by the fact that Gemma would be returning to her life which was familiar and comforting to her — even if she didn't always notice that it was. The things I missed were the things that for years I had taken for granted.

When Tigger arrived that evening, the whole hotel knew about it. 'Spuddiieee!' he called out in a loud and very English accent, and threw his arms round me in a wave of beery smells. He had been at a rugby match all day and was suitably well oiled, but it was good to see him. Tigger was an old friend and a familiar face.

Another pint topped up Tigger's flagging beer level, and he strode around the bar with great strides, his brogues clipping the floor in a noisy fashion. After only ten minutes he had badgered some of the locals into giving donations, and was even more self congratulatory. After the gentle people we had been meeting he was so hyperactive, and I wondered how I was going to cope with irrepressible Tigger after conscientious Gemma.

As the evening progressed, Tigger wanted to party as he might in London. 'Stay and talk to me. Let's have a drink. Don't go to bed,' he slurred.

'I have to Tigger. I can't bear walking when I'm tired, jaded and overhung.'

'Don't be so boring.!'

Tigger lit an umpteenth silk cut and ran his hands through his hair in a cool way. He lurched around, bombarding me with peer pressure and teasing me for being so sensible. I was tired and sensitive and his teasing hit a raw nerve. I stayed up to convince us both that I wasn't becoming boring and 'fuddy duddy' — but perhaps I was?

Was the whole experience changing me? Would I ever return to a less regimented as well as more sedentary life? Was I now very boring? And would I ever regain contact with those friends I never talked to?

I went to bed and woke up feeling terrible. Ahead were twenty long miles of road walking. I stewed over how boring I was; then dreamt of my bed, and remembered a time when I was lambing and had been so tired that I slept scrunched up on a single bale. I was that tired I could have slept anywhere, and now I closed my eyes as my legs carried me. I was just nearing sleep walking when the tooting of a car woke me up.

We met Tigger as the full moon rose over the Five Sisters of Kintail. He had lost some of his tiggerishness and we talked about how boring I had become. 'Of course the walk's bound to rule your life for now,' Tigger reassured.

'I just know if I don't stick to the routine everything will fall apart —' I tried.

'I appreciate that.'

'I can't just not walk one day because I don't feel like it.'

'Spuddiee! Relax!' Tigger put his arms round me; but I wasn't convinced.

Tigger was so confident with people and himself; he could cope with any situation. I was feeling less and less like that and felt more and more at home in the hills. I loved their peace and lack of pretensions.

The next day we walked down the other side of Loch Duich, looking across to Eilean Donnan Castle perched out on its almost-island hillock of rock, before plunging into a dense coniferous forest. The path was steep and my hamstrings tweaked in a now familiar way. I just accepted that they did this, and could see no way of avoiding it. Tess chased several forms of wildlife hidden by the trees, but returned on her own. The risks I had taken in leaving her to find me had been worth it.

The forest took us to Glenelg, and we spent the remainder of the afternoon on the road, passing Sandaig, Gavin Maxwell's home where he lived with the otters and wrote *Ring of Bright Water*. As we scurried on towards Corran, the weather deteriorated completely.

The wind became so strong that every step felt like twenty, making me put my head down and so putting pressure on my back. As I staggered into the torrent, the only vehicle we had seen for the last few miles stopped alongside us. The farmer wound down his window just enough to speak, and letting in as little rain as possible, and said 'Jump on the back,' taking it for granted I would. Tess looked wistfully up at the man and the rain stung my face.

It was almost dark, and as the blue truck with its bemused driver disappeared into the deluge, I thought how easy it would have been to jump on the back. Easy but impossible. We were offered more lifts on such quiet Scottish roads than anywhere else.

Corran consists of about four houses, and the nearest village is Glenelg, twelve miles away. After that it is ten miles to Shiel Bridge, over a road frequently cut off by snow, and then twenty further miles to Kyle of Lochalsh. It is another world.

The Spudtruck was parked next door to Billy's caravan. I had spoken to Billy the previous night, and he had organised for the fish farm to ferry us across Loch Hourn to Knoydart, which is only accessible by boat, or on foot (which involves camping). We would be dropped in the middle of nowhere and would have to spend a night in Inverie.

Billy came into the Spudtruck for a dram. He was in his thirties and had piercing blue eyes which would have melted even the coldest of hearts as he sat across the table from me. Tess snuggled up to him, while Tigger bounded around the Spudtruck as if he had all the space in the world.

Billy was originally from Corran and had returned after several years working away. He talked about the scene which greeted him: 'There just isn't any accommodation here now. The houses are priced right out of the reach of the locals.'

I had passed empty holiday cottages on an almost daily basis. 'What about jobs?'

'The only thing is fish farming, but many of those jobs are taken by incomers.'

'What do you do?'

'Any part time work I can. I make ends meet, but I really want to stay here. I'd like to get my own place.'

Even amongst the hills and glens of Scotland there is no escaping the social problems usually more evident in urban areas. Yet the people here retain a cheerfulness which is humbling, certainly to me. I feel sure that the strength I derived from the hills plays a large part in the way the locals tackle everything with such cheerful equanimity.

In the eerie morning light we came across the now familiar sight of the men preparing to feed the fish. Tess had her usual breakfast of pink salmon feed, and I donned the rubber suit and boarded the boat. 'We'll see you in Mallaig tomorrow. And go steady in the Spudtruck!' I told Tigger.

Tigger drove the Spudtruck as you might a Porsche, flicking it in and out of gears and belting around corners before slamming on the old brakes – riding a cart horse as you might a Derby winner. He now faced a monumental drive via Fort William to Mallaig, but had twenty four hours to do this.

The boat left us like castaways on an island. The weak sun had come out, and the dried heather, bog myrtle and bracken turned the hills a brilliant orange colour. The walking was easy along the flat land of the coast.

It was a magical day of peace, and when we joined the road the narrow stretch of tarmac weaved over the hills ahead of us, breaking up the orange colour as if it had been rolled out onto the surface of the land. Not a car disturbed us and I felt like Dorothy; 'We're off to see The Wizard, the wonderful Wizard of Oz, because because because, because . . . because of the wonderful things he does!' Toto the dog weaved from one side of the road to another, and I even managed a shuffled Dorothy-type skip.

We stopped to eat our sandwiches on a pile of timber, and when they had been demolished Tess retired to a nearby metal container where she sat like a child in a Wendy house. Lunches away from the Spudtruck were cold affairs, but had often been unavoidable over the last six weeks. Usually we ate as we walked, and often the rain made the sandwiches soggy before we had eaten them. But food was food.

Little did I know that our stay in glorious Inverie would be memorable for its culinary delights! The small Pier House Guest House, situated in the middle of the single line of houses which make up Inverie, put us up for the night, and flatly refused money for either the accommodation or the melt-in-the-mouth dinner of superbly fresh langoustine. I sat on my own, unselfconsciously extracting every morsel: while Tess was in my room suffering the consequences of too much fish food breakfast — her stomach had swelled like fully inflated bag pipes. It was a rackety night.

In the morning we caught the estate boat to Mallaig, where the fishermen were mending their nets on the quayside. The engines of several boats were running and crew were filling up their ice containers and reloading nets. While I was watching one boat below me, I noticed a dog on it. It was Tess! She had jumped down onto the boat at the high bow, and run along the deck. She looked up saying 'aren't we going on this one now?' I could imagine the boat setting off with Tess in her normal figurehead position, bound for the open seas and a week of fishing.

As we walked south, the rain became more persistent and the landscape changed from low headlands breaking up the white beaches of Arisaig, to being more rugged again. The burns were rising at an alarming rate in the sudden deluge, and white water made gashes in the hillsides, breaking up the sodden vegetation in its winter colours. The noise from even small and seemingly far away burns filled the air, giving the deceptive impression of wide and powerful rivers.

This landscape, its vegetation, rivers, burns and lochs, rely on the notorious Scottish rain. To be part of this landscape during a downpour, and to bear witness to the sheer volume of water around you, is an experience not to be missed. A long time ago I was told that white water emulates negative ions which are therapeutic for your mind and inner self. In contrast positive ions (given off by pollution) aggravate the spirit causing impatience and aggression.

Why else do waterfalls have such a magnetic appeal, yet we aren't affected by their deafening noise? And why is it that for centuries bards have written by the shores of foaming rivers and waterfalls? Could it be possible that the laid back nature of the west coasters is a result of the abundance of negative ions in their environment?

We walked through these downpours on the main road, passed by little traffic. By 2pm it felt dark, and by 3.30pm there was no daylight left. We rounded Loch Ailort with our heads down and Christy More playing, and on the south shore of the Sound of Arisaig we arrived in Glenuig in torrential rain. And so now we have come full circle.

Ahead of us rises Glenuig hill and to replenish our energy we enter the green tin shack. As I stand dripping water, eating my chocolate bar and chatting to the proprietor, I have no idea that in exactly one year's time this will be my local shop, where Tess helps herself to carrots from the box on the floor. Across the road the whitewashed pub will be our mail delivery point, where the first rejection letter arrives; and where many a session will be had and tunes enjoyed. And that out on the small headland is an ideally simple cottage, served by no road and no electricity, but with stunning views over the islands of Rhum and Eigg and the Arisaig Peninsula. And here I scribble with pen and paper, pausing occasionally to peer through binoculars at seals, porpoise and sometimes otters out to sea. Perhaps if I had known all this I would have ground to a halt.

CHAPTER NINE

The single track road along the edge of Loch Sunart is definitely not designed for campervans, especially with inadequate windscreen wipers on a night which saw a good deal of this area's 140 inch annual rainfall. The back of the Spudtruck rolled from side to side, making the pots and pans waltz in their various compartments.

'The plates have a tendency to fly out,' I told Steve, who I had just picked up from Fort William. 'Though amazingly we haven't smashed one yet.'

'Have you had much trouble with the Spudtruck?'

'Not mechanically.'

No sooner were the words out then the Spudtruck ground to a halt on a small hill. We gave the old girl several rests, and sat in the gloom talking of nothing in particular. Finally she restarted — reluctantly, and after a bit we regained momentum. The plates continued their dance, and on one particularly vicious corner they shot out — and one smashed. None of this was proving to be a very good omen.

From Kinlochmoidart we climbed a hill through woodland in the dreary dampness of morning, disturbing the first two deer of the day. The road was winding and felt softer underfoot then the previous day's walking along double track road. We weaved left, then right and up and down; passing grey bungalows, Highland cattle in barely fenced fields, a family of ducks, and sheep taking breakfast from the wide verges.

Each bend in the road brought something different, until we branched off to find a path along the north coast of Ardnamurchan Peninsula, and a lovely signpost reading 'Ockle, up the brae' assured me we were heading in the right direction. We continued up the brae through boulder strewn landscape, and, except for the fact that it was the start of another stretch of tarmac, we would have been forgiven for not noticing we had arrived in Ockle.

These hamlets on Ardnamurchan are some of the most isolated in Scotland. Despite the fact that they are serviced by a road (of sorts), it is twenty miles to the main road, where you might find a garage or small shop, and more than the same distance again to any sizeable place. Ardnamurchan feels much more isolated then even Knoydart.

Passing some of the cleanest and whitest beaches in Britain, we reached Ardnamurchan lighthouse, where the sea roaring around the base of the rocks was justifying the name 'Ardnamurchan' which translates as Point of the Ocean. It is Britain's most westerly point, reaching out twenty miles further than Land's End.

That night we were virtually blown off a lay-by overlooking Macleans Nose, and the next morning things continued to deteriorate. I walked alone along a lane which clings to the edge of Loch Sunart. Flanking me on each side were naked oaks, among which mosses took in more water than they could hold. The rain water dripped from every branch and every leaf. I walked through the puddles, which I always imagined offered some cushioning to my feet — I wasn't going to get any wetter by doing so.

I got bored of the oaks, the mosses and the shiny holly bushes. At least if they hadn't been there I would have been able to see something else, anything but the monotonous tarmac and the continual stream of water pouring from the edge of my hood. There were no deer, no birds, no Tess — and barely a glimpse of the water. My feet seemed to be detached from me, they looked like someone else's at the bottom of my legs. I wished they were.

At lunchtime we parked beside a public phone box and I took my mug of soup into the phone, wondering why Steve couldn't have made the phone calls. The people I needed to call were never there, and I was sick of standing in draughty red boxes. We were trying to contact Johnny, a journalist from the Big Issue magazine in Edinburgh, who was joining us for a day. I left a soggy message. I hated answer phones.

My speed picked up and by 3pm I had completed the twenty miles, and we were in Strontian — which is not the place to be on a wet December day. Steve had BORED written all over his face, and I felt absurdly responsible. He was an old friend who had been dragged from a warm office in Bristol, and the wet Highlands clearly weren't suiting him. 'Right Steve, let's cheer this place up!' I said, as I hung up my wet clothes, stuffed my wet boots with wet paper, and went next door to the only glimmer of life — the village shop.

Chocolate hobnobs declared 'buy me', and near the counter there was tinsel, streamers, false snow and Father Christmas baubles. I took back my cynicism of Fort William, where the tired false snow had been ridiculously offset by the very real beauty of the snowy Highlands, and bought some of each.

I thought the Spudtruck looked just fine with its new festive air, but Steve didn't look so convinced. 'What's wrong Steve?'

'Nothing.'

'I'm sorry about the weather.'

'It's hardly your fault.' I still felt responsible.

Steve still had 'bored and pissed off' written all over his face the next morning. I hated seeing him like this, but there wasn't a great deal I could do, as Tess and I set off along the south shore of Loch Sunart. It was raining — again.

We passed Laudale House, and passed a salmon farm which was the last sign of civilisation. A forestry commission track took us on, and Tess was soon hunting among the dense trees. After a while I called her back, and saw there was blood on her leg. The blood then began to pour from a deep gash.

I bandaged the cut with medications which had been at the bottom of my rucksack since Tower Bridge, but knew that she needed stitches. We turned round to retrace our tracks to the fish farm, and Tess limped behind me in the rain, stopping occasionally and lifting up her leg. 'I'm sorry Tess, but you're too heavy!' I chatted to her. I was beginning to think she might have damaged the bone.

A guy from the fish farm gave us a lift to the road. 'Where's the nearest vet?' I asked.

'Fort William. But there might be someone round here who can stitch. We'll stop at our other fish farm. Someone there'll know.'

At the other fish farm the lads gathered around the wounded dog, who dropped her head and lifted her eyes in a look of complete self pity, which worked on me. The lads were not taking things as seriously. 'I could have a go with a needle and thread,' one piped up, and they all laughed. 'Aye. If we could find a needle and cotton I'd have a go too!'

They all laughed again, and I joined them to be polite. 'Perhaps a knife would be better. I know someone who's good with a knife!'

'Aye, I think there's no hope for her!' Ha ha ha ha.

I thanked them all for their kind offers, and ascertained that it would be quicker to go to Mull, via the ferry at Lochaline. 'You couldn't just give us a ride over the top of the main road could you? We should find our home up there — somewhere. If not . . .' I trailed off. If not we'd walk or hitch or swim or something.

The road was being progressively covered in a thin layer of snow. The wheel marks from a previous car were being obliterated by the minute. The sky was white, the hills were white, the road was white, and the Spudtruck was white, but again its orange footprints stood out. Steve saw us at the last moment.

I carried Tess into the cold Spudtruck, letting snow in at the same time, and told Steve we were off to Mull. 'What about Johnny?'

I had forgotten about Johnny, the Big Issue journalist. All I cared about was getting Tess to the vet and I couldn't have cared less if we never saw Johnny. 'He'll find us.'

'I'll stay here and wait for him.'

'What? In the snow? In the middle of nowhere?'

I had just presumed that Steve would come with us. I had no idea if we would even be able to get back that day, but I remembered that we were staying with people. 'You can always go to the house.'

We left Steve, a forlorn figure on a white and empty road some height above sea level, and set off loudly thanking him for the lack of support. Tess' leg was priority, and nothing else mattered; but without noticing I had followed Steve's example and had refrained from communicating. Instead of asking him to come with me I expected him to offer, then cursed him when he didn't.

I hoped to find the vet at the end of a dead end road on the way to Tobermory. My directions had been about as vague as that, and the road I found was certainly dead. I parked the Spudtruck outside the last house and waited for the vet to return, thinking that the isolation I had so often enjoyed was now against me. I jumped from the driver's seat to the back of the Spudtruck to check on Tess periodically; I put music on, but turned it off. I was wallowing in my loneliness, and I could not have felt more alone.

I had a dog in shock who might have really damaged her leg; a silent driver who was probably getting hypothermia; I had seen no sign of life on the whole of Mull; there was snow on all the roads; and if we disap-

peared no one would know where we were. I felt close to tears. Tears of
loneliness and tears of frustration. I wished I was a vet; I wished I had
called Tess back sooner; I wished I had any of the other drivers with me;
and I wished I was at home.

I thought of the phone, which hadn't worked for the past six weeks,
and in an attempt to find some sort of human contact I turned it on. By
some quirk of science it worked, (the only time it did on the entire
north west coast). I dialled through to home, realising that the chance of
finding Pops there was pretty slim. He was. Someone was looking after
us, even if it was sometimes at the last possible moment.

Four hours after Tess cut herself, the vet stitched her up. The cut
was clean and there was no other damage. 'The stitches should be in for
two weeks,' the vet said. 'She should have a week off walking.' He packed
us off with antibiotics, refusing any money.

Back on the ferry I brewed up some tea, and was disturbed by a face
at the window. Reluctantly I wound the window down and let the cold
air in. 'Hi! I'm Johnny!'

'Oh, come in!' I let him in through the side door.

'How's Tess?'

'How did you hear?'

'The lady at the kiosk in Lochaline told me.'

Johnny sat in the passenger seat and we drunk tea and ate brownies
as the ferry took us back to Lochaline, where the snow had turned to
ice. I felt that I now had Johnny as well as Tess and Steve to look after,
when we turned up at our host's in the dark. I wasn't sure what Steve
had done all day, but wished that he would say something, express some
sort of emotion, rather than just silence.

Our hosts warned me that the middle section of the nine mile path
running over the hill from Lochaline no longer existed. 'Take care,'
they told me, as I set off in my usual 'I'm invincible' frame of mind.

As the path climbed higher, the snow started again and began to
camouflage the path in its white sameness. I dug out my compass, which
I had managed to use more successfully since the north coast, and set it
to a distinctive long and skinny loch.

I was soon in the middle of a snow storm, and the path disappeared
completely. I couldn't make out any hills; the sky merged with the land
a matter of yards from where I walked, and the snow settled on my
hood, arms and boots. I kicked through the snow and caught flakes in
my mouth. A deafeningly silent white blanket had been thrown over
the hills. I had never been skiing, but supposed I was in the midst of

what I had heard called a 'white out'. I was relying entirely on that compass needle.

I reached a loch and felt pleased with myself. As I began to walk along the shore of it I realised that it was not long and skinny and there was an island on it. It was not the right loch. My mind went blank — for a brief moment I had no idea where I was. Was this a dream? Was I in New Zealand? Where was Tess? It was an instantaneous thing, a matter of seconds which I suppose was sheer panic, during which the white blanket closed in more.

I stopped and took a deep breath. Under normal circumstances I would have reassured myself with the sound of my own voice, but now I was silent. Over to my right I made out outlines of hills which shouldn't be there, but they disappeared again. Perhaps they should be there? Between where I thought I was, and where the right loch should be, was a slight hill; but not such a tall hill as that!

I pushed everything from my mind except for the direction which I was going to have to trust. If it proved wrong then I would start again, but then I wouldn't know where I was again?! I set off to the other side of the loch and climbed a hill which I couldn't see the top of. I might climb and climb and climb and never reach the top. It might be like one of those bad dreams when you fall and fall and fall and never reach the bottom.

I thought of all this. Things went through my mind in a matter of seconds. I thought of Ranulph Fiennes, who I have always admired, and who now gained even more of my respect. I wondered how you made snow caves. I wondered how long I would survive up here. I wondered what I would do when I realised that I was really lost. Would I keep walking, somewhere? Would I stop? Would anyone find me? Would Tess sniff me out?!

The hill reached a summit and I started blindly down the other side, stumbling on uneven ground beneath the snow. Out of the whiteness appeared a loch. It was long and skinny and very clearly the one I had missed.

A glen opened up in front, and I descended to the edge of the suffocating white blanket; the white monster which had spat me out in disgust. I wished I would never find myself in that situation again. My voice sounded hoarse and the air I took in was cold — it was as though I had forgotten to breath during my panic.

We parked for the night on the edge of Loch Linnhe. Everything in the Spudtruck was wet: Sweatshirts hung from every available place; the shower was full of dripping socks and rank smelling clothes; the wallpaper expelled water when pressed; the cupboards had warped and were home to sprouting vegetables, confused by the damp and dark conditions; the cushions we sat on were wet, and we spread anything dry on them before sitting down. Only the tinsel was unconcerned by the damp.

But Steve seemed happier, as he sat hunched on the seat, his glasses misty with condensation. 'What was wrong?' I asked.

'Nothing.'

I dropped the subject, and we laughed a supported the whisky industry again. But I felt exhausted. I was certainly relying on the drivers for more than just getting the Spudtruck from A to B.

Immediately across Loch Linnhe was our destination the next day. It rained again and my clothes hadn't dried for five days. I felt like a sponge which had reached saturation point. Under my layers I couldn't even feel my pedometer, as I walked another twenty miles; then another twenty miles. It rained again.

The only difference with the second twenty miles was that I was on the south side of Loch Linnhe, and the road was busy. Trucks and cars sprayed me with filthy water. I was busy spelling the names of places; B . . a . . l . . l . . a . . c . . h . . u . . l . . i . . s . . h.

I counted the rain drops as they dripped off my hood. I counted the cars. I put on my favourite tape — a mixture of walking songs which a friend had made up: The words of the Proclaimers *'I would walk 500 Miles'* were appropriate, and I liked *'Take a walk on the wild side'*. At the end of the tape was *'The long and winding road.'* Occasionally I stopped to rearrange the tongue of my right boot which was slipping round and rubbing the now swollen ankle bone. In this way I walked to the bridge over Loch Etive, where I was brought out of my wet world of self pity.

I caught up with a slight and hunched figure walking in the same direction as me. She had a pink bundle thrown over her shoulder, and wore well worn light blue tracksuit bottoms spattered in puddle water, an old knee length coat, and an Oxfam woolly hat. On her feet were a pair of tatty gym shoes. Her name is Margaret and she is seventy.

I carried her weightless blanket bundle for her, and we tried to walk together, but the bridge was narrow and we walked awkwardly, continually splashed by the stream of traffic. 'Where are you off to?'

'Towards Oban. I've been to see my sister-in-law back there, but she's no good. She drinks a lot.' Her accent was really thick.

'Where do you sleep?'

'Under bridges, on benches or in empty sheds — anywhere really.'

Her face was sad and red, and her skin and lips very dry. 'How long have you slept out?'

'Three months. My husband died and I was forced out of the house.'

'Do you have any other family?'

'A sister and a brother. I don't see them. They don't know my situation.'

Her purposeless steps were painfully slow, but we came to the end of the bridge and walked to a junction where I was turning left. I took one of Margaret's hands, which were crooked and frail with nails worn down to the quick. It was like holding a sculptured piece of ice. I gave her five pounds and my gloves. 'They're a bit wet but tuck them into your trousers and they'll warm up.' This was a trick I had learnt.

Margaret's eyes were watery from the cold, and she took my hands in her now gloved hands. 'Look after yourself.' I said.

'When will you come back?'

'I don't live round here.'

'But you'll come back one day. Won't you?'

'It's a long way —'

'But you'll come back?'

'I'll try.'

I gave her her bundle and watched as her small frame set off inland. I couldn't imagine sleeping out that night; I couldn't imagine sleeping out any night in Scotland. I vowed never to complain about the Spudtruck again. I vowed never to complain about anything again.

Relief appeared from dark Oban station that night in the form of a tall rucksack, an oversized hat, and a small black dog resembling a shadow. Ruth materialised from under the rucksack and hat, and Stobbie, a hardy looking Battersea Dogs Home *bitsa*, was the one on the lead.

Between us we manhandled the rucksack into the Spudtruck and Stobbie sniffed around our home 'I hope he doesn't get cold and need a coat,' I said. Ruth laughed, and Stobbie looked indignant. Two days later he was sporting the local pet shop best.

Being Scottish, I presumed that Ruth would want a whisky. 'I'd better tell you that I'm pregnant!' she said cheerily. Ruth always has a smile just waiting round the corner from her face. 'Or do you think it will be good for the baby?' We decided that, following good Highland tradition, it would be medicinal in moderation.

I felt that I had been sapped of energy over the last week — not just physically but mentally too; as if a vacuum had drawn every ounce from me. I now dropped everything onto Ruth's lap, and she caught it.

The jagged edge of the coast south of Oban took us north as well as south. At times we had to resort to the main road, and south of Ardfern the coast is impassable due to dense forest and rugged hills, so I kept inland and passed through an area thick with standing stones, burial chambers, cairns and forts of Celtic origin. These culminate at the central Dunadd Fort which was the focal point of the Tolkein sounding kingdom of Dalriada.

From here the country becomes flat, and my hamstrings rejoiced. I walked lonely straight roads and missed Tess greatly. It felt pointless to walk without a dog — like driving a car with no destination, or shopping with no money; but she had had her week off and she joined me from Crinan. Ahead of us was seventeen miles of road which would eventually peter out.

At first the road was sheltered by forestry, but then it opened out and the wind and rain came at us face on. 'It's raining it's pouring the old man —' I sung, and watched Tess' ears as they reacted to the changing tones. I then sung carols, shouting silently as the wind whipped away my words. Unlike when I played carols on my penny whistle, Tess didn't join in.

'Rain rain go to Spain and come back another day — another day when I'm tucked up in bed somewhere.' My hips ached, my knees ached and my feet moaned about the concrete. There wasn't even the consolatory view; just wind and rain.

We passed scattered cottages and I looked enviously through their windows to open fires, Christmas trees, fairy lights, Christmas cards and baubles. I felt like a voyeur from my own wet and grey world.

I listened to Gregorian Chants which were the closest thing I had to Christmas music. I kept postponing my sandwiches, telling myself to reach one more landmark, then one more. When I did find them, they became soggy before I could eat them, as did the ginger cake. 'What the hell, it all gets soggy in our stomachs anyway!' Tess didn't care what condition they were in, and I tried to eat the cake without her noticing so that I didn't have to share it, but she was too astute for that trick.

At Kilmory we rounded the corner and started north to Achahoish with the wind and rain on our backs. With three miles to go the rain stopped, and we walked along a track boarded by rhododendron bushes which smelt of fertile vegetation; the leaves were shiny and clean. I pushed my hood off and gulped the clear air. There was a sky after all! I took off Tess' coat and my leggings and hung them to dry on the back of my rucksack.

We went to bed at eight thirty that night, accompanied by the smell of something Stobbie had rolled in, and woke to the sound of rain and wind — again. I turned over, and wished I was on a desert island.

My throat hurt and my limbs were achey with a fluey feeling I had been trying to ignore; the thought of yet another day of rain was more than I could take, and, although I had had ten hours of sleep, I still felt tired. I thought of Glasgow and pulled the lead limbs, which seemed to be my body, out of bed. Underfoot the carpet was damp and I felt the knotted muscles in my feet. My ankle bone was protruding from my foot where the tongue still rubbed; but Ruth was making porridge and I had no option but to face another day.

We were on another single track road to Kilberry. Between eight and nine in the morning we shared the road with a handful of cars taking people to school or work. When this *rush hour* had passed we were left to the road for the day, passed by the occasional car, or the Spudtruck, with its baubles and tinsel swinging gaily in the back window, until the second *rush hour*.

In Kilberry, an old man was pushing a wheel barrow load of fire wood down the middle of the road. 'You've got a good load there!' I said.

'Och. Aye!' he said, putting the barrow down. 'I always collect my own wood, several times a day. I generate more heat by fetching it than I ever do by burning it!'

He was wearing a tie and a well worn jacket patched at the elbows. On his head was a beret. 'It's beautiful down here.' I said.

'Beautiful but isolated,' my eccentric told me, and went on to talk about the declining community. 'There's no public transport here any more. If you need to go to the doctor in Tarbert you have to catch a taxi, which'll cost you £26.'

Only the rich, healthy or resilient could realistically continue to live in this village, which must represent so many dwindling hamlets. 'How many live in this village?'

'Nine.'

'I see you've still got a pub though!'

'Aye. We managed to keep it open. It stays open until seven o'clock each night.' He had a real twinkle in his eye and looked incongruously smart in his tie and beret.

As we set off he said, 'I live on my own and I've been looking for someone to come and live with me. If you meet any homeless people tell them to come here!' I thought of Margaret and wondered whether I could do a little match making.

Near Tarbert I saw my first field. After the free range Highlands it looked so claustrophobic and possessive. Likewise, the thickly forested hills looked tamed, harnessed into productivity. I also saw my first sign to Glasgow in Tarbert, but between here and Glasgow were some of the biggest detours we had faced anywhere on the west coast.

I crossed Loch Fyne at Lochgilphead to avoid one of the longest diversions, and set off across country the other side. My achey limbs had matured into flu which made my hips, knees, back and neck ache, and no matter how much I thought of kneeing someone in the groin, my legs refused to lift up. To reach Tighnabruaich, we covered thirteen slow cross-country miles in five hours.

We took to the road again around Loch Riddon, and the following day joined a path down the east shore of Loch Striven, where, six days earlier, the body of a murdered lady had been found. 'I'll be alright with my big fierce dog — hey Tessie?' Tess had put on some weight due to her enforced rest, and we would take out her stitches in Dunoon.

We reached Toward Point and sat down to have our sandwiches. Naughty Tess had munched the first delicious batch, and the replacements had been hastily made with stale bread. Tess now had the audacity to want some of these. There was no end to her nerve sometimes.

The sandwiches went her way anyway, and in Innellan I bought a snickers bar and a doughnut, neither of which replenished my lost energy. Out to my right the redshank, curlew, oystercatchers, and dunlin, all of whom had been absent for a while, turned a blind eye to the temperature which refused to rise above freezing. Beyond them and the Firth of Clyde was Gourock, where we would start the long haul south after Christmas; but for now we had to delve northwards into the snow.

I had mis-planned these last few days, and that evening saw me shivering and sneezing as I walked up to the top of Holy Loch on an icy road. Glasgow was the light at the end of a very long tunnel which, no matter how much I willed it, refused to come any closer.

William had taken over from Ruth. He is the brother of Mike (of Border notoriety), and was unflustered by anything. The Spudtruck roof had reached saturation point so that the waterfall effect of it filling the light fitting and overflowing onto the table meant that we would have required an umbrella. The offending patch of roof had been replaced; but the incurable seepage remained.

Meanwhile, the water pump had frozen up and there was no chance of hot water — in fact no water at all. We drank whisky instead, which numbed my numb limbs even more and made me sleep.

The temperature plummeted to -8°c overnight and the familiar frozen condensation greeted us the next morning. I packed up sandwiches and we arranged to meet at the top of the Rest and be Thankful road — the highest point of the A83 which separates Glen Croe from Glen Kinglas.

I walked like a zombie; counting anything I saw; ticking off every slow landmark; watching my pedometer; taking off and replacing my hat as I alternated between sweating and shivering; following Tess' familiar gait; and dreaming of Glasgow.

Up Loch Long, then left up Loch Goil, and only another six miles to go. The paths had been frozen into rutted bogs, and now the roads were sheet ice; the forests enclosed us on each side, threatening and cold, and as we started up the long hill to reach Rest and be Thankful the snow started. The road ahead became whiter and whiter, and the flakes larger and larger. It was hard to walk up hill on the new snow but I pushed myself harder and harder to reach the Spudtruck, despite being convinced that it would be stuck in a snowdrift. Tess took on a puppy playfulness in the snow, becoming an excited blue blob in the virgin snow.

A car skidded towards us — once down in Lochgoilhead it would not be able to get out. It was the last car I saw. The snow became too deep for cars, and our footprints were quickly filled in.

The white world levelled out, and I made out some orange footprints. The Spudtruck was the last vehicle to make it up the hill. Although it annoyed me to miss out a section, there was no choice but to get off that hill as quickly as possible.

We inched onto the road, where we were the only ones heading south. There were still cars and trucks trying to ascend the hill, and they emerged out of the whiteness in a slow motion film, until a truck ground to a halt, blocking the other side of the road entirely.

We reached the bottom and skated into a lay-by on Loch Long, just as the radio declared 'the Rest and be Thankful road has just been closed.' My race up hill had been worthwhile, but my fluey sweat had turned cold and there was no hot water on the horizon.

I wondered whether I would have carried on if Glasgow wasn't now so close. At the moment the *boss* was winning the battle over my body, but I wondered at what point my body would take over and simply refuse to move.

I thought of George Orwell's *Down and out in Paris and London*. It always occurred to me that his story might be different without the knowledge that he had a home to return to. I was in a similar position. I was exposing myself to pain and cold, but in my mind I knew there was a warm home to return to. If there had been no warm hearth, might I have given up?

I had a goal and it was Glasgow. The distance between myself and this goal was a little over forty miles. The first twenty six miles were along a filthy and frantic road, where rain camouflaged icy puddles, and my sore left shin returned. Sometimes there was a pavement, sometimes there wasn't. Where there wasn't, trucks passed so close I could have touched them.

A friend joined us for the final stretch through Glasgow's suburbs; the obsolete canal, the industrial works, out-of-town shopping centres and congested roads. I was like an alien being submerged in the chaos of civilisation for the first time.

The persistent noise and drills which drowned every other sound, the farting fumes, the relentless traffic and scurrying people, the advertisements and abundance of them, the glarey lights, and the parasitic shopping arcades, all hit me in one intensive shock. For three months I had seen no town bigger than Fort William, and had spent all my daylight hours in the company of the hills and wildlife. The chaos grated on my tired nerves.

For three months, and more, hardly a human had passed without some verbal communication. Now here I was amongst all these people trying to keep up my 'hellos' to each nameless person; each replied with a blank stare. In the end I accepted my insignificance and gave up, realising that I was the one who was weird. But I was saddened by the lack of human interaction and warmth.

Tess also wagged her tail at everyone, but soon discovered that, if she didn't want to wag it right off, she couldn't keep on top of things. Nevertheless, she adapted to city walking much better, making the most of overflowing rubbish bins and avoiding broken glass.

At 2pm on 23rd December we arrived in festive Georges Square, accompanied by the Scottish rugby player, Rob Wainwright. I had arrived in Glasgow and felt relief; but not elation. I was numbed by fatigue and flu.

We went to a pub in the Square and I put down a sweatshirt in the corner for Tess. She curled up angelically, her eyes closing. I watched her out of the corner of my eye — my faithful friend.

'Sorry. You'll have to take that dog outside,' a voice said. The others began to complain. 'That dog's walked over 2,200 miles!' But it was fruitless. We were certainly back in a city.

I roused the sleeping Tess and took her back to the Spudtruck, tucking her under plenty of layers. But as I left the truck her brow furrowed and her big brown eyes looked worried as they did every time I went off without her. She didn't know we had reached the half way point of the walk; and if I had asked her to she would have joined me and walked wherever I led her that afternoon.

But we weren't walking anywhere. Tess and I were being lent a flat in Glasgow until we went home on Boxing Day. I needed time on my own. Time to reflect without the metronome thoughts which marched through my mind when I was walking. I just needed to STOP; stop walking; stop talking; stop aching; and stop thinking . . .

CHAPTER TEN

The streets of Glasgow were empty on Christmas morning. Behind each tightly shut door children ripped into stockings; and elder sisters and brothers shattered the myth of Father Christmas. I imagined big break-fasts and Christmas dinner preparations. I wondered how many turkeys were being squeezed into ovens, and how many people had suddenly realised that they didn't have enough silver foil. I thought of mother-in-laws getting ready to descend on grandchildren; and vicars getting ready for morning services.

Yet I saw nothing, and took a certain enjoyment from my detach-ment. I would be going home on Boxing Day, when Christmas would duly be celebrated. Some would not be so lucky.

I had decided to spend Christmas Day with those for whom we were walking, and had put my name down as a volunteer at the Wayside Club for homeless people. This was also giving me a chance to be Spud rather than The Walk.

The Wayside Club is a nondescript building beneath a railway bridge. It is, perhaps surprisingly, solely for men. This is because there are pro-portionately fewer women on the street, and they find adequate sup-port centres.

The head volunteer, Bob, greeted the men with familiarity, and the men responded — that is the old men who were as cheery and cheeky as their situation allowed, but I was struck by the despair of the few young guys. Although there weren't many, Bob told me the reason. 'It's not because there aren't many young on the streets, but because they find it hard to come here; they don't like to admit their position by accepting what they see as charity.' All over Glasgow there were young guys spending Christmas alone, possibly hungry and probably pissed.

I found myself in the kitchen among a large band of volunteers and mountains of donated food. The head volunteer was a large man with a grey beard who was stirring vats of soup over the oven. He told me about Christmas Day here. 'All the centres agree on when they are providing hot meals. That way there is a hot meal to be found every day. We're doing a Christmas dinner tomorrow.'

We buttered and stirred and mixed and poured, until soup by the gallon, turkey rolls by the hundreds, pies, biscuits, fruit, chocolate bars, sausage rolls (not to mention vast vats of milky tea) flowed out of the kitchen in a continuous stream.

Upstairs, the men sat around formica topped tables smoking, drinking tea and making a dent in the quantities of food. It wasn't the time or the place to find out why these guys were homeless, in the same way as no one asked about my obviously very English and alone presence. I was Spud, and they were Jimmy, Reg, Bill etc. No questions; no answers. To these guys, Christmas Day was just another day.

I returned to the flat at 7pm that night and ate my deli samosa Christmas dinner. I had lifted myself out of the walk and at seven o'clock on Boxing Day morning Tess and I set off in a hire car back to Wiltshire, leaving the Spudtruck still festively decorated but hemmed into a barn by sheet ice and snow.

Returning to Glasgow was like returning to school after the holidays. The drive up was interminable, and the weather progressively colder. We may have been half way through the Walk, but we weren't necessarily half way through winter.

It felt as though I had been hanging onto the whole thing by a tenuous thread prior to Christmas. We had had every element and ailment thrown at us during those nightmare days before Glasgow; every obstacle which threatened me psychologically. I now felt refreshed; but half way was only half way, and when Mike (of Border notoriety) dropped us off at a roundabout near Old Kilpatrick, where roads, towns and ports cling tightly onto the south shore of the River Clyde, it felt as though I hadn't been anywhere, or had any time off. My body was in pain, the walking was grim and I felt suddenly abandoned. But once the Spudtruck was gone, I had no option but to go and find it. I was like a dog whose owner exercises it by making it run behind the car.

We found a few fields to trespass across, and had only gone two miles when the M8 motorway squeezed us right up against the Clyde, leaving no option but to cross it. Luckily Tess didn't choose this moment to relieve herself as she had once done when crossing a road!

Finding the shortest way through cities meant finding ourselves on such estuary shores, which gave me a biased view of the city, not least Glasgow whose Clyde River, once so important, is now bordered by run down shipyards, industries and warehouses. Central Glasgow may have been 1990 European city of Culture, but Port Glasgow missed out.

We found our way along roads parallel to the main road, where grim sixties flats loomed over shops whose windows were boarded up and decorated with graffiti so that, until we walked past the doorway, it appeared that the shop no longer existed. The pubs were similar. Their only sign of trade were the blue Tennant beer signs hanging above the dingy doorways; and throughout Port Glasgow I was stared at by loitering, bored looking youths. I saw and was seen, but never involved. My body took orders from the *boss*.

The following day we rounded the corner to Gourock. The clouds were threatening to soak us with another Scottish downpour, but as we looked across to Holy Loch and Dunoon, and the drizzle shrouded hills beyond, I could feel only sadness at leaving the hills.

The rain began to fall, and the road became reality. We turned left to head south and found a small road running inland through undulating hills which stretched the sore muscles on the fronts of my legs. The country here was suburban compared to the hills, and the fields so small — their hedges declaring 'this is mine, and that's yours'. The hedgerows themselves were black and lifeless in their wet winter garb.

I had arranged to meet Mike in the first pub on the left in Largs. It would be cosy with a roaring fire and cheery locals; and it was. After sixteen miles we negotiated the final puddles and entered Ye Olde Anchor Inn. Tess shook herself heartily, spraying the small bar and handful of drinkers.

I draped our waterproofs as near the fire as possible without them actually catching fire, and salvaged some damp tobacco which was just smokeable if you sucked hard enough. I sat by the fire, drifting off into a land of whisky and warmth.

Eventually Mike strode into the pub, hunched up in his familiar ankle length grey coat. He looked very fed up and smiled a wry smile; 'My first day and I've spent five hours in a campervan centre!' (On top of the broken water pump and various other ailments, Mike had just discovered that we had been driving on illegal tyres for five months.)

More rain had fallen in the first few days of January than was normal for the whole of January, and record floods were reported down south. This weather was apparently heading our way; but the snow stayed out on the islands of Great Cumbrae and Bute, and the heavy black clouds obediently worked their way inland up the country. It was about time the weather was on our side.

Once past this area's last remaining coal mine, the shoreline is comprised of stunning red sandstone, also evident in all the buildings. Its rich colour gives the narrow and patchy beaches a feeling of cleanliness.

On one beach we waded through a mound of finely shredded seaweed resembling tea leaves. The seaweed comes from the Outer Hebrides to end up in the alginic acid processing plant — used in jellies — and then discarded on this beach. We walked through the dog walkers of Saltcoats and Troon, and came off the beach in Ayr: it only takes a few minutes to learn that Robert Burns was born here.

In fact, Burns pilgrims need only glance at the map to learn where to find Burns Cottage and the Land O Burns centre; while Burns Street and Burns Tavern are unmissable. The Burns pilgrimage stretches down to Dumfries where Burns farmed (unsuccessfully), and in the surrounds of Dumfries you can visit the farm; drink in his pub; visit his grave; visit the church where he was married; visit shrines which inspired certain works; visit the well where he attempted to cure himself; and culminate the tour at the Robert Burns Centre. This is Burns mania.

From Ayr we took to trespassing in strangely empty fields. The grass was as short as when the last sheep or cow had grazed it the previous autumn, and the fields always sloped down to the right, as they had over the last five months. Even on the roads we kept to the right, where the camber slopes to the right; and all this was to illustrate itself later. But there is one stretch of road where the camber is inconsequential.

The optical illusion of the stretch of road called Croy Brae (or Electric Brae) has become something of a tourist attraction, and we arrived with our empty coke can to test the theory. The stretch of road looks as though it slopes downhill, but is actually uphill; and with a little persuasion our coke can followed the route uphill of its predecessors.

Tess, meanwhile, was more interested in a large stick which she had dragged onto the road. I wasn't prepared to humour her so she dropped it in the middle of the road. This had happened before, and I'm afraid to say that I never walked back to push them onto the verge. But it does offer an explanation to all the times you see branches in the middle of a

road, despite the fact that there may be no trees in sight; obviously they
have been deposited there by just such a walking dog! Also, I removed
numerous branches and several exhausts from roads. When driving, I
had often wondered who manages to stop in time to remove such obstacles, but now I know that it is charity walkers! Such thoughts made
huge amounts of sense to me.

We passed Culzean Castle, and at Girvan were forced onto the
Stranraer road which is permanently busy with ferry traffic. I motored
along in my world of H.E. Bates' *Fair Blew the Wind from France*. Anything to do with wind was appropriate. The snow and floods may have
avoided us, but the wind was making up for it. The strong headwind
would stay with us for the next few days; making Tess' ears fly back like
Piglet's, and exhausting me and bringing on back pains.

Inland, expansive fields of weed-less grass led the eye to open moorland, while to my right the coast dropped away to a nondescript rocky
edge. Across Loch Ryan was the top of the hammer head mass of the
Rhins of Galloway, and at the base of Loch Ryan is Stranraer where I
deposited Mike and picked up Geoffrey.

Geoffrey had been preceded by his reputation. 'Geoffrey's with you
for two weeks?! My God! It'll be interesting anyway! He can't boil an
egg, and can't change a light bulb without electrocuting himself —' were
the words of my sister, who is Geoffrey's partner in an art gallery.

Geoffrey climbed into the Spudtruck, curling up his long skinny
legs to fit in. 'Now tell me Spuddle, what do I have to do?' he began,
furrowing his brow in worry. 'Well, the most important thing is that
our battery has gone — again.' This was the beginning of ten troublesome days which would culminate in Carlisle.

Geoffrey ran his hand through his dishevelled hair in a flustered
manner, and I tried to convince him that he could cope, but it was easy
to be blasé on driver number seventeen. 'You'll be alright Geoffrey,
whatever PC might say!' Geoffrey laughed and remonstrated that none
of what she said was remotely true.

Whether or not it was true remained to be seen, but Geoffrey had
been involved from the start of the Walk and his enthusiasm and natural
ability to laugh at himself meant more than any cordon bleu or elec-
tronic wizardry; despite pettiness brought on by fatigue.

The northern part of the Rhins of Galloway is perfectly green and gently undulating, like rolling lawns, but the tracks were deep mud and
large areas of bog forced us onto lanes.

We were found on one rainy lane by the local paper, and climbed
into the back of the cramped but dry van. The usual questions then

followed, including the ones asked by every single reporter: 'Has any-one ever threatened you?' and 'Have you had any near misses on the road? Almost been run over?' they would say, rubbing their hands to-gether with gleeful anticipation.

I was appalled by their morbidity and desire to know the bleak as-pects of the walk. Why did they never ever ask about all the good, gen-erous, selfless Brits who had made possible our trip so far? Isn't there enough bad news in the world anyway?

The other question which I now found equally hard was the usual, 'Why?'

'Well,' I began, and then stopped. 'I was shocked at how many peo-ple were sleeping on the street —' I didn't sound shocked at all! I had said it so many times that it had lost its meaning; it sounded shallow and contrived. It certainly had been the original reason, and was still the motivating factor; but the *other reason*, the one I was still trying to un-derstand, was much too hard to explain.

The shelter of the red van disappeared and I promised Tess we would find somewhere dry to eat our sandwiches. That somewhere was an empty farm cottage. We squeezed through the front door which hung off its hinges, and inside there were arm chairs, sofas, tables and old chests of drawers — all of which was covered in a thick layer of wet dust and white birdshit. I perched on the edge of a now white plastic sofa and thought of blue-eyed Billy and his caravan, and of Margaret. In such country I passed empty cottages on a daily basis. The irony of the situa-tion made my legs ache more and the rain feel wetter.

Nevertheless, the first signs of Spring were catching my waiting eye. Snowdrops weren't worried that frost and snow might return, or by the continual wind; and daffodil tips bravely showed themselves over the next week. It was only mid-January but I was further cheered by seeing my first field of lambs three days later.

We skirted a large bombing range and joined a main road running along a ledge of flat land on the mainland; I had finally found a piece of reclaimed coast. Perhaps my theory was right, and we would collide with Ireland? Having seen the lights of Ireland across the water from Portpatrick I was even more convinced.

That night the radio cheerily told us: 'Gales of up to 100mph will hit most parts of the west coast of Scotland tonight,' and we found as much shelter as an umbrella would give in a hurricane on a stretch of coast designed for a wind farm. 'Geoffrey, I think we should move,' I said nervously several times, to which he replied 'where to?'

He was right. Short of going far inland there was no where to go, so I posted myself into bed and woke to an eerie silence. Only the sea was still shambolic, as if brooding over the previous night's argument.

By the side of the road I came across the ruins of small Chapel Finian, which once offered a place of refuge for Irish pilgrims landing here on their way to visit the shrine of St Ninians — the first foothold of Christianity in Scotland. The exact location of the original 400AD St Ninian shrine is a matter fiercely debated between the villages of Whithorn, and Isle of Whithorn situated on the tip of The Machars peninsula.

Isle of Whithorn is a charming village with a natural harbour enclosed by grassy headlands. Being low tide, the fishing boats were stranded at lopsided angles on the sand; and behind them a couple of houses are built with their walls dropping straight onto the sand, so that their views would be similar to looking out from a boat.

Geoffrey shuffled his business-like steps towards us. 'Poor Spuddle. You must be exhausted and starving!'

I had walked twenty one miles without anything to eat, but I was thinking of Geoffrey's patience with the again ailing Spudtruck. Like everyone else he had given up valuable holiday and I wanted him to enjoy himself. 'Poor Geoffrey! You must be really pissed off!'

But fatigue surfaced once in the Spudtruck. Fallen pasta and raspberry ripple teabags lay strewn around, along with several day old newspapers scrunched up by Tess' claws and Geoffrey's unorthodox method of reading them. The disorder threatened my routine.

I found bread, and the lid of the honey came off in my hand and I dropped the jar. I should have learnt by now that lids simply don't have a place in Geoffrey's vocabulary, but all this still irritated me.

I was tired and sore and had completed another walking marathon. Returning to the Spudtruck was like suddenly scaling down my life, from the immense panorama I shared only with Tess and the wildlife, to a space barely allowing two people to stand up; and where, even if you were on your own, the simplest movements needed some manoeuvring. It was hardly surprising that I felt permanently on top of the other person.

But I hated myself for these pathetic grievances. They weren't worth the breath. What did it really matter? We were here, and in one piece. If I wasn't careful I would end up like a pernickety spinster.

Outside my scaled down world, Isle of Whithorn was catching the last of the sun. Thin grey clouds were dragged through the sky from the west, teasing out the orange glow in constantly changing patterns, and the grassy headland with its ruined St Ninian's Chapel was silhouetted jet black against the orange. Looking around the familiar 180° sweep of sea, it felt as though we were on the tip of the world. This was reality.

In the Steam Packet Inn the party of locals mingled sociably, and we chatted to a vociferous lady about the area; 'This is the road to nowhere. No one comes here unless they're making a specific journey to Isle of Whithorn. There used to be lots of dairy farming round here, but it's a long way for the milk tankers. They've closed down along with numerous distilleries and every other industry. The communication simply isn't here. The area's been left behind.'

I did notice that virtually every car on the road was a Lada (except for a BMW whose stroppy owner was the first person in five months to order me off land). But the area didn't declare poverty. The fertile looking farms were well kept and the livestock fat and healthy. I decided that Isle of Whithorn was worth the specific journey.

In the morning, as the approaching orange glow silhouetted skeletal trees on the horizon, we were joined by the livestock. We were always the first sign of humanity, and the cattle and sheep came up to the fencelines as we passed, noisily demanding their silage. 'Sorry lads. I haven't got what you want!' I tried to pacify them, but they would have none of it.

A little later the first sounds of tractors indicating that breakfast was imminent increased the decibels among our companions, and they jostled each other for prime gateside positions.

When the sun rose it revealed grassy Galloway and Dumfrieshire stretching away, and the next peninsula feeling its way out to sea and culminating in fingers of rock which grew longer as the tide went out. My friends the birds flew across Wigtown Bay, reaching my evening's destination in a matter of minutes.

Wigtown Bay channelled in to the River Cree, and, beyond the mud banks rising sharply like smooth and shiny slides, the other side was so close but yet so far. Creetown lay one mile across the channel, but involved eleven miles of walking.

By 5pm we had walked twenty eight miles, and approached Creetown as the light was disappearing. The days were getting longer; they certainly felt long in the ten hours between sunrise and sunset. The rushes on the glistening banks were tinted mauve by the various evening blues and purples, and the call of the curlew resounded off every bull rush. A full moon appeared and a severe frost set in.

I climbed into the Spudtruck and shed my boots. My toes were suffering from the road walking and my ankle bone was still swollen. But I still hadn't had a blister. Contrary to people's advice, keeping my feet soft was preventing blisters, and I anointed them with peppermint foot lotion and arnica cream.

I sat down to write my diary, and beside me Tess gave a big sigh and fell asleep. I never tired of evenings in the Spudtruck. The thought of them kept me going through the day. As long as we continued to park on a slope (battery problems), the Spudtruck would materialise like a refuge, symbolising warmth, friendship, food, sleep and normality.

'What's for supper?' I asked, guessing it would either be pasta or sausages. I had made the fateful mistake of telling Geoffrey that these were the two easiest things to cook. 'Sausages —' this was the third night in a row.

'Shall we jazz them up somehow?'

'Yup. I thought I'd cook baked beans with them.' That sounded pretty jazzy!

Food was something which filled my mind on a Sunday, when we walked like the Bisto kids, moving from roast to roast across the country, and trying to forget the prospect of sandwiches — again.

I felt the discipline of our schedule more strongly on a Sunday. I thought of everyone taking lie-ins, preparing lunch, and being with family. I began David Niven's *The Moon's a Balloon*, and was soon having a good chuckle.

Kirkcudbright Bay forced us inland again. I liked the name Kirkcudbright (pronounced 'Kirkoobree'); K . . i . . r . . k . . c . . u . . d . . b . . r . . i . . g . . h . . t was thirteen strides and took us a little closer to the end of the day. I looked everything up on the map; tracks, farms and features out on the estuaries. Names such as Devil's Thrashing Floor obviously marked a hidden mud bank, and even a tiny rock had been named — Frenchman's Rock. Other features included Sugarloaf, Goat Well Bay and Gipsy Point.

To avoid an MOD range east of Kircudbright, we turned inland and followed the River Dee to Castle Douglas and Dalbeattie. There were no beaches, no redshank or dunlin, no metronome-type waves and no wind. Instead we kept to our respective sides of a yellow road bordered by tall blackthorn hedges which weren't blown into comical shapes by the wind.

But we were drawn back to the sea as if by instinct. The sea filled me with its presence even when it wasn't wild and noisy. Inland I felt unbalanced. 'Come on Tessie. To the sea; to the sea!'

The small village of Kippford Scaur marked our return to the sea, which was now the Solway Firth. I hadn't eaten my sandwiches after eighteen miles, and the sight of an open pub persuaded me that it would be well to wash them down with a final pint of Scottish beer. In three days time we would be leaving Scotland.

Tess came up to the bar, jumping up with her front paws. The barman peered over the bar at her. 'Do you want a pint then?!' Tess wagged her tail in agreement. She had become a great enthusiast for Scottish Eighty Shillings, and took great gulps from my pint to prove this, to the amazement of the barman.

We ate our sandwiches watching the sun begin to dip over the narrow channel of Urr Waterfoot, and then made our way to our hosts, Norman and Tessa, who live a mile inland in a house hidden by thick forestry. After half an hour Geoffrey arrived at the house, looking as though he had been in a Dumfrieshire pub brawl. As usual his clothes managed to look as though they had been put on the wrong limb, and the right knee of his trousers displayed a large rip.

'Oh! I've been having a terrible time,' he began. 'I thought you were lost, so came to look for you. Then I got lost and . . !'

'What happened to your knee?'

'Well, I came here first and Macduff took an instant dislike to me!'

Geoffrey and Macduff the Scotty regarded each other with suspicion. It could only happen to Geoffrey; the man who once securely locked the Spudtruck, but left the window wide open!

We trudged northwards for the final inland detour of Dumfrieshire. Criffel hill was supposed to rise up on our left, but was obliterated by rain. The farmers were busy muck spreading and the muck was being spread equally well along the roads as in the fields. Muck spreading felt like a very English thing to do! Even the hedgerows looked English; beech hedges, blackthorn, and sycamore were coming into bud.

New Abbey is a small village dominated by the Abbey, which is anything but new, and is romantically known as Sweetheart Abbey. The story of its construction in 1273 is a tale of devotion: Devorgilla Balliol (Lady of Galloway) built the abbey in memory of her deceased husband. Taking devotion to the extreme, she carried her husband's embalmed heart around with her until her own death in 1290, when she and the heart were buried together at Sweetheart Abbey.

The Abbey was built from a rich red stone, but it is in ruins now. We parked alone beneath the red masonry, unhindered by tourist season regulations, and the night wrapped the Spudtruck in its blanket, so that the old van could have been transferred anywhere else in Britain.

The lights began to dim and I stole a look at the electric board. Sure enough the ominous red light had returned. 'Geoffrey! Didn't they hook the auxiliary battery back onto the main battery?!'

'I don't know,' Geoffrey giggled weakly. 'What's the auxiliary battery got to do with the main one anyway?'

'What?!!'

After ten days of campervan battery education, I couldn't believe my ears. It had started on Girvan church driveway, at 10am one Sunday morning, when the congregation had had to pick their way round the Spudtruck and an AA van, and from then on our friendship with Dumfrieshire and Galloway AA had grown. Geoffrey had also learnt to park on slopes, so that he could at least jump start the old girl — a term he always used with an air of great knowledge, as though he had said 'carburettor', or 'alternator', or 'prop shaft', instead of simply 'jump start'.

We had finally purchased a new battery, which had led to the red light, and Geoffrey's confession. I buried my head in my arms on the table. 'We'll have to find another mechanic, and this time I'll come too!' I chided.

'Sorry Spuddle. I'll cook you a good supper to make up for it!'

'Oh yes?'

Geoffrey opened the rotten smelling fridge and declared with a triumphant air, 'sausages . . . and beans!'

I was beginning to feel like a sausage, and was certainly familiar with the smell which hung determinedly in the recess of my bedroom. I don't particularly even like sausages.

Our last full day in Scotland started with an avenue of two hundred year old Scots pine trees on the outskirts of New Abbey. They rose tall above me, so that I felt like a ten year old Man. United footy fan parading off the home pitch through the tunnel of idolised players. I gazed up at them and the sun appeared.

I could now see Criffel Hill, which, at 569 metres, is the tallest hill in the area and would be a landmark until Whitehaven. But for now it was behind me, as I walked twelve miles north to Dumfries to cross the River Nith. Although I was sad to be leaving Scotland, I was willing Carlisle and to be turning southwards.

I thought of everything Carlisle meant to me. Its name was synonymous with overnight stops on the way to family holidays in Scotland; small bed and breakfasts, where the sheets were purple nylon, the carpets swirly orange flowers, and the curtains clashing. The landladies were always small, grey haired, meticulous, and smelt of home cooking.

These night stops had always been a big excitement, but I'm sure that four children on a long car journey was not something my mother was ever very excited about. It was almost ten years since mum died, and not for the first time I wondered whether she was witnessing the walk from a comfortable cloud. She was definitely with me — somewhere — and often her words came back to me: What you put into life, you get out of life.

I wanted to put everything into each place we walked through, but our visits were so fleeting. One minute we were walking into Dumfries, then we were crossing the river, and after half an hour Dumfries was a jumble of buildings in our wake. All I knew was that it had magnificent old bridges, grassy riverside paths, and good doughnuts.

We turned left at Caerlaverock Nature Reserve, and the shore took us east up the north bank of the Solway Firth. The railway line and main roads began to bear down, skirting the hills and searching for the most direct route to England. Like the tortoise and the hare, we were making our own slow but steady way along the flood plain.

The road ran straight for five miles and I followed Tess' familiar pacing gait. 'Perhaps we should put the pedometer on you Tessie?' I wondered how I would set it to her stride — how long was one of her strides? When she was pacing it would be easy to set it — until she went off after wildlife, when the pedometer would go berserk.

From Ruthwell, home to Scotland's first ever Savings Bank (now there isn't even a shop there, let alone a bank), we walked on to Powfoot, and the following day set off to England.

I had mixed feelings about returning to England. I had grown such an affinity for Scotland, and out of the six months we had been walking, over four months had been spent in Scotland. Now we only had two weeks of populated England before we would branch out into Wales.

The weather did nothing for my morale, and when we met Geoffrey at the border, the River Sark, it was a grey greeting. The small road out of Gretna crosses the river with little ceremony — in fact there isn't even a sign declaring the border.

This time there were no pipers and whoops of joy, but it was still our landmark, and at 12.30 on 20th January we crossed the River Sark after 2,525 miles. I then put my most purposeful pace on in the knowledge that we could no longer walk wherever we pleased. Straight away this meant joining the frantic A74 for over a mile.

We walked on the expansive verge decorated with service station sandwich wrappers and coke bottles, feeling the draw of wind as the lorries passed. The exhaust fumes filled my lungs with each breath. 'Oh misery Tess. What a welcome!' Tess didn't respond. She was pulling me on and for once I didn't yank her back. I could have done with the skateboard.

Deciding to claim ignorance of English trespass laws, we walked down a small sliproad to a gate. But the gate was heavily fortified with rolled up barbed wire which also barricaded the fences on each side. There was no way we would ever be able to negotiate that. Also on the gate was a board on which was written in big red letters; 'Any person found trespassing on this land will be prosecuted immediately.' As far as I was concerned this was the sign which read 'Welcome to England'.

I turned the dejected Tess round, and we rejoined the A74, the pylons and the railway line towards Carlisle.

CHAPTER ELEVEN

We found England in such villages as Drumburgh, on the rubble that was once Hadrian's Wall: the churches, the manor houses, the greens opening up from muddy farmyards, the blossom, the bulbs, the bridleways and footpaths, and the suddenly *quaint* stiles which Tess leapt like the superfit athlete that she was, displaying happiness with her usual innocent and envious panache.

As the sun began to disappear a car pulled up and an elderly woman wound down the window. 'Are you . . . Spud?' She said 'Spud' hesitantly, worried that if I was the wrong person I might take affront at being referred to as a vegetable. 'Oh, I'm so pleased I've found you. I'm Millicent,' she said, putting her hand out of the window and shaking mine enthusiastically. 'I spoke to your driver and the Parish have arranged a bed for you in Bowness.'

Millicent pointed us in the right direction for Mrs Chattle's B&B and drove off with lots of good wishes.

There was no sign of Geoffrey in Bowness, but I found the appropriate bungalow. A wave of hot air came out of the hallway and Mrs Chattle stood there, eyeing Tess suspiciously and shuffling from foot to foot in her blue fluffy slippers. The carpet inside looked as though it had just arrived from the shop, and only a perfect cyclamen adorned the well polished table in the hall. 'You can come in. But your dog can't. He'll have to stay outside,' she finally said.

There was simply no way I could leave Tess outside in the cold while I warmed up in the house, so we exchanged warmth behind Mrs Chattle's empty flower bed until Geoffrey turned up. That night I opted to stay in the Spudtruck, as did Geoffrey, declaring that he slept better in the Spudtruck than he did in his own bed.

This wasn't the only time we opted for the perhaps unsavoury Spudtruck. Over the last week we had been grudgingly offered two hotel rooms. But the grudge definitely took the pleasure out of the treat, and had led to Geoffrey's lesson of the week: 'If there's one thing I've learnt since I've been with you,' he had said, 'is that if you're going to give at all, give with a good grace. Otherwise don't give at all.'

Back on the coast at Silloth, I bent my head down into the strong southerly wind and began a relentless march intended purely to get us to our destination. The beach, the sea, the dunes and occasionally a fleeting glance of Tess as she chased the spume, were blown in and out of my view as we notched up the miles and the landmarks to Maryport.

We were back in coal mining area, which is the apparent reason behind the familiar grey colour of the sea; the colour I had witnessed due east from here four months previously. Between the railway and the shingle beach we followed a coal black path overgrown with autumnal grass which swayed and sung in the wind. Trapped among the vegetation, the ubiquitous railway plastic rustled harmoniously.

But apart from the railway line, nothing else joined us on the coast. The sea had been put 'in Coventry'. Even Maryport was shrinking away from the sea, leaving the deserted harbour and handful of boats to yet another building site of exclusive residential developments. As usual this one was empty, so exclusive are they in price as well as construction.

But Whitehaven was different. Whitehaven was populated, where Maryport wasn't; and in Whitehaven I saw collieries transformed to industrial parks which were actually in use.

Whitehaven harbour is geometrically intricate, with small harbours within the main one. At one stage it was the third largest port in Britain after Glasgow and Bristol, with a thriving ship building industry and smuggling trade. During one raid, a band of smugglers took refuge in a cave, where their only sustenance was rum, butter and sugar. They lived off this until the coast was clear, and the resulting Cumbrian delicacy of rum butter still exists as proof of the tale.

South of Whitehaven, St Bees is a headland of red sandstone which stood firm while the coast to the north and south receded. The legend behind its name is that St Bega, a seventh century Irish maiden, was shipwrecked here and became the guest of Lord Egremont. During her stay, she pleaded with him to give her some land to set up a nunnery. It was midsummer's day, but Lord Egremont said she could have as much land as was covered with snow the next day. The following day snow lay on a small patch of ground. He kept to his word and helped her establish the nunnery.

South of St Bees we took to small lanes and tracks to Sellafield. Despite my green tendencies I was looking forward to looking round a nuclear power station.

Shirley the PR lady was smartly dressed in what I considered to be a power suit, and ushered us out of the wind and into the reception hall, where we sat on a sofa for the photos. Tess jumped up to join us, leaving muddy pawprints on the executive suit. I grappled with Tess and tied us both up in her lead, sweating in the false heat. 'Could you just get a little closer?' the photographer requested the usual agony of restraining Tess and smiling politely, while Shirley and I politely fought for the cheque.

Such ordeals were definitely alleviated by Tess' continual disregard for human pretensions; and I was always struck by my own similarity to Mr Bean! Something about enclosed places and false heat now brought out the worst clumsiness in me, and many a shop had been vacated by our Laurel and Hardy performance.

The ordeal over, we set off to look round the visitor's centre. At the moment, Britain produces one fifth of its electricity from the seventeen nuclear power stations. Cosmetically, nuclear power appears cleaner than fossil fuels, and a minimal amount of uranium is needed for the process. But the daily transportation of spent fuel, reprocessed fuel, and radioactive waste around the country; not to mention the danger of radiation seepage or a full scale Chernobyl accident, barely balance out the advantages. I arrived at Sellafield with an open mind, and left genuinely impressed — but not convinced.

Tess and I used Sellafield's private railway line to cross rivers and avoid MOD land over the next couple of days, hoping that we wouldn't be steam rollered by a train load of spent fuel. As it was we crossed six bridges and met only one train, and lived to tell the tale.

For the rest of the time footpaths and farm tracks skirted the snowy and cloud shadowed hills of the Lake District, and led us through Cumbria's rich farming country. The walls and buildings here are built with beautifully rounded boulders interspersed with slate to become works of art. The colours of the stones range from pinks to greys to blues.

The other thing which characterises this area are the grey, squat, herdwick sheep, which appear to have been dragged through burnt vegetation. Their lambs were under the watchful eyes of territorial collies who raced out of their farmyards when they smelt Tess, hounding her on to the domain of the next one.

At Millom we rounded the corner to head north and round Duddon Sands. The wind was now on our backs; but the relief was temporary. The wind had been with us for days. It sneaked into every hole in the Spudtruck, and under any part of untucked clothing or bedding. Not a single piece of rubbish or feather was spared its sweeping effect.

Turning southwards into it again towards Barrow-in-Furness, the exposed marshes defeated me and we sought shelter on a series of tracks which took us to the outskirts of Barrow, where the buildings gave us protection. But on Barrow's stoloniferous pavements the ball muscle of my right foot made itself known. It was perpetually knotted, as though I had a lump of solid plaster in my boot, and the pain shot to the end of my middle toes. To alleviate this I walked without bending my foot. The result was somewhat flat footed, but it was a walk I was to resort to many times between here and Tower Bridge.

'Thwack . . . thwack . . . thwack . . .' my feet on the pavement sounded like a one legged duck. I began a chant which started with my left foot and went in time to my strides. It made a little pavement disappear; 'Left . . left . . left, right, left . . My pack's too heavy, my boots are too tight and my boobs are swinging from left to right . . left . . left . . left, right, left . . My pack's too heavy, my boots are too . . .'etc. In this way we passed the steamy loo paper factory and arrived in Barrow centre. Within minutes, a snowstorm had sent Barrow High Street scurrying for cover, and back on the coast it settled on beaches and low cliffs. So much for it never snowing on the coast.

We had decided to stay on Roa Island for the novelty factor, but now it was a struggle simply getting there, as I staggered from lamp post to lamp post up the half mile causeway. The one road which runs the length of the three hundred yard long island is bordered by the houses which are home to the sixty inhabitants of the island, and the houses act as a wind tunnel. At the end of the wind tunnel was the Spudtruck and Peregrine, who had rejoined us in Whitehaven.

In search once more for water, we were taken under the wing of Sue and Anton who run Roa's cafe. They confirmed our suspicions. 'Roa Island is the windiest place in Britain. It's notorious!' Anton declared triumphantly.

'I heard on the radio there are winds of 60 knots forecast tonight,' I told them. Anton and Sue laughed. 'That's nothing! Where are you off to tomorrow?'

Anton gave us each a beer which slipped down a treat after the dehydrating wind. 'Towards Grange-over-Sands.'

'Not across the sands I hope! Those routes can only be taken if you're with a guide. [There are actually public rights of way marked across the seven miles of sand.] The fishermen know the sands and how they shift and they'll take you at certain times of year. It used to be the main route used during the nineteenth century, to prevent the large detour inland. Stories abound of the coaches and horses which vanished entirely.' What a slow and suffocating death!

I had once been told what to do if you find yourself in quicksand; 'Lie down and swim for it!'

'I'd say you say a final prayer!' Anton laughed. Respect for the sands was the answer; and for the tides, which race in faster than a man can run.

The Spudtruck was now parked within the shelter of the cafe, and across Morecambe Bay the lights of Blackpool twinkled that night. The following morning we turned our backs on Blackpool and walked north to cross the Rivers Leven and Crake.

The road felt hard and unforgiving. 'Left . . left . . left, right, left . . my pack's too heavy. .' I passed two newborn lambs which were still wet but were already drinking heartily, encouraged by their very vocal mother.

A short section of footpaths saved us a few miles of road before we crossed the river at Greenodd and walked through skeletal oak woodlands and through patches of snowdrops. Adding a splash of deep green at the edge of the wood was an evergreen oak.

Tess was skitish after her morning off and when I stopped to rearrange the tongue of my boot for the umpteenth time, she ran off with a glove. She shook it viciously from side to side until I picked up a stick and threw that for her. She dropped the glove. 'See. I get you every time!' Tess didn't care. As long as she had something I didn't have she was happy.

We walked inland to Cark, where we stayed for the night. Our hostess opened the door in a mass of flowing white material which floated gracefully around her feet, and under which you could have fitted several dogs of Tess' size without even noticing. 'Darlings! Come in.'

She waved her hands around and smoked a cigarette in an elegant way. 'You must be exhausted. Sit down. Where have you walked from today? You must be thirsty. I've got some bubbles here. Pink champagne. I love pink champagne. You'll have some won't you?'

A glass of pink champagne was thrust into my hand. Tess shoved her snout up the billowing material and was duly rewarded by a steady supply of peanuts. The champagne went to my head, until I was swallowed up by the biggest and most bubbly bath. A bathroom all of my own. No sneaking through a flimsy plywood door to douse myself in a hosepipe dribble. No self conscious dressing with as much room to move as there was under my bed during children's games of hide and seek.

I anointed myself completely, and walked round the room with no clothes on for the novelty factor, swinging my arms to prove the space; then slept soundly from one gastronomic feast to the next. Cumbrian sausages were a delicacy not to be missed — even by someone who had been inundated with sausages for two weeks.

The wind had eased a little, but the day was smothered in a low grey mist which dispensed pathetic drizzle. The sky was within reach of my hand — if it could be called sky. I remembered a New Zealander saying to me that the 'sky in Britain is so low.' This sky was so low that it decapitated even the smaller hills.

I repeated the word 'sky' until it made no sense. I thought of any song I could think of which had 'sky' in it. I thought of the saying 'the sky's the limit', and decided that if that was the case, then the limit was pretty low on an average British day. It was the sort of day which is guaranteed to greet you when you fly back into England after a holiday, and your first view of Blighty is the second before you touch down.

Grange-over-Sands brought us around to the River Kent, where I spotted an unusual looking island out on the estuary. It took form to become twenty sheep huddled together, and the in-coming tide lapped at their feet as I watched.

It is uncommon for sheep to be pleased to see a human, but these sheep looked at me across the water as if I was their saviour sent. I sped off northwards to the nearest house.

A man and his son opened the door, but took one look and smell of me, and almost shut the door. I had fallen in a slurry pit that morning, and my once red left leg was now a thick and glutinous brown from my big toe to my bum. The slurry was seeping through to my knickers, and was squelching its way round my boots. I wasn't a pretty sight, but then I wasn't particularly comfortable either.

At lunchtime, Peregrine reluctantly let me into the Spudtruck which was decoratively strewn with wet washing, soon to become slurry perfumed washing. He had bought some chips from a nearby cafe and we had chip butties washed down with several cups of blackcurrant bracers and apple zingers. My body had long since rejected coffee, and was fuelled by such colourful sounding but insipid tasting herbal teas.

'Any luck with the water pump?' The thought of still not being able to have a shower was appalling to us both now. 'Sort of.'

Peregrine went over the new pump procedures, involving a complicated sequence of taps, switches, pumps and water cooling systems, the sound of which would have caused Geoffrey sleepless nights. Nevertheless, it worked, and when we fell asleep to the sound of the tide lapping Arnside esplanade that evening, the smell of slurry had all but disappeared.

At the end of the esplanade we passed through a beech wood, and well watered snowdrops, before being joined by Sunday. In Silverdale the serious walkers appeared, sporting colourful lycra leggings which had Tess confused as to which red legs were mine, new boots, fleeces emblazoned with brandnames, map cases and daypacks. We were also joined by mountain bikes which buck their way noiselessly along tracks; and a group of rock climbers surveying one of the many limestone escarpments which make up this area.

The presence of so many companions hit me. This was our coast! What were they all doing here? We had walked the coast alone for six months, through the worst of the winter, and where had they been then?! To say I felt indignant would be an understatement. I felt as though we had intruders in our home as we rounded Morecambe Bay and entered Lancashire.

Our bright-eyed outdoor enthusiasts had more sense then to walk along the A5105 into Morecambe, and in Morecambe our companions changed to the ambling promenaders with their coat clad Yorkys. After a few hundred yards I saw a familiar sign: 'Beware of Sea Born oil pollution. Keep pets off beach.' Such signs had been a daily occurrence on sections of the east coast.

A tanker had recently (legally) rinsed its tanks of a supposedly 'harmless' chemical outside the legal twelve mile limit, but the result had still been massive pollution and the deaths of hundreds of seabirds. As a result, the twelve mile coastal limit and discharge laws were being reviewed; but, as always, it had taken large scale pollution to expose what had been going on legally for some time. The cumulative affects of such pollution has perhaps been uncovered by a recent report connecting the increasing number of children being born with limb defects, who live on the coast, and pollution. Areas such as Ayrshire and Hartlepool have been named. Although the correlation is not fully confirmed, the evidence strongly suggests the horrific effect of the pollution I was witnessing.

At least the River Lune is honest about its pollution. A sign next door to the jetty, used by water skiers and jet skiers in the summer, warns of the dangers of swimming here. We spent two nights on the River Lune, parked in the car park of The Golden Ball. It is a pub with liberal licensing laws, because it is only accessible at low tide.

On Monday my sister Charles returned, and the tide let us out. We crossed the river and skirted Lancaster to join the Lancashire Coastal Way. There was water everywhere; at intervals the path was submerged in water, the roads to Glasson were flooded, and several boats were sinking. It was a scene of desolation.

The area was experiencing ten metre tides due to the wind, rain and time of the month. As far as we were concerned I hadn't noticed the rain, which always just avoided us, but I was sick of the wind. Like the pains which came and went, each of which I swore was worse and made me will back the last, each meteorological element was worse than the last. It was the grass is greener theory which made me cry: 'Bring back the snow and rain!' As usual my call was ignored.

But what a glorious morning it was at Cockersand Abbey, when the stillness woke me with its novelty. I shook my head and looked through my curtain. Sure enough, stretching up from the marshes was a mass of still blue sky daubed with only the odd whispy cloud.

I lifted my bandana and exposed my forehead to the sun for the first time in 1994. Like a plant reaching up to the sunshine to photosynthesise after a long winter, I walked tall and looked up without having my eyeballs sucked out by the wind.

'The sun has got his hat on, hip hip hip hooray, the sun has got his hat on and is coming out to play,' I sung to Tess, as we cheekily began a stretch of severely grazed sea wall which wasn't a footpath. Before Scotland I would never have even put a big toe off a footpath, but since then we had been known to stray.

We climbed a stile into a field full of horses, and immediately a bow-legged man came racing towards me like a bull to a matador. 'What are you doing in here? This is private land! Get out!'

'Is it? Oh, sorry. I just presumed that the sea wall was a path.'

It was a pathetic excuse, and I knew it, but I smiled sweetly at the irate man as he frog marched us across the field. 'Nice horses,' I said, determined not to have my good mood dampened on any account. 'Are they yours?'

'Hmm.' He wasn't overly chatty.

'Beautiful day isn't it?'

'Hmm.'

'Do you compete your horses?'

'My daughter does.' Things were getting better.

'My dog and I have walked over 2,700 miles. We're . . . I'm sorry about trespassing.'

'Hmm. Well, if everyone did it there wouldn't be much room for other people.'

I wasn't sure what he was getting at. I wasn't greatly worried I was starting a trend in walking Britain's coast.

We reached the gate. 'It's beautiful country round here. Nice and flat too for walking!' I was determined to work a smile out of this man, or at least something other than a monosyllabic grunt. 'Oh well. I'm sorry again. Bye —' we set off down the road.

'Good luck with the rest of the walk.' I turned round at his words and gave him a cheeky grin, which was returned by the merest hint of a smile. Even so, I decided to conform and stop my wanderings, and we returned to public footpaths to Knott End-on-Sea.

From Fleetwood the promenade stretched ahead of us; mile after mile of concrete backed by residential houses, parkland, mini golf courses, hotels, schools and even a small rifle range. Twenty miles of this would bring us to Blackpool and then on to the River Ribble. We strode out, unselfconsciously making a tape and passing skateboards, grannies, lonesome philosophers, yorkies, poodles and even a horse.

A gathering ahead materialised into a cluster of telescopes focused onto the shingle. I pulled up next door to them, and was told, during a lull in twitching, that we were looking at a juvenile kentish plover.

'Here. Have a look through these love,' a broad Lancashire accent offered. 'It's the one on its own. It's smaller and the black collar doesn't go right round its neck.'

'Oh. I see it!' It is quite catching this twitching. 'Where's it come from?'

'At this time of year it should be way down in southern Europe. There was one here last year too.'

'Oohh. Are you doing that now?' Another twitcher had seen the sign on my back. He didn't have the musical 'oohh's and 'ahh's of the Lancashire accent, and I realised that not all of these twitchers sung the same tune. 'Where have you all come from?'

'All over.'

'To see this bird?!' It seemed incredible.

I wondered who had been the first to spot it on these miles of shingle, and I imagined the internet's Bird Line or The Times nature section which says things like 'little bunting at Colchester; ring-necked duck at Leeds; spotted crake at Sittingbourne' — and now 'kentish plover at Blackpool.'

I was thrilled to be in Blackpool — the Mecca of holiday resorts and world famous for its Britishness. Behind North Pier (used by the Victorian middle classes to eye up the marriage prospects!) stands the 500 foot Blackpool Tower — Blackpool's biggest landmark — and below this is Blackpool's ballroom. Here, surrounded by Victorian hotels, signs such as 'The fun starts here' let you know that you have arrived in Blackpool proper. As far as I was concerned, the fun ended here.

An early morning stillness preceded an increasing rush of easterly wind which brought with it a snowy blizzard of angular flakes which rested on my hood and Tess' coat. I thought of the hot and claustrophobic hotel room we had just left, (the box within a box where I had felt trapped without the sound of the birds, the rain, and, dare I say it, the wind); and almost wished we were back there.

Through the horizontal flakes, posters declared 'Showaddywadddy playing here live in March', and 'Star guest Johnnie Casson here in April'; and we were joined only by two guilty looking council workers taking refuge in their truck.

There was only one point when I made myself look up, and that was to see the newest crowd puller in Blackpool, which was then still under construction — the tallest roller coaster in Europe. The snow stung my face and the top of the roller coaster was invisible. I wasn't surprised to hear that it had had to be approved by civil aviation.

Below this, new versions of old seaside entertainments awaited the opening of the crowd puller — The Coaster Tavern, The Coaster Amusement Arcade and I would imagine plenty of Coaster rock and Coaster candy floss.

The snow blanketed the world in a silence it was hard to break. Even the cars slushed through the wet roads in a muffled fashion. I thought of Jimmy and his sleeping bag; and then of the other reason for the Walk.

In every one of us there is the yearn for a challenge. Some channel this energy into the sports field, or at work, but for those not satisfied with this other challenges beckon. Because the world has become so much smaller, people resort to weird and whacky firsts. I wasn't interested in being a first; but I needed a big enough challenge, and walking was the only option. I seemed to be able to walk myself into a state of mental well-being, and believed more and more that man has only tempo-rarily curbed his nomadic instinct.

But nomads can't just stop because of the weather and sore feet! And, despite both these, my mental well-being was fine as long as I was walk-ing. The time it wavered was when I stopped. Then, my mind stopped, the pains surfaced, and the weather got the better of me. But at least then I had a band of fantastic drivers — as well as the knowledge that one day it would come to an end.

But that was a long way off, and I returned to one step at a time, and the concrete pounding my feet, and the sleety snow brought by the cold easterly wind we walked into, as we turned inland up the River Ribble. At this point nature called.

The cold and the exercise played havoc with my bladder. We were in a residential zone which meant that it was either a rarely found public loo, a barely concealed gateway, or parked lorries and cars. With legs crossed, I found a public loo; 'These public conveniences are shut dur-ing the winter. The nearest are Fairhaven Lake.' I should have been used to this by now and, not for the first time, I wondered whether people generally needed to pee less during the winter.

I dragged Tess at a run to Fairhaven Lake, only to come face to face with another sign; 'Please insert 5p into the slot.' In a final surge of bladder control, followed by a stroke of good luck, I found an elusive 5p. The most painful moments of the walk had not been due to blisters, but thanks to more basic matters.

Previously I had avoided public loos like the plague, thinking that one needed galoshes to enter them, and that once inside all that you learnt was that Brian was a 'good shag,' but I had found the majority of loos clean and well kept. The best public loos on Britain's coast are found in Mumbles (Gower Peninsula, Wales), where carpets, pictures and pot plants turn natures call into a positive experience for a bladder-weary coastal walker!

It was easy to contemplate such mundanities of life in Britain, as the cars sloshed through the sleety roads, and the water of the River Ribble bucked and pranced as the tide brought it upstream, and the wind pushed it back downstream. Even bird baths would have suffered tidal waves that day.

That night we stayed with a friend in Moss Side, which is a new suburb of Leyland. Although the houses were identical, their gardens were all different; tall and shrubby gardens teetered dangerously over the fences of the juxtaposed neatly prepared earth gardens, where any plant over a foot high and more than fifteen centimetres wide is considered messy. Most gardens boasted daffodil bulbs, but even these reflected the orderliness of the household. Linda's garden housed chickens.

'Ohh, ehh. How're you getting on then Spuddy?' Linda's voice sang along in a strong Lancashire lilt, and her whacky disposition shone out in Moss Side. As we shut up the Spudtruck, Linda's neighbour drove up. Out of the corner of her mouth Linda said 'ohh look out, here comes Mrs Glum,' and turning to Mrs Glum she gave her neighbourly greeting. 'This is my friend, Spud. She's walking . . .'

'Mm. Not much of a day for anything really is it?' said Mrs Glum, looking up to where the sky should have been.

Despite knowing exactly what we were doing, people often said 'you haven't picked the right weather for it,' or 'it's a lovely day for a walk.' Often I had as much difficulty with perspective as these people had. It seemed that the more miles we walked, the smaller the total sounded. 2,800 miles sounded like nothing; and anything less than twenty miles a day felt like a stroll in the park.

I imagine that Southport beach was once magnificent, but it has largely been desecrated by a sand extracting plant — the sand is sent to the Middle East. The dunes have all but disappeared, and the expansive beach is dreadfully eroded so that in places the underlying clay is exposed. These patches are intent on swallowing ankles.

Near Formby the world bounced into Saturday action, as though emerging from winter hibernation. Children kicked footballs and walked (eagerly or otherwise) along the beach with families, while their dogs raced in excited circles. A couple of fluffy muddy ponies had been cajoled into action; microlights used the mile deep beach as runway; and kites stayed momentarily airborne.

The vastness of the beach spread out these activities, but even at high tide the sea is still some half a mile from the dunes — more evidence of Britain moving westwards? There were certainly no sea walls or groynes here.

The beach ended at Crosby, and five miles of pavement would take us to Liverpool. We took to a dead straight road running parallel to the docks. The docks boomed during the eighteenth century until they stretched in an uninterrupted line for seven miles. The seven miles remain, but the picture is a sad one now.

I looked down each side street with a morose fascination, and the empty docks stared back at us and their gloom seeped eastwards. Our street was bad enough. I didn't see a single working industry or open business; warehouses were either boarded up, or in a state of semi-demolition; while other razed factories were fenced off by high netting. I peered through the netting of one such demolished building, and from out of the rubble charged a slavering and snarling rottweiler which would have easily munched Tess and I in one go. It jumped up at the fence, which sagged under its weight.

I was wallowing in the despair of my surroundings, and felt weighed down by the oppressiveness of the street. It is clear why Merseyside has the unenviable reputation of being one of the poorest regions in Europe. Recent attempts to lift the area from the doldrums appear to have been cosmetic, and are certainly based around the city centre. On my road, 'For Sale' signs were in as much disrepair as the buildings themselves.

The thin stream of cars turned their lights on as the day progressed. I willed Liverpool centre. Like Christopher Robin I concentrated on not walking on the lines of the pavement, but had to look up to cross the side roads, though there was never anything coming. There was little reason to turn right to the docks.

The empty industrial part of town gave way to a more residential zone; but still the people we passed could have been counted on one hand. A family ahead of us were leaving a small terraced house. The young parents were manoeuvring a toddler in a push chair and three other children. All four children were girls, and the oldest must have been seven. It was a squeeze for them all to fit into the patch of garden weeds before they spilt out onto the pavement and came towards us.

Four daughters. I am one of four daughters, and I wondered whether I would be here now if I had been born in that house in Liverpool? I wondered too what I would be like if there had been a baby mix up when I was born, and I had ended up here instead of with my real family. Would I be different? Would I be settled in a steady job, or would the restless streak still be there?

The family said nothing as we passed. I smiled an embarrassed smile, and the children stared blatantly. I wondered where they were going and wished, in a funny sort of way, that I could go with them.

CHAPTER TWELVE

PUFFIN ISLAND
ANGLESEY
GREAT ORMES HEAD
LLANDUDNO
COLWYN BAY
POINT OF AYR
WIRRAL   LIVERPOOL
DINAS DINLLEN
CAERNARFON
BANGOR
DWYGYFYLCHI
CONWY
LLANDUDNO
RHYL
PRESTATYN
LLEYN PENINSULA
TREFOR
MORFA NEFYN
PWLLHELI
RIVER CONWAY
RIVER DWYRYD
HELL'S MOUTH
BARDSEY ISLAND
CRICCIETH
MORFA BYCHAN
PORTHMADOG
PORTMEIRION
SHELL ISLAND
HARLECH
LLANBEDR
RIVER DEE
BARMOUTH
RIVER MAWDDACH
LIVERPOOL
TO
ABERYSTWYTH
223.3 MILES
TOTAL: 3,032.1 MILES
TYWYN
ABERDOVEY
YNYSLAS
RIVER DOVEY
ABERYSTWYTH

The lights went down and the show started; Liverpool's population came to life on Saturday night as if inherently nocturnal. Buskers occupied every street corner, and the Liverpudlians filled their hats with drunken abandon; a born again Christian rap band was busy spreading the word; restaurants bulged; drunken party goers spilled out of nightclubs; and a queue of people, young and old, stretching the length of an alley and spilling out onto a main road heralded the Cavern Club — where the Beatles started their rise to fame. Whatever the economic doom and gloom which blankets Merseyside, the Liverpudlians are, quite rightly, determined to continue their nightlife.

The following morning we made our way back through the silent, sleazy streets to a service at the new Anglican Cathedral. Like so many of the buildings in Liverpool, this Cathedral is outrageously large. Its foundation stone was laid in 1904, and 64 years later the red sandstone cathedral was completed. The result is magnificent, if somewhat costly — it costs £2,500 per day to run!

The sixty odd people attending the service cowered in one tiny part of the Cathedral. At the beginning of the service a young guy walked in whose strange assortment of clothes and lank hair declared 'homeless.' He sat between two ladies in front of us and a smell became apparent. The shoulders of the ladies tipped away, and they both looked at fascinating things on opposite walls for the remainder of the service.

Would anyone ask if he was alright? Perhaps they would give him a share of the offertory money which he was eyeing up as it passed? But nothing happened, and as we left, guilty as the rest, I wondered at the sense and justice of building such a needlessly large Cathedral (the largest church in this country, and the fourth largest in Europe), and then daily pouring such money into its upkeep.

It hardly comes as a surprise that one of Europe's poorest regions has a homeless problem. It is mainly young people who end up on the streets, and for this reason Shelter have set up a Housing Aid Centre aimed specifically for young people. Some of the money we raised was coming here.

Back at the hotel, the next driver, David, had arrived and was doing the Guardian crossword. People who did cryptic crosswords terrified me with their intelligence. 'Did you have a good trip up?'

I had apparently met David once before in a pub two years previously, but either drunkenness or memory loss prevented me from remembering this. He had come to drive in place of someone else. 'No. Nightmare! I'd only been driving for an hour when this lump of concrete flew up off the road at me!'

I thought of our beloved home, and hoped there wouldn't be any flying lumps of concrete along the lanes of North Wales. (It was only one year after this incident that I learnt the flying concrete had in fact been the very static kerb).

David went back to the crossword. He smoked an endless stream of cigarettes and from time to time fired clues at us. We scratched our heads in thoughtful and intelligent fashions, but came up with no solutions. He then began to talk about the numerous books he read, and the two degrees he had. David seemed arrogant and much too donnish for me, and I wondered how we would both cope with my end-of-day mindlessness. In fact, I fell asleep wondering whether we would get on at all. Little did I know.

There seemed to be some confusion as to where the Welsh border actually was, but we had finally arranged with Shelter Cymru to use the River Dee as the border. Having rounded the golf courses and beaches of Liverpool's suburbs which encompass The Wirral, we covered the seventeen miles to the border with plenty of time.

Shelter Cymru is entirely separate from Shelter England and Scotland so all the money we raised here would be kept separate. Owen from Shelter's headquarters in Swansea met us at the bridge, and gave us revised editions of our literature and sponsor forms — they were all in Welsh.

From here, the A548 was determined to stick as close as possible to the River Dee, and to shut myself off from it I began a new book — George Orwell's *Down and out in Paris and London*. It was appropriate because we were walking for homeless people, but it also made me remember the small Scottish village of Ardfern, south of Oban. George Orwell went up to this part of Scotland for the clean air, and lived on nearby Jura. His sister had married a farmer with one leg from Ardfern, and when George died in 1950 they adopted his son.

Really things haven't changed much since Orwell subjected himself to life on the streets in 1933. The one thing I did notice was that all the men he met were old; there obviously weren't the same mass of young people who end up on the streets in 1994.

The end of the River Dee was heralded by the first Welsh colliery, situated on the Point of Ayr, and running eight miles under the river/ sea. A footpath took us through the slag pits and over the railway line, where we joined the beach to Prestatyn.

One linear caravan site stretches from Prestatyn to Colwyn Bay, and we walked between the deserted mobile homes and the sea. I imagined the beach crowded with colourful windbreaks and excited children building Welsh sandcastles, and in Rhyl I pictured the Carousel Arcade brightly lit and noisy, and the mini golf course with players rather then the couple of bored gulls perched on yellow flags. Rhyl was waiting patiently for the first hint of summer when it would emerge from its winter chrysalis.

I liked the names of the Welsh towns. They would be a challenge for my spelling, and I liked trying to pronounce them. Owen had chided us for calling Llandudno 'Landudno' — it is 'Clandudno', and the 'Cl' has to be said as though you have a big globule of spit in your mouth which you are half heartedly trying to get rid of. If you manage the desired pronunciation both the 'c' and the 'l' should disappear into the spittle, but the spittle should preferably stay in your mouth.

I practised this on Llanddulas, and alone on the promenade it didn't matter how much spittle I gathered. But I stopped this pastime when I saw we had the dog walkers of North Wales as company.

The first was a rotund girl with spikey shocking pink hair who was accompanied by an Alsation with a shocking pink collar. As we neared them the girl turned round and gave a little shriek, before grabbing the pink collared Alsation. 'Euh —' she gave several more shrieks at the sight of Tess. 'I'm terrified of dogs!' she declared in a strong Mancunian accent. She eyed Tess warily. *A pink haired alsation owner terrified of dogs? Hmm.*

Then there was the particularly randy Labrador who was forcing precious toy pooches into their worried owner's arms, but the sturdy booted, barbour clad owner of Matt the Labrador was oblivious, and was more interested in Tess' breeding. This was a typical introduction between us dog walkers. 'She's got Boxer in her hasn't she?'

Before long we were talking about Matt's favourite toys (newspapers) and Tess' favourite toys (socks, gloves and fluffy toys). We then covered their scatological habits and exercise routines. Labrador owners are particularly chatty, but of all dog owners, the bereaved are the most verbose.

In front of us on Colwyn Bay sea wall was a bent double figure wearing a track suit and sneakers. When she saw Tess she went into raptures. 'Hello darling,' she drooled. 'Ooh, aren't you lovely. Yes, yes. You are, I know.'

Tess gave the lady several hearty licks. 'I know darling. Yes, you are lovely. Just like my Amy was —' This was my cue. 'Well, Amy was a *bitsa* really. A rescue dog, you know. But a good deal of collie. Oh she was lovely. I miss her terribly.'

Amy had died six and a half months ago, and I felt positively guilty for having the very much alive Tess at my feet. 'She saved my life you know.' (The life saving stories often went with the bereaved dog owner.) 'A small fire started in the house one night. Amy usually slept in my room, you know — on the seat in the corner. It was her bed. It's still there —' there was a pause. 'Anyway, one night this fire started in the sitting room — the electric heater had been left on. I heard Amy get up and leave the room, but I went back to sleep. She sometimes did that, you know, just to have a wander around. But this time she was persistent. In the end I took the hint and got up —' I wondered if I would have an heroic tale to tell of Tess.

Remembering the lady's bent double position, I asked her what she was looking for. 'Fish hooks,' she replied matter-of-factly.

'Fish hooks?'

'Oh yes. The fishermen are careless you know.'

'Are you a keen fisherwomen?'

'Goodness no! It's just that they're such lethal things — for children and dogs, and other wildlife. I used to come out here every day with Amy. I still come, and always find several.' This began an in depth discussion on fish hooks, from where the potential was limitless.

The ice cream colours of pinks, blues and yellows which highlight the Victorian facades of Llandudno are not swamped by garishness. The well preserved, elegant buildings look gracefully seawards over the wide and barely shelving bay, enclosed by the headlands of Great Orme and Little Orme.

The sand exposed at low tide had been moulded into orderly ridges and troughs by the now non-existent waves, and at the end of the beach we shed sand onto the carpet of the Grand Butlins hotel. Here, stetsons, tassled jackets, cowboy boots and glittery trousers confirmed the fact that we had walked in on the Country and Western week. Leaving Spud snoring in bed (her day was over when the walking was over), David and I shook collecting tins round the cowgirls and cowboys.

I was pleased that the fundraising was picking up. At times during the winter I had questioned the economics of the Walk. I knew we had to raise over a certain amount of money to justify the whole thing — (although I wasn't sure what that amount was.) Consequently, wearing the sweatshirt, shaking tins, and waving leaflets had become something of an obsession. At least with every step further south I knew that if the running of the Spudtruck became impossible or too uneconomic, Tess and I could camp. I fully expected the Spudtruck to give up. So far it had only held together by sheer strength of character, as well as a few rusty bolts.

As if to confirm my optimism, the limestone headland of Great Orme Head beckoned in brilliant sunshine the next morning. A tramway runs to the top, parallel to the very steep lane which we used, and the views from the top are magnificent. Looking inland we saw the snowy hills of Snowdonia, increasing in size and severity as they move away from the coast; while westwards was Puffin Island and Anglesey and below us was our next destination, Conwy. On the other side of Conwy I had two options — the A55 dual carriageway which hogs the shore, or a diversion inland through the Welsh valleys. I chose the latter.

The road was quiet and ran along the bottom of a valley floor, before climbing to reach Sychnant Pass. In every direction the countryside swallowed us up; a blanket of greenness diluted only by the black winter hedgerows and trees. The blue half of my world returned at the village of Dwygyfylchi, which gave my spelling its biggest test so far.

Here the sound of the trucks racing to Holyhead greeted me, as they disappeared through a rabbit burrow at the base of a towering hill dropping severely to the sea. At first glance it looked as though we would have to swim.

There was, however, a path around the hill. It was reached by crossing the main road and its slalom of roadworks; and the path itself was concrete, stepped and narrow. None of this had deterred the local council from erecting a sign reading; 'This path is open to horses, carriages and pedestrians' — there was even a mounting block beneath the sign!

Just to get a horse across the main road would have been an achievement.

The road moved away from the coast, and Anglesey came closer. We took a grassy track to Bangor, following a fenceline constructed of pieces of slate of varying mauves and greys dug into the ground in the same way as the flagstones of Caithness. Each piece of slate is less then a foot in width so that half a mile of this fencing used literally hundreds of pieces. I guess there is no shortage of slate in Wales!

The road became quieter past Bangor, and this took us to Caernarfon, which was bustling with a Saturday air. I went in to a newsagent to buy a paper and for the first time realised I was really in another country.

A few locals moved away from the counter but continued to chat in alien Welsh, as I made for the gap with my paper. 'Just that?' the shop assistant slipped into English with that infuriating ease which bi-lingual people manage, then returned to Welsh. I obviously had English written all over my face.

After centuries of repression the Welsh language is currently experiencing a revival, (during the nineteenth century, any child caught speaking Welsh was made to wear a sign around their neck saying 'Welsh Not'!) Not only is Welsh now part of the compulsory national curriculum in Wales, but a growing number of schools are teaching the entire curriculum in Welsh. This is also true of Gaelic in Scotland.

I found the Spudtruck cowering beneath the impenetrable walls of Caernarfon Castle, which was built as a symbol of English power after the defeat of the last native Prince (rather sadly called Llewellyn the Last) in 1283. Since then the Principality of Wales became incorporated with England, and all male heirs to the throne have since become Prince of Wales, and are invested in Caernarfon.

The doors of the Spudtruck were thrown open in the sunshine, and David was looking very pleased with himself. I was enjoying David's company now. He was a mine of information, and on only night three I had admitted I found him initially arrogant. I had no doubt the Spudtruck could make enemies just as quickly, but fully intended never to find out.

'Good news. Two pieces,' he said, drawing in his breath in a manner which I now knew indicated importance. 'Yeah?' I dumped my rucksack on the front seat and sat down with a groan. 'Yup. Huge success with the supermarket, thanks to the Welsh literature.'

This was good news, and my stomach grumbled in agreement, but I couldn't find the same enthusiasm. David put a mug of cinnamon surprise in front of me and added nonchalantly, 'Oh, and a guy sponsored you 35p a mile.'

'You what?'

'35p a mile! Well, it was thanks to Tess —'

I had estimated that the Welsh coast would be between 600 and 700 miles, which would mean a total from this guy of around £250. Perhaps I could just leave the whole thing to David and Tess?

I felt in fine form after this piece of good news. It was Saturday, we had left behind the roads of North Wales, and ahead of us was the Lleyn Peninsula. The day after tomorrow was a day off, and then I would be joined by my oldest sister, PC, who was coming from Ireland to drive the Spudtruck. I was only sad that she wasn't bringing my two nephews.

Instead she was bringing number three, which was due sometime in the summer. Inspired by thoughts of my family, I made a tape for them in the still winter sunshine, following the sun westwards until we dropped down onto the firm sand of expansive Dinas Dinlle beach.

The sun setting out to sea underlined the small waves with pencil-thin black shadows the moment before they broke, and glistened on the wet sand, along which fishermen cast out their long lines. At the end of the beach, a collection of earth moving machines were building a protective groyne. As the sun dropped lower, the JCB's became silhouettes against the sunset, their arms lifting and dropping, resembling prehistoric creatures in their featureless blackness.

After two weeks of walking at sea level, I now huffed and puffed through the heather of the Lleyn Peninsula, passing old slate mines, and dreaming of the peace we would find at the top of the Yr Eifl hills. We were pioneers again.

The vague path levelled out and ahead of us were Lleyn's rugged hills which have been placed on the landscape in no particular order. Footpaths and gravel tracks took over, and the smell of roasts guided us to Morfa Nefyn. We had reached another red pin.

That night, as the frost descended, the man who, on his first night, had declared that he 'never drunk spirits,' was the first to produce the whisky bottle, declaring that it was 'purely medicinal.' While David cooked, I hovered over his crossword in an attempt to look intelligent. As usual it failed. 'You know, it's funny I get so mentally exhausted during the day,' I mused.

'Walking doesn't mean your brain stops.'

'Far from it. But I think people find it hard to appreciate.'

I began to write my diary. 'I spell words when I'm walking. Does that sound weird?'

'How do you mean?'

'Well, I pick a word and spell it in time to my steps.'

'A sort of meditation.

'I suppose so. When I spell, my mind's clear of everything else.'

Tess stirred, sniffed the curry and went back to sleep. 'I also run through conversations. Either ones I've had or ones I might have, perhaps a phone call I've got to make. Something like that. Sometimes I pick a conversation I've had and then change it! Then I spell the words in the conversation too.' David gave me a weird look. 'Perhaps I'm cracking up!'

'Do you get lonely when you're walking?'

'Not really. I sometimes think it would be nice to have a companion, but the times I have had other people I've missed my solitude. I think I'd find it hard with a companion. Anyway, I've got Tess to talk to.'

'Definitely cracking up!'

It was hard to convey what exactly my days were like, and on the whole I never wanted to talk about them. They could be so long anyway that relating the day would make them longer still.

We began to talk about Australia, where we had both been, then moved onto pirates, life and death. So much for first impressions — there was definitely a thin thread of chemistry growing between us.

The grey rendered houses and bungalows of Welsh Morfa Nefyn were being buffeted by the bitter wind which whistled down the streets the next day, and the smoke which rose from the chimneys had no option but to join the wind in an easterly direction. We took refuge in Morfa's only pub, which was soon resembling so many other *offices* we had used on Britain's coast.

We were found in this way by PC, Mary and Moira. Mary is PC's husband's Irish aunt, whom we had stayed with several days previously, and who had driven PC from Holyhead. Moira was her equally jovial friend. Together they made an impromptu party which continued in the Spudtruck, where the duty free whisky bottle elicited a succession of 'whell now, just a wee one's from the Irish contingent. The Spudtruck had never known such a party.

At some point during the evening, Moira rallied Mary into action and asked David if he wanted a lift to Bangor. David looked reluctant, as well as a little worse for wear. 'I don't really want to go!'

'Well stay!' PC and I chorused. That was enough. He swayed a little, and as soon as Mary and Moira had gone he passed out on the now collapsed table.

Meanwhile I had given PC my letter box bed, but five months through her pregnancy she was already fairly large. She looked as though she was wedged between the roof and the bed, and was bright red in the face from uncontrollable giggles. 'I don't think I'll ever move from here!' she cried, tears streaming down her face.

I never saw PC extricate herself the next morning. I ringed an isolated lunchtime parking spot on the map, and left David nursing his head self pityingly and PC wondering on her next move.

I stumbled along low rocky cliffs, following a frozen path and admiring dagger-like icicles, wonderfully sculpted stalactites which hung like chandeliers from rocky headlands enclosing small beaches. The sea had taken on an identical cold grey colour to the sky, and was broken only by the shadows of shags.

Much of the tip of the Lleyn Peninsula (or the Land's End of North Wales) is owned by the National Trust, and consequently there are plenty of footpaths criss-crossing the fields divided by turf banks. Rocky outcrops litter the landscape and produce sheer drops to the sea.

Two and a half miles out from the very tip of Lleyn, Bardsey Island rises up dramatically, and not a single white horse disturbed the intervening stretch of deep blue sea. But in Welsh this island is called Ynys Enlli which means Isle of the Currents or Tide Race Island, which says a lot for these deceptively calm waters. In AD 615 a monastic community was founded on Bardsey Island, and pilgrims journeyed here with the knowledge that three pilgrimages to Bardsey Island equalled one to Rome! Nowadays Bardsey Island is privately owned by an environmental trust.

All evidence showed that this coastline is used to bearing the full brunt of the prevailing wind — one reason why it will surely remain unspoilt. The only vegetation is ever resilient and ever-green gorse bushes, and stalky blackberry bushes so flattened by the wind that they smother whole hillsides. Tidal currents, cliffs, triphid brambles and frighteningly named Hell's Mouth Bay — this is not a coast for the faint hearted.

The soft sand of Hell's Mouth Bay shelved steeply into a cruel sea; a sea which has been the graveyard for many ships over the years. We trespassed our way along the low, slumping cliffs backing the beach, safe in the knowledge that it was too windy and wet for anyone to be after trespassers. At the end of the bay the paths returned, and a holiday coastline runs to Pwllheli.

Mobile homes looked out with blinkered eyes over the rough sea, their net curtains pulled shut for their winter hibernation, and only a few colourful crocuses providing any colour. The grey blanket of weather weighed me down, and I could feel myself tipping my body too far forwards and letting my legs shuffle. The weather was my back's worst enemy.

On the outskirts of Pwllheli the Butlins loudspeakers could be heard advising the holidaymakers on the afternoon's activities. We had stayed there the previous night, among 5,000 half termers, and now, in the grey cold, I dreamt of the sub-tropical pool with its rapids and whirl-pools, and thought jealously of people watching films, or lounging in the jacuzzi. I also thought jealously of David sitting on the warm train.

I was compiling a list of spoiling experiences for myself sometime in the future. (I never thought about giving them to myself at the end of the Walk, because the end of the Walk was not something that even crossed my mind: I just thought of them 'sometime in the future'.)

Apart from jacuzzis, massages, open fires, roasts (each one of the few roast potatoes I had eaten over the last six months received at least three rapturous lines in my diary), lie-ins, and sunshine, was added a long train journey. We had followed so many stretches of railway that the thought of lazily watching the countryside from a train had blown itself out of all proportion. I had to take a train journey!

I followed the railway line east, along largely flat and boring marshland where the track offered crossings over countless dykes, and passed a very closed Criccieth Castle. Sand dunes took us to through Morfa Bychan to Borth-y-Geest, from where it is half a mile to Porthmadog.

During the nineteenth century an MP, William Madoch, put Porthmadog on the map when he planned a mail route to Ireland via Porthdinllaen (on the north shore of the Lleyn Peninsula). Because the train route would pass through Porthmadog, the potential for tourism in Porthmadog was great.

In anticipation of this great scheme he built a dam at the mouth of the River Glaslyn, along which the railway line would run. But Holyhead became the main port, and Porthmadog remained a quiet town with 7,000 acres of extra land, and the Cob, along which the road and a nar-row gauge railway line now run.

The Ffestiniog railway was built in 1836 to transport slate from Blaenau Ffestiniog. It now carries tourists, and is the oldest narrow gauge railway in the world — a train spotter's delight.

On the other side of the Cob we climbed a hill through oaks and ashes, whose branches criss-crossed above and around us in a gnarled fashion, throwing shadows across our path. Shadows were a novelty. This path took us to Portmeirion.

Visiting Portmeirion is literally like stepping straight into Italy, which was the desired effect of the architect, Clough Williams-Ellis. The village, which overlooks the sand flats of the River Dwyryd, was built between 1925 and 1972 and consists of ornate mellow colour-washed buildings, columns, statues and fountains, all of which are interlaced by vehicle free paths. Sadly there are no cafés or bars where we could munch a pizza and drink a little Valpolicella, but I was perfecting daydreams.

On the south shore of the River Dwyryd, we followed pancake flat reclaimed land along a deep protruding spit. Britain is definitely making a gradual move westwards! And at Harlech the waves which once lapped the base of the hilltop Castle are now some half a mile from it.

In the car park of Harlech Castle, amid squeals of ever emotional greetings, we were joined by Dee. Many years ago, Dee had the unenviable task of looking after my sisters and myself, when she herself was at the ripe age of seventeen. Apart from weddings and funerals we hardly see Dee, but she had come to walk with us for a few days.

We kept on the road to Llanbedr, where we set off across the sand dunes to Shell Island and the beach south. The tide was out again. 'Do you know Dee, we always seem to hit the beaches at low tide! I never plan to but . . .'

Dee fell in alongside, and humoured me by responding to my drivel, which continued . . . and continued. I talked about sand dunes, birds, Shrewsbury biscuits, pollution, nephews, and a whole range of equally unrelated and inconsequential subjects which had built up over seven months. Meanwhile, Dee concentrated on walking, and developed several healthy blisters.

The Spudtruck was parked among the dunes, and I sat down to write my diary. Somewhere on the beach we had crossed our 3,000th mile; yet 3,000 miles sounded like nothing. The further we walked, the less the mileage meant.

I knew that from now on the success of the walk would depend on sustaining the mental equilibrium and strength. In John Merrill's book (the first person to walk Britain's coast), he wrote 'I firmly believe that marathon walking as I practise is principally a mental exercise'. He was right. Physical fitness alone wouldn't have got us this far.

While I wrote, I listened to PC and Dee and enjoyed their familiarity. The Spudtruck shook to girly giggles and stories of our childhood. 'You used to kick us under the table when we were naughty Dee!' PC began.

'I never did!'

Dee was always defending this one, and gave PC a friendly boot under the table. 'Then there was murder in the dark,' PC continued. 'And finding you in my bedroom with some man!'

'No way!'

Dee had been the object of admiration of any man who had come to our house. 'And then there was Kenny! He really had the hots for you!'

The stories and reminisces went on into the night, until I decided to clear the deck and leave PC and Dee to sort out their shared bed. As I drifted off to sleep I heard them declaring what a funny thing it was that we had found ourselves in a campervan in North Wales on a February night.

The next morning it was perfectly clear who had won the battle for the narrow bed. PC stretched and yawned in a satisfactory way. 'I was just having the most fantastic dream. I was eating lobster!'

'No wonder you were making such a racket!' Came Dee's voice, wedged against the back wall.

PC got up and disappeared into the loo, which she declared was like a 'blimmin' broom cupboard,' and from here the conversation continued. They were off again.

Through my curtain I could see the day dawning in a very Welsh fashion. Low grey clouds skidded across the sky, threatening rain but seemingly not stopping in one place long enough for this to happen. We ate porridge and Dee set off with us again. She didn't appear to be feeling the blisters.

After five miles, the hills found the sea, squeezing the railway line and main road up against the shore, and reducing the beach to a narrow strip backed by some rocks and Barmouth esplanade. Here we were met by Bill from Barmouth, a Shelter supporter.

Barmouth is a gorgeous town on the mouth of the River Mawddach. Wedged between spectacular hills, the river, and a groyned beach, it provides a little bit of everything for its plentiful tourists. But the Barmouth we found was enjoying its winter vacation, as Bill ushered us along the main street, introducing us to anyone and everyone and paying royalty type visits to select shops.

The people of Barmouth listened to Bill's garrulous enthusiasm with good humoured patience, and responded to the collecting tin which Dee held out as Oliver had done when he asked for more. Bill then joined us across the River Mawddach, giving us a running commentary on the area; the gold found in the river, the thwarted plans for a marina, and, with just a hint of pride, the presence of the tourist railway which terminates at the station with the longest name in the world.

We found Gorsafawddachaidraigddanheddogleddollonpenrhynareur
... gion Station — but even Bill from Barmouth couldn't pronounce it.

By mid-afternoon Bill had turned back, and Dee had been unable to
conceal her pain any longer. The state of her feet would have made the
most intrepid foot explorer proud — there was barely an inch which
wasn't covered in blisters and lumpy swellings. Dee had to leave the
next day. The muscle of her foot had been ripped away from the bone,
and it only began to heal four months later.

Everyone who had walked with us, whether it be for an hour or a
day, had suffered some ailment. I felt responsible, but didn't need the
responsibility. I told myself that from now on I would be bossy and
dissuade people from being too ambitious. Resolutions are grand things.

We walked along a small road to Tywyn. The clouds still slid over
the hills inland, covering them then revealing them again, each time
showing me the hills from a slightly different angle. However slow our
progress might be, it was still progress. Aberdovey would finally arrive
in our path.

I remembered Aberdovey from an Outward Bound course I had been
on aged fifteen. We had canoed in the River Dovey, camped on Cader
Idris, abseiled, made rafts to cross the river, and been daily subjected to
an assault course where I had finally wet myself from laughter!

Now Aberdovey was heralded by the blue figure of Dee. PC had
long since gone on to make the large river detour, so Dee had spent
several hours in a small café, exposing her feet to the people of Aberdovey.
The sympathy vote had won, and she had received numerous donations
as well as securing us a lift across the river with Tommy.

Tommy hopped from foot to foot in a relaxed fashion. He had curly
hair which was crusty with salt, and the beginnings of a beard. His face
had a healthy glow from a life at sea. He had fallen under Dee's charm,
and smiled a twinkling smile through blue eyes. 'We'd better get going
then. At low tide you can't get the boats in or out.'

Tommy's boat was already a long way below the top of the jetty. He
was a prawns, whelk and lobster fishermen, although, like most fishermen, he declared that he'd fish for 'whatever was about.'

There were so many people who had helped in so many ways, and it
is often hard to show sufficient appreciation when you are more deeply
grateful. 'Ah. It's no bother,' Tommy said cheerily, flashing a look at
Dee. 'Good luck. And I hope the feet get better!'

We watched Tommy's boat draw away from our sand bank, until it
looked the size of a matchbox compared to the sand banks which had
now risen from the estuary like vast whale's backs. Another friend had
come and gone.

We joined the road at Ynyslas, where we hoped PC and the Spudtruck would find us. It was getting dark, and I had walked twenty four long and interrupted miles. We found a sheltered seat in the bus stop. The energy went from me immediately, and the cold seeped through my additional layers.

Where's the Spudtruck? I thought of tea; great big steaming mugs of strong and milky tea to wrap my hands round, and these became vats of tea to quench my thirst. The pleasure of the cushioned seat added to the vision of tea, and I shifted my weight on the cold wooden seat.

Where's the Spudtruck? I felt irrational, and sat there building up my end of day treats like building blocks. Tea, a seat, removal of boots and then food. Tea and the end of day cigarette. Each one became an obsession.

A gloomy light enveloped the bus stop, and the headlights of the cars hit us face on. Each one had to be the Spudtruck, but wasn't. When it finally turned up I was swimming in tea and munching my way through mountains of biscuits.

PC had been on a hunt for a place for our family to stay that weekend, and had found a converted barn which had a wood burner, arm chairs and enough beds to accommodate all thirty drivers if they had wanted to join us.

I wrapped my hands round the real mug of tea, ate a banana and had my end of day cigarette. I had come home again.

Our elevated letter-box bed.

CHAPTER THIRTEEN

The Mayor of Aberystwyth's wife wore a sensible mackintosh, and a very determined look. I decided that I wouldn't like to cross her in a WI meeting. She was joined outside the town hall by other women in sensible mackintoshes, who clearly held her in awe, and then by Mrs Thomas.

Mrs Thomas' sensible mackintosh was red and done tightly up to her chin. She wore a fluffy tea cosy hat, and had a kind face and a smile which efficiently hid any teeth problems. She had been actively supporting Shelter for twenty five years.

'Mrs Thomas isn't in the photograph! She should be,' the Mayoress cried, asserting her position. 'Oh, no. Don't worry,' Mrs Thomas herself chuckled, and her fluffy hat was ruffled by a gust of wind. 'Of course you must Mrs Thomas,' cried others. There was great consternation.

The photographer gave a sigh of barely concealed irritation. He had decided that Mrs Thomas wasn't an important component; but she was. We pulled Mrs Thomas into the photo and the Mayoress looked mollified.

The Mayor crouched lower to Tess, gingerly patting her as if she was a red hot coal, and his chain glinted in the sunshine. The proximity of such importance was too much, and Tess launched herself at his face. I grappled with Tess, the Mayor backed away again and patted more gingerly than before, and the photographer repeated his request 'a little closer please.' I bit my tongue. Tess was definitely the ring leader in our juvenile pact.

From Aberystwyth, we walked along the side of the hills, through small livestock farms linked by barely used footpaths. We disturbed snipe and walked through fields of lambs, who approached Tess with an interest not tainted by the introduction of sheep dogs into their lives. My legs were on auto pilot and I made no attempt to channel my thoughts. I let them do their own thing, as they flitted from Tess, to Shelter, to a shag out to sea, to an isolated farm which I built into my home. We stopped in Aberaeron.

We had been joined by PC's husband, Patch, and were found in Aberaeron by a friend from agricultural college, Chris. That night, three inches of snow fell on Scarborough beach, and I pulled my most colourful hat firmly down over my ears as Chris and I set off the next morning.

Even though Chris was fit and kept up with us, everything took longer with two people; things like climbing fences, having a pee, or twitching. We also had a rendezvous to keep in Newquay.

Although Newquay is essentially a quiet fishing village, it has a special attraction for summer visitors because Cardigan Bay is home to one of Britain's main populations of bottlenose dolphins. Consequently, Newquay was the first place to be awarded Heritage Coast status out to sea, a status which extends for one mile offshore. But this important population may soon be under threat, as both oil and gas development have been licensed within Cardigan Bay.

We were greeted in Newquay by a group of blue faced people huddled behind stacked lobster pots. Stalactite drips on noses indicated that a stage of numbness had been reached, and their hats rammed firmly on their heads and hands thrust deep in pockets were doing nothing to deter the increasing wind, which would have lifted the most determined of tweed skirts.

Overpowering the group in presence was a flamboyantly dressed lady with peroxide blond hair, who introduced herself as Dot and gave us both an all-embracing hug. Having flattened the mouse-like Vera, Tess was now shoving her snout up Dot's fly-away skirt, and was rewarded by a big cuddle. At this level Dot's pendulous water melon earrings became the next target.

Dot has been a Shelter supporter for years and, over mugs of hot chocolate in the steamy Mariners Cafe, we then met Eve. It transpired that Eve had been homeless.

Eve was a very young forty five, dark skinned, short and slim. She had lived on the streets of London when she was about twenty. 'I managed to get a job, though,' she said. 'I worked in a cafe and used to sleep wherever I could, cleaning myself up in the mornings and going to work. Eventually I saved enough to put a deposit on a flat. But it's not so easy these days; it's harder on the streets. There was a certain camaraderie when I was homeless. Everyone looked after each other. It's not like that now.'

Even in the warm and faraway Mariners Cafe in Newquay, Eve's memories were no less clear. I was struck by the number of unsung heroes who play their own parts in exposing homelessness. They were all an inspiration.

From Newquay we took to cliffs which have been compressed, folded and refolded, and subsequently weathered, so that their layered strata and sheer fractures are clearly visible. In some places the crinkling is so intense that the rocks appear tangibly pliable, and they belie their true 450 million years. They were formed when Britain as we know it today was part of a massive continent far from this spot; and they have borne the thunderous tread of dinosaurs.

We alternately put on and took off waterproofs, as we dropped, and climbed, and dropped, and climbed; following a coastal path, then taking to a sheltered lane. 'You know, Chris, by walking anticlockwise we're always walking across hills and cambers which slope to the right.' I called Tess over to illustrate this.

Tess' left toenails on her left paws were more worn down than her right toenails; and my left boots were much more worn down than my right boots.

'Now you come to mention it Spud,' Chris began in his mock serious way. 'You've obviously got used to compensating for the hills, because you're leaning over to the left even on the flat!! You'll have to walk the coast the other way, to balance your body!'

'Hm.'

'We'll have to make a prop for you to lean against when you're on the flat!'

'A portable one —' we giggled as the images went on.

We found the chaotic Spudtruck in Aberporth, and Patch waving a bag of rubbish around. 'I can't find a rubbish bin!' There were signs around the car park telling people to take their rubbish home, but this would have been a little hard for us.

Litter bins, like public loos, were a diversion of mine. In Scotland I had been impressed by the amount of litter bins found in even the quietest lay-bys; whereas in Wales the request to take your litter home is common, and consequently litter bins are scarce. In England, however, we have come up with the perfect solution — the self emptying litter bin. These are made from netting with holes big enough to allow kleenex tissues, chocolate wrappers and even determined chip paper through. They are quite ingenious.

Patch returned, rubbish-less, and I went to find refuge in the shower; but discovered that the gas had been left on since Patch's morning ablutions. The water was cold — again. 'Patch!'

'Oh! Sorry Spuddle!'

Patch's hand shot up to his head in flustered vagueness, and he chuckled guiltily, secretly. In two days we had got through one gas cylinder, which normally lasted ten days! I would often see Patch, out of the corner of my eye, turning every cooker gas knob on and waving the igniter around like a magician with a wand. When I enquired if he was really trying to blow us up, he would simply reply, 'Oh Spuddle! It's such fun!' Memories of Geoffrey came flooding back. All we needed was a Macduff.

If Patch wasn't blowing us up, it was guaranteed he had lost something. He was the only person who could scuttle in the Spudtruck — and scuttle he did, there and back, rummaging under things, scratching his head and saying 'Bother' in a Mad Hatter fashion. On this particular night he had lost his newspapers, until I found The Times, February 22nd 1994 scrunched up, soggy and just a little cheesy in my boots.

It was still raining when Chris and I set off the next morning, and the inside of my coat felt familiarly cold and clammy. Once we were walking I relinquished the map to Chris, who had just been helping a group of school children on an orienteering exercise in the Brecon Beacons. If anyone could map read, Chris could.

We set off round Aberporth airport in search of a path which ran half a mile inland. I kept wanting to look at a map, in the same way as you might check the time despite not wearing your watch that day.

We began scrambling across country and battling through bramble hedges and over sheep netting. 'The path should be somewhere here,' Chris said as though he was forging a track through dense jungle. Then ahead of us appeared what looked like an airport. 'There can't be another airport here! Let me look at the map,' I demanded. Chris laughed and looked guilty. We had gone in a circle and were lost.

We came to a farm track and a lonesome farmer, and enquired as to where we were. 'Well, this is . . .' His thoughtful words reminded me of so many Highland farmers.

'Where's that on the map?' Chris asked, holding out the map.

The farmer put his foot up on a nearby stone and scratched his head under the hood of his waterproof. He held the O/S map upside down, then turned it round the right way.

'Well . . .' he waved his farming finger over the map as though casting a spell on it. Well . . . Perhaps here somewhere.' His finger had landed a long way from where even I knew us to be. 'But tell me now, where are you trying to get to?'

'We're trying to follow the coast to Cardigan.'

'Oooh. Ahh. Well . . .' he gave his head another scratch, and changed feet. 'It's not the best place to be starting from!'

We thanked the farmer, who appeared to have strayed from Ireland. 'No problem,' he replied, relaxing his furrowed brow and looking suitably pleased with himself.

We followed our noses and instinct, and after a healthy diversion found the right way. This was the first and last time I trusted anyone else with the map; the children in Brecon did not know how lucky they had been.

From Cardigan it would be impossible to get lost, thanks to the Pembrokeshire Path, and at Cemaes Head one of the most spectacular coastal stretches in Britain started. The ancient cliffs are again sheer and folded into weird and wonderful sculptures, and we followed their tops, climbing up to between 300 and 500 feet before dropping back to sea level at every insignificant stream.

I hooked my thumbs into the straps of my rucksack, and tried not to lean forwards too much up the hill. 'One more stride, and one more stride, and one more stride; I'll stop at the top,' I told myself, taking my thumbs out from the straps, and pushing down on my knees with each stride. 'One, two, one, two, one . . .' My thumbs went back to the straps.

The path was very muddy. I wore gaiters and had long since abandoned any idea of staying clean. But, with my eyes on an acrobatic chough, I missed my footing on a down hill section, landed on my bottom and slid.

The next minute Tess had jumped on my shoulders, sharing her own mud with me. 'Tessie! No!' I giggled weakly again, but then felt like crying.

I stayed sitting as the mud seeped through my trousers. Pulling my rucksack off I found a chocolate bar which I had been saving for just such an emergency. Sharing the bar (nearly) fairly, we sat in the mud where I had fallen. 'Happiness is a snickers bar in the mud!' Then I looked at the next proud hill, and felt like crying again.

But no one was going to find us. I pushed myself to my feet and the mud squelched through my fingers. I now had mud everywhere; it was beginning to get dark; and we had to reach Newport.

I put on a tape of Van Morrison (getting mud on my walkman), and walked in time to the music. I liked Van Morrison — it reminded me of Scotland. These hills also reminded me of Scotland, except for the presence of a path. It was the path which made it so muddy.

After twenty five exhausting miles we arrived in Newport in the dark.

The thirteen miles to Goodwick felt like a turn around the garden, from where the sky, the sea, the clouds and the rain merged into one grey and damp sphere; a claustrophobic mass. It was broken only by the red, yellow and black form of a goldfinch, and the piercing white strobe of Strumble Head lighthouse. A solitary buzzard which disappeared into the murk with three flaps of its wings was the only other sign of life that day. The harmony of rain and crashing sea resumed.

The waves built up, gathering pace and momentum from miles out in the Atlantic; the sound of water being pushed and pulled, increasing and increasing, until it reached the crescendo — the point of no return — when the force of that carefully built wave was spent on the resilient rocks.

The spray flew up, was momentarily suspended when it reached its highest point, then succumbed to gravity. The white water left by the broken wave jostled around the rocks like a great frothy cauldron; but already, as it began to disperse, here was another wave, building up and building up.

I watched wave after white topped wave come out of a grey nothingness. It was exhilarating, but damp — and still muddy. I tried to dig my boots into the mud, but in doing this I inadvertently put pressure on my back. There were two consolations; the hills weren't nearly as high as they had been the previous day, and the wind wasn't too strong. There was always a worst scenario.

The rain and cloud lay low over the numerous rocky outcrops of iron age forts, such as Garn Fawr, which was also an historic radar site in World War II. In between these two points in history, this inhospitable and still inaccessible coast has provided valuable communications and transport of goods for agriculture.

In Abercastle a stone lime kiln can be identified near the small harbour. Lime was shipped into many places in Britain to improve surrounding farmland, and had to be processed on arrival. Culm was also manufactured in such ports to be used as fuel. It was produced from local anthrocite dust and clay, mixed together into balls.

But, perhaps more amazingly, villages such as Abercastle were home to shipbuilding enterprises during the late eighteenth and early nineteenth centuries. This supplemented the usual fishing and smuggling (the latter in the not too distant past); as did brick works, and granite and slate quarrying. In villages such as Abercastle and Porthgain, the cottages can now be counted on two hands; yet the quays remain, withstanding the ever unpredictable sea as well now as they did up to four hundred years ago.

Trevine appeared after seventeen solitary miles. Not a single article of my clothing had been spared the drenching, and I hung them in every available Spudtruck corner. The rain battered us from every angle, and began its slow seepage down the inside walls; but Patch appeared blissfully unconcerned. He lay on the seat, pulled a blanket over him, and went to sleep.

Before I fell asleep I inspected the mould inches from my nose. Although I visibly noticed the damp, I never noticed it at night. Instead, I enjoyed my nights; even these stormy ones. It was extraordinary to have heavy rain only two feet above my head, and no more then a few inches in front of my nose. Even a tent wouldn't bring you as close to the falling rain.

I enjoyed the knowledge that the great outdoors was just *there* — my world of wind, rain, birds; as we progressed from winter into emerging spring

I dreamt that the world was flooding, and in the morning I pulled back the flimsy curtain and pushed my nose up against the cracked plastic window. The wind had dropped and the rain stopped, but there was a surreal mist. In a small bush on which buds were just appearing, a tiny wren sung its song of enormous magnitude.

The birds were definitely emerging. The fulmars swooped and glided with more urgency, and paired up on their rocky ledges where they kissed and squawked to each other in fulmar courting. I had seen oystercatchers similarly welcoming spring; and thrushes and blackbirds materialised.

After forty miles of not seeing a single person on the path, other people joined our coastline near St David's Head. Despite feeling my familiar indignation, any sign of spring was welcome. Luckily I wasn't to know quite how far away spring still was, and that this was Britain's first spring — the one that makes us winter-weary Brits capable of lasting until the real one arrives.

St David's, the smallest city in Britain, shone in all its glory on March 1st, when it comes alive to celebrate the country's Patron Saint, and the founder of the magnificent twelfth century Cathedral which dwarfs the small valley within which it is built. It is like finding Canterbury Cathedral on a village green.

But St David's Day sticks in my mind for its colourfulness, largely thanks to the children in their Welsh dress. A picture comes to mind.

The little boys are wearing waistcoats and plus fours of deep red, and some wear flat caps perched on their heads at jaunty angles. The girls wear capes of the same red, over patterned skirts and little lace aprons, and some wear the traditional stiff and tall black hats, with a fringe of lace hanging from within them. But most of these hats are several sizes too big and absolutely refuse to stay on the backs of their heads.

Scattered amongst the reds, greens and blacks are the bright yellows of hundreds of daffodils, pinned onto hats and capes. The shocking weather of the last few days has been forgotten, as the sunshine catches the yellow daffodils, the red capes, the verdent green of the mown lawn, and the mellowed stone of the Cathedral.

Enthusiastic mothers are beginning to arrange their children in front of the Cathedral. 'Let's just have you all sitting on the grass —' a photographer tries to get some order.

The colourful rabble congregates and I position myself and Tess on the grass, feeling not dissimilar to Gulliver in the land of Lilliput.

'No, Jasmine. You stay there!' Jasmine's mother is trying to take photos, as are twenty other children's mothers. Jasmine's two year old face screws up, indicating that tears are imminent. 'Tommy, hold her hand!' Tommy takes Jasmine's hand, and holds on very tightly, displaying early signs of chivalry; but Jasmine's hat falls irrecoverably over her eyes. 'Tommy, pull her hat off her face!'

But now Jasmine really starts to ball, and on hearing this wondrous sound Tess sees it as her duty to jump on Jasmine. She launches herself over me, while I struggle with my bunch of half worn daffodils, and try not to fall backwards, so flattening the ramrod straight children behind me.

It is too late. Tess has leapt me, and would have flattened Jasmine, if Jasmine herself hadn't made the final dash for her mother. Tommy pushes his own hat off his head and looks rejected. He must be all of three.

'Here. Ellon can take Jasmine's place,' another eager mum pipes up, and another traditionally dressed two year old is propelled forwards.

Ellon's hat is already over her eyes, but she is clearly confused into silence. I grimace at the cameras as I try to control Tess, while the little boy on my left is picking his nose and eating it, and beyond him an angelic looking girl has her chin lifted determinedly and is smiling with all her might. The scattered yellows of the daffodils look dog eared, but this time both Ellon and Tess stay put. Children and animals . . .

The following day we set out southwards to Solva. In geographical terms, Solva is a drowned valley which protrudes deep inland providing a safe haven from the weather and customs men. During the nineteenth century as many as thirty trading ships were based here; but it is now home to a small fleet of fishing boats, and is often ignored by people with their minds set on St David's, or their buckets and spades ready for Newgale Sands.

The two mile crescent of Newgale Sands is the first beach of St Brides Bay. The cliffpath which runs behind the beach is black under foot, which is the only evidence that this area mined coal until 1905. After this time it became more profitable to import people, and now this is the elitist destination of bucket and spade holidaymakers who rent scattered cottages and take bracing walks.

The location of Pembrokeshire alone makes a trip here something of an event. There is no town of any size on the coast, and the only railway line serving this area arrives in Milford Haven, which would do little to persuade anybody that such a beautiful area lies so close.

A circuitous route took us on a narrow path which negotiates every single promontory beyond St Brides. Below the red sandstone and shale cliffs, small and inaccessible beaches appear at low tide, left to the world of rock pools and gulls, fulmars and choughs. Up, down, round, west, south, east. Skomer Island appeared, and then disappeared, and we arrived on the Dale Peninsula.

The Dale Peninsula is tethered to the mainland by a gully which is part of a trench running east from here, making up the deep channel of Milford Haven. After the coast of natural beauty, came flooded Milford Haven with its mish mash of human interference.

The coast path sticks determinedly to the shore and so we found ourselves in a mile square, terraced, gorse wasteland, dotted with chimneys and served by cracked concrete tracks. This is the remains of the Esso refinery, which closed down in 1983. Although the majority of the refinery was dismantled, the jetties were never removed and these redundant structures creaked as we walked under them. They stretch almost a mile into the estuary as if saying 'we're still here; we won't be forgotten; we're indestructible'.

They are eerie and sad. They are industrial museum pieces. Perhaps in two hundred years time these twentieth century ruins might be viewed with the same nostalgia with which I viewed the old ports?

Also sharing Milford Haven are the Texaco refinery, swallowing two miles of shore; the Gulf refinery which lay in our path; and, a mile inland, the Amoco refinery. Docks, power stations and nameless works exaggerate the intensity of the invasion. Although I had been through this channel on a ferry, nothing prepared me for the scale of industry experienced during that thirty mile detour of Milford Haven.

The Texaco refinery pushed us right down onto the shore line, from where the huge black bulk of a tanker obliterated any other view. It was unbelievable that so vast an island could sit in such shallow water.

I was used to feeling vulnerable; but this was different. This was scary. It was the mad professor experimenting again. How could we, such microscopic dots, manufacture these things which tower above the landscape itself. Will it all one day get out of hand? But I had changed a little. I could now find an awesome respect for our progress. I likened ourselves to termites; building edifices completely out of proportion to our size.

Around the corner, Angle peninsula looked as though it was another world away from its twentieth century neighbours, and a pair of beautiful curlews reassured me that where there was progress there was also life.

Spring seemed to be gaining confidence. Yellow was the predominant colour. The roadsides were flecked with flowering gorse; daffodils were opening; primroses, celandines and marsh marigolds carpeted areas. In neighbouring fields the grass was taking on the lime green of new growth, and later on that day (March 5th) I smelt my first cut grass.

The following day spring showed itself in the caravan parks for the first time in 1994. Somewhere there were DIY shops doing a roaring trade, thanks to the spring mania of cleaning and nest making in preparation for spring fever, which the animal kingdom has agreed is crucial for its survival. Even the Spudtruck had a vigorous clean, thanks to my Australian aunt, Jane, who had now joined us.

In celebration of spring I optimistically discarded my red trousers, which I had lived in for five months, and put on my blue shorts and purple leggings. We were edging our way round the circle.

From the quicksand of expansive Freshwater West Beach, we took to a quiet road to avoid the MOD range at Castlemartin. In an attempt to fill my mind with constructive thoughts, I resolved to learn poetry, and began with Thomas Masefield's *Sea Fever* which conjured up so many of my feelings with the sea as such an integral part of my life.

The only side effect of reading and walking was that when I looked up each time I felt off balance, while Tess found the repetitions as painful as amateur musical instrument practice. But by the time we reached the sea again I had learnt the entire poem.

We were on sheer, flat topped limestone cliffs, and after a little way came across a spectacular chasm known as Huntsman's Leap. The story goes that a huntsman unwittingly jumped the 130 foot deep chasm on his horse, but when he turned to see the obstacle he had just negotiated he died of fright! I kept Tess firmly away in case she had ideas of changing its name, and made towards a trickle of people disappearing over the edge of the cliff, where we knew there to be (of all things) a chapel.

Thirteenth century St Govan's Chapel is wedged between rocks on the shore, and is reached via some haphazard steps. Inside, there is one bare stone room and a single window looking out to the sea, which must beat mercilessly against it on a rough night. The original chapel was built by the sixth century Celtic saint — Govan — who lived the life of a hermit here.

The Saturday brigade ambled with us towards Stackpole Warren, where they decided they had walked enough. All of them missed beautiful and unspoilt Barfundle Bay, shielded from the outside world by rocky headlands.

From here the coast ahead rises and falls in a series of continual waves. The rock strata are so carefully defined, as if painted on to the rock faces with a fine paint brush; yellow rock sandwiched between red sandstone and black rock. But the scene deflated me. Somehow we had to get seven miles along the top of those cliffs, and no one was going to do it for us. Tess waited for orders and I wondered why she couldn't lead the way. Surely she knew which way we were going by now?

I stuck my thumbs into my rucksack straps and set off up the first hill. The hills were steep, and I couldn't recite *Sea Fever* without wasting precious breath. The perfect morning's walking seemed days away; my hamstrings pulled with every step up; and the ball of my foot felt as though it was on fire.

Tess trotted dutifully, but when she got in my way I growled at her, then apologised and cursed myself for taking my misery out on poor faithful Tess.

By the time we reached Manorbier I was closer to tears than I had ever felt. There was a final hill up from the shore to the Spudtruck; but I wondered if I could physically manage it. I wasn't sure if my legs would take any more punishment. I bent down to help them, and pushed hard on each knee as it hoisted the other leg up the grassy track.

That night I wrote in my diary: 'Heading along to Manorbier — muscles complaining like mad — couldn't even listen to music and felt very down to think of everyone on a Saturday evening, getting ready to hit the town, feeling fit, lively and chatty. I just feel frazzled — physically and mentally.'

I woke the next morning at the routine hour of seven, got dressed, had some cereal and set off without thinking about the misery or pain of the previous day. After a couple of miles the pain resurfaced, but by then it was too late. I would have to reach the Spudtruck again.

My usual Sunday consolation was that I never had a hangover, and it cheered me to think smugly of all the people feeling awful! Such are the thoughts of a coastal walker.

Tenby Beach looked as though it had been meticulously rolled. Dotted along the length of the beach were Lowry type figures walking predominantly in pairs, and at the other end of the beach the houses and hotels of Tenby perched on the clifftop are smartly painted in white, mellow yellows and blues. They add the perfect back drop to the beach.

Up in the town itself, we wandered through the streets trying to find the right way out. I loved the narrow cobbled streets which occasionally allow secret glimpses of sections of the old walls of the town. One day I would return to Tenby, but for now the next place was fixed in my mind — Saundersfoot.

The path to Saundersfoot continued to run either uphill or downhill, but at least this was wooded so that I wasn't constantly looking ahead to where we were going. Looking ahead to the next bit of coast was like looking forward to something — it meant that you ignored the time (and places) in between.

Saundersfoot was once a mining town supporting around nine collieries in the surrounding area. The last mine was closed in 1930, and nowadays there is little evidence of the industry except for a remaining stretch of claustrophobic tunnel running from Saundersfoot to Wisemans Bridge, through which the 'miners express' once travelled.

At the other end of the tunnel, the Pembrokeshire Coastal Path comes to an end. We had followed the path for 180 miles of some of the most beautiful coast, as well as some of the most industrialised. It was quite a relief to walk on the mud-less road we were now forced on to by the eight mile stretch of MOD owned Pendine Sands — used by Amy Johnson for her first flight, and since used for land speed records. The five mile beach between Saundersfoot and Amroth was used for a full scale dress rehearsal of the Normandy landings.

I also had no choice but to join the main road to negotiate the Rivers Taf and Tywi, and reach Carmarthen, where Jane was leaving and Susie was taking over. Susie had phoned the previous night and the conversation had gone something like this: 'I won't be Caernarfon till late Spud.'

She had a relaxed way of talking, and I didn't spot the mistake. 'I have to change umpteen times.' She was only coming from Warwickshire.

'To Carmarthen?' There was a pause.

'Caernarfon?'

I could see Susie arriving in North Wales, and wondering where on earth we were. I hoped that this didn't bode too badly for a week in which we had numerous appointments with Mayors. Our first Mayoral meeting was in Carmarthen.

The Council Offices were easy to find and Tess and I entered as two bedraggled figures. 'We've come to see the Mayor.'

'Name please?' the receptionist asked.

'Spud.' As usual the receptionist was reluctant to tell the Mayor that a vegetable had arrived.

Beautifully carpeted stairs finally led us up to the Mayor, where a sea of strange but smiling faces greeted us: 'Where've you come from today?'

'How're the feet?'

'How are Tess' feet?'

'Where are you going next?'

'Have you enjoyed Wales?'

They handed over cheques as well as notes of good luck, and tended to our every need. But it was Tess who was the star. She could look as though butter could melt in her mouth, and she did her enthusiastic bottom shuffle (carried out when she had been told to sit but still decided she could change positions), across the beautiful carpet to get as close as possible to the food. 'Here. Have a sandwich,' Tess wolfed that and bottom shuffled to the next. 'No wonder you're hungry! Have a piece of cake.'

I wished I could be so uninhibited and tuck into the goodies with such gusto; in the same way as only that morning Tess had flirted outrageously on my behalf with a very good looking farmer. Again I wondered whether I should try her tactics — pounce on him and lick his face and ears?

How would I have survived such ordeals without Tess?

CHAPTER FOURTEEN

The rain was beating down on the shell of the Spudtruck, and seeping down the back walls and dispersing by osmosis into the foam cushions on which I sat. Our back garden for the night was an area of gravel between us and the road. Ragwort, plastic bag bushes, thistles and tin can shrubs grew here, enclosed by a saggy fence of wire; the area of 'no mans land' which is compulsory at every station in Britain — but none looks so depressing as Carmarthen station on a bleak, rainy Monday evening. I wouldn't have blamed Susie if she had gone to Caernarfon instead.

Susie is a friend of my sister's, while Florence was her King Charles Spaniel puppy who fitted neatly into Tess' mouth. It was quite clear that Susie and Florence would soon be winning 'the dog most like its owner' competition. When Susie grinned, Florence grinned, and when I commented on the fact that Florence would soon be needing a coat, I received two identical looks of disdain. I was right.

The next day the blanket of drizzle had dropped even lower, as we set off on the merry-go-round of Carmarthen's roundabouts. Water ran off every stalk and bud; it created puddles on the tops of walls; and ran in streams down the sides of roads and paths. Further away than that, I couldn't see what it was doing or where we were going as we bulldozed our way across country, through thick bramble hedges and gateways so deep in cowshit that Tess' body appeared truncated. A few extra miles were notched up before we resorted to the small lanes moated by brown rivers.

Sometimes I walked in the rivers, damming them up with my boots and watching the increased volume of water as I removed the dam. I still felt that walking in the water was softer than walking on drier tarmac; in a similar way as the tarmac of small lanes was softer than the tarmac of main roads.

After Kidwelly I was forced alone onto a main road which took a constant stream of cars to Llanelli. The cars prevented the water from settling on the road, but sent it continually flying with a 'swish, swish'. Meanwhile, I was listening to *Wuthering Heights* and was willing Catherine and Heathcliff to get their act together.

Industrial Llanelli swallowed us up, then spat us out at the River Loughor, leaving us to begin the Gower Peninsula. The one thing that was immediately noticeable from the map was that a great deal of Gower is owned by the National Trust.

It would be impossible to walk Britain's coast without appreciating the tremendous work of the National Trust. A lot of National Trust owned land was acquired through a scheme called Enterprise Neptune, launched in 1965 specifically to preserve our coast.

North Gower was the first piece of coast purchased under the scheme, and the Trust now owns a total of 11% of Gower — some 5,000 acres of stunning cliffs, headlands, bays beaches and downland. The importance of this protected land on such a beautiful peninsula can not be overstated.

Through Enterprise Neptune, the Trust has acquired a total of 520 miles of coastline. This land cannot be sold — except by the express will of Parliament, so that it is safe for years to come. On top of this land, much of our coastline has been designated Heritage Coast and is being protected and managed by the Countryside Commission and local authorities — though the land remains privately owned. Since the beginning of this scheme in 1973, 850 miles, or 31% of our coast, has been designated Heritage Coast. Long may these schemes be supported. Our beautiful coast is the only one we will have!

On the roads of Gower the principle traffic is sheep and ponies. In Llangennith a small group of ponies had congregated at the centre of the village and were looking wistfully over a small wall into someone's garden. Another pair were ambling out of the car park of the Kings Arms, where I found Susie.

Perhaps it was this which prompted Susie's observation that night, as she cooked supper with an artistic vagueness. 'You know. I think this is like a British safari!'

'What, driving the Spudtruck?'

'Mm. Sort of finding your way round; doing the chores, which take so long; and just sort of 'surviving'!'

Susie lived in Kenya and should know about these things. I thought it was a very apt description, and was secretly pleased that she likened it to something which suggested such adventure!

Adventure or not, Susie and Florence hated the mornings and determinedly ignored the alarm. But in the car park of the Kings Arms the next morning I couldn't ignore it. Gower Belly had kicked in. I scurried down the ladder and into the cupboard. 'Ahhh. No. The loo's full.' Susie laughed from under her cover. But this wasn't funny.

I went outside in my pyjamas. But we were in the middle of a village which was too small to have a PC, but too big to make a dash for the countryside. Instead, there was a muddy ditch bordering the car park. The fact that it was overlooked by various windows was tough. But it was too late.

I had a dual belly ache from Gower Belly and period pains, I felt weak and sick, and had lost any self respect I had once had during the first half hour of the day. I then gave Tess an earful for nothing, and set off in a foul mood; cursing the fact that Susie hadn't emptied the loo, and wondering how she could possibly be so cheery while I was in such pain.

At least back on the beach there were ample dunes. This made me relax a little more and I apologised to everybody. 'I hate being like this Tessie. I can see why real expeditions often end up in strained relationships.' I talked at length to Tess, even though a good deal of the time she was in the dunes. Sometimes it was also hard to differentiate between what I thought and what I said anyway.

Rhossili Beach runs for three uninterrupted miles and we had the finely planed sand to ourselves. The sea, however, is inevitably affected by the human sink of the Bristol Channel and I was appalled to hear of one surfer who visits Rhossili Beach who takes a course of antibiotics to prevent picking up an infection. I heard more of this on the other side of the Bristol Channel, in Newquay, where surfers regularly compete with condoms and shit. Often the water is so brown that they can't see their feet from their boards. As a result, the surfers have set up an organisation called SAS (Surfers Against Sewage); while the EU has also set a series of directives aimed at updating Britain's Victorian sewage systems. Happily I saw these being implemented on several occasions, such as Salcombe.

Gower is a microcosm of the Welsh coastline. It has estuarine marshes, glorious beaches (of which Threecliff Bay is the most beautiful), and cliffs. The limestone cliffs on the south shore are craggy and disorganised as they tumble down to the sea. Up on the clifftops, fields of cauliflowers and cabbages were being manually harvested and filled the air with their smell. I like the smell of brassicas. It is a truly vegetative smell which encompasses the soil, the rain and the growing plant.

We squelched round the muddy fields and through the gateways, and came across a ewe which had just had two lambs in the muddiest part of a field. The lambs already resembled mud wrestlers, but were sucking heartily all the same. The fact that we had witnessed our first lambs in January in Cumbria linked up the coast and the continuing seasons.

We found the Spudtruck at Port Eynon, from where Devon was visible for the first time, and spent the rest of the day in Swansea, in the hands of Owen from Shelter.

The Guildhall is a large and pillared building, and the rooms inside are no less grandiose. But it was always the carpets which I noticed. The one in the Lord Mayor's spacious room was a deep green and the length of newly cut grass — at least in my eyes it was. Clods of Gower mud came off my boots, and Florence shed her fine white spaniel hairs with equal abandon.

The Lord Mayor had sincere eyes and a strong handshake. 'How are your feet?' he asked. Everyone asked about my feet, which were, on the whole, fine; but no one ever asked about my legs, which were sore.

We stood round sipping orange juice from wine glasses and talking about Tess and Florence in the same way that babies dominate conversations. Two days previously Tess had met the first Ukrainian Mayor in Britain, the Mayor of Llanelli. Not content with dominating the conversation and then cleaning his ears, a blanket had then been laid out for her on the meticulously polished parlour table, and Tess had been invited to lie on it while we grouped round her like disciples for the photos. Tess was becoming positively blasé about such treatment.

The Lord Mayor called a hush. 'Spud, and Tess. I'd just like to say a few words of welcome to you.' I shuffled my feet and didn't know whether to smile or look serious. 'It's great to see you in Swansea, but most of all it's a fantastic thing you're . . .'

The Lord Mayor continued, and looked at me with those sincere eyes as his words hit me in a wave of nauseous emotion. I blinked like mad to hold back tears. It was only when I remembered my terrible morning in a muddy ditch and thought *If only they had seen me then*, that the quivering eye was replaced by a sharply bit lip. How quickly my tattered and volatile emotions could switch from tears to laughter.

Our day in Swansea also included an interview on SC4 (the Welsh national TV station), for which we were joined by Welsh speaking Claris from Shelter.

The building was brightly lit and bustling with activity, and after a few minutes a lady whisked us off to the make-up room where Tess and I both had our shiny noses toned down with the help of a little powder. Tess rose to the occasion like a super model, as she then did on the chat-show setting. She sat bolt upright between Claris and I on the all-con-suming sofa and looked at the camera in a haughty fashion. Having lulled me into thinking she was behaving, she noticed the proximity of Claris and had soon left an unpowdered streak across Claris' face.

Despite the fact that Owen had been teaching me the Welsh for 'good afternoon' all day, at the end of the interview it slipped my mind. The only words I was familiar with were ones I saw every day on the map or on the roadsides — words such as 'aber' (river); 'cwm' (valley); 'pont' (bridge); 'maes parcio' (car park); and 'croeso' or 'croeso y Cymru' (wel-come — to Wales'). None of these phrases was very conducive to a conversation.

We parked for the night on Mumbles Head, which faces Swansea Bay on one side and the Bristol Channel on the other side, and we were surrounded by an increasingly boisterous sea. The only building in sight was an angular white building, which could have been mistaken for a very large public loo — probably witness to the occasional amorous car rendezvous. In fact we had backed the Spudtruck up to Neptune's Nitespot.

When the first party goers arrived at 9.30, we were in bed, and just as Michele was screaming at Michael to 'bloody wait for me' I fell asleep.

But at two o'clock in the morning we really were in the firing range. It was as though we had pitched a tent at the exit gates to the winning World Cup team. 'Whatshish'en Steve, Shelter Coastal Walk — Spud and Tess,' woke me up with its drunken Welsh slur.

'Never 'eard of them. Who are they?'

'Dunno. Reckon they're in there?'

A bottle smashed, followed by another one. There was hysterics from what sounded like a group of girls in much too high stilettos. A hand slapped the Spudtruck bonnet, and another inquisitive drunkard asked if anyone knew who Spud and Tess were. Their voices were unnaturally loud and unnaturally deliberate. The snippets of conversations streamed past like trailers of people's lives. 'So, I said to him 'no way! Get it yourself —'

'Quite right —'

'Hey Ange!' reverberated across Mumbles Head. 'Wanna come back to my place?'

Loud giggles as the supremely confident propositioner was egged on by his entourage of drunkenly egotistic males. 'Piss off Steve — we all know where you've been!' Loud giggles from Ange's corner.

More bottles smashed, more arguments were raged and more liaisons were confirmed — until the place went deathly quiet as if a tornado had just passed through.

The next morning, a half bottle of Newcastle Brown sat on the bonnet of the Spudtruck like a car mascot. Neptune's Nitespot was having a lie-in. Across Swansea Bay I could see industrial Port Talbot, where we were off to that day. It wasn't a particularly cheery sight.

A new bridge was under construction over the River Neath, and this had thrown the area into a chaotic maze of workman's Portakabins, temporary gravel roads, bollards, scaffolding and towering red cranes. The traffic whizzed past me, unaware of the energy going into the bridge which would enable them to reach their destination all the quicker in the future.

From the middle of the existing bridge I watched the disruption of the scene below. Squeezed between the two bridges was a small marina, where a few sailing boats doggedly retained their berths. Next door to this was a boarded up pub brandishing a rather hopeful For Sale sign. But the only sign of life on the toy looking wasteland was a gypsy tending his piebald pony. As I continued watching I saw another pony nearby, lying stretched out on its side. The gypsy's dog went up and sniffed the motionless animal, and only then did I realise that it was dead.

In front of me was old and new, life and death; and in that moment I felt the full force of our mortality and the imbalance that we create for ourselves during this mayhem we call civilisation.

The imbalance is between our surroundings and us as individuals, and there it was; the giant structure of the new bridge, the deserted old buildings of the partially invisible village below; the invisible gypsy, the unaware drivers whizzing past; the dead horse, and non committal dog. I was witnessing a world which increasingly squeezes out the race which creates it.

I jumped on the conveyor belt of my legs through Port Talbot. I ran across main roads, hopping across crash barriers; I jay walked across quieter roads taking the most direct route possible. Sometimes there was a pavement, but at other times there wasn't and then I walked along the concrete curb with my arms outstretched like a tight rope artist — but all the time I kept up the pace.

Past three miles of British Steel works, across the thickly bunched cats cradle of railway tracks, and back to the sea. When we turned east, it was easy to forget the presence of Port Talbot and Swansea, as the beach ran in front of us for five miles, backed by two mile deep dunes. I stopped to look back once, and the fiery chimneys of the steel works continued to add splashes of red/orange to the grey sky, throwing out their warning as beacon towers once did to warn the country of invasion.

Apart from the dunlins, we were only watched by a couple of very possessive looking courting swans who were gracefully gliding around in a pool of a river, cutting their way through a surface thick with debris consisting of driftwood, and air filled plastic bags.

Among the beach debris we witnessed, the predominant articles were things such as gloves, hats, spade handles, brushes, u-bends, the ubiquitous plastic detergent bottles, oil drums, Tupperwares, nylon ropes, plastic mugs, paint tins, paint brushes; on one occasion we had found a large chest freezer, and on another a container the size of a van had been thrown high up onto the base of cliffs as though it was its matchbox equivalent. On this beach Tess found a carrot.

The only other thing we found on this beach was a solitary gannet. Gannets are normally found on rocky coastlines, and although there was nothing visibly wrong with this one, it was clearly unable to fly. But, like the oil covered cormorant, this goose-sized bird was eyeballing me in an unnerving way, and its bill looked in perfect working order. There was nothing I could do.

In Porthcawl I came across the beach I had often joked about finding — a concrete beach. It shelves gently down from the sea wall to the water's edge, in the same way as a swimming pool might have a tiled *beach*. I supposed that tennis balls and graffiti art would take the place of the more usual sandcastles, but there were no shops open to discover what they might sell in the line of beach games.

We skirted the River Ogmore via ankle shaping dunes, (I had once been told that walking in soft sand shapes the ankles, and always consoled myself with this trivial vanity during such painful stretches!), which made the subsequent tarmac on small lanes make me feel as though I was walking on air.

The coast we returned to at Dunraven Bay must be one of the little known coastlines in Britain, but it is truly spectacular. The red sandstone cliffs we followed are stacked like plates of rust coloured pancakes, and they have eroded uniformly so that they fall in a sheer drop to the sea.

The country inland was relatively flat, and even the cliffs were gentle after the hills of the Pembrokeshire Coastal Path; yet my hamstrings were getting worse. I had a love/hate relationship with hills because for four months my hamstring muscles had nagged. Although I had been told how to stretch them, the cure hadn't been instantaneous and I had quickly given up! I was also much too keen to sit down every evening to start inflicting more pain on myself.

Someone else had advised me to take smaller steps, and when I reminded myself to walk as though I was wearing a too tight pencil skirt, the nagging did lessen. But largely I accepted it as a side effect. I kept them warm, and slept with my hot water bottle on them at night. I rubbed in plenty of tiger balm and had popped arnica pills to the extent that they had made me feel sick.

I called Tess over as I rested one leg and then the other on a stile. I picked up one of her back legs and pressed the pad. The muscles in her hindquarters sometimes flinched when I did this — an indication she was tired; but now they didn't. She had gained a new lease for life, or had crossed a fatigue barrier.

In Barry Country Park we were joined by the dog walkers. An elderly lady with a Chihuahua on a retractable lead pressed the button when she saw Tess. The Chihuahua was reeled in like a prize fish. Further on, a large and hairy black mongrel was not so protected. It belonged to a young and clearly in love couple who were busy throwing a tennis ball, which Tess had soon stolen.

The hairy black mongrel found himself a stick, which made Tess drop the ball. A tug-of-war ensued, until the stick was ripped into pieces and they each went off with one. Each looked very pleased about their victory. Even in the dog world there is sharing.

We passed other dogs; Boxers, mongrels, shy ones, timid ones — they were all there, practising for 'the dog most like its owner'.

In a similar suburban patch in Penarth I came across a sign reading 'Please make sure your dog uses the Dog Toilet.' There was nothing that looked remotely like a toilet — but then I didn't know what I was looking for. Anyway, how on earth were you supposed to make your dog use a toilet?

I finally came across a railed in area of foul looking earth. A large sign across the top said 'Dog Toilet', but I for one would never have that much control over my dog. Dog Toilets. I ask you! What would we expect our pooches to do next? Talk? 'Hey Tessie?'

'Yes Spud?'

'Not far to go now. Nearly home.'

I put Tess on the lead and swung inland to Cardiff, where we ate and slept. In the morning we fled, and it only took two miles to reach grassy estuary walls which were beginning to come together with Somerset.

The estuary walls were measured in hours, not miles. I listened to a new tape from a friend in New Zealand twice, and made one back to her. It made me feel homesick for the life I had left behind, and envious of the sunshine, but we had got rid of nearly four hours and were leaving Newport. A train trundled past pulling carriage after carriage of imported coal. Coals to Newport.

We set off around the last corner of Wales, the drained land of the Caldicot levels. I felt that it would be different to be back in England; that perhaps my energy levels would pick up because, in a way, we would be on the home straight. Or so I thought. It was enough to humour myself with such thoughts, and I arrived in Redwick in a fine mood, considering it was the end of a day. We found the Spudtruck parked between the Red Rose pub and the village hall.

Redwick is a beautiful peaceful village, hemmed into position by the M4 motorway, a four mile stretch of steel works, Newport and the Severn estuary. Perhaps it is because of its unenviable setting that it feels undiscovered and unspoilt. What hidden gems lie behind the South Wales industrial corridor!

Another evening of business and pleasure passed in the Red Rose pub; sweatshirts were sold, 'if only to pacify the missus, so as she can't shout at me when I'm late home!' (which was a common sales promotion); donations were made; cider was drunk; and the usual jokes were cracked. 'I bet your dog hates the word walk now!' and 'I bet she was a Great Dane before!' and (the most favourite one of all) 'couldn't you find a car?!'

After a night of peace, Tess sensed my anticipation the next morning and we set off singing 'the sun has got his hat on' which was a mandatory way of greeting even a glimmer of sun. The motorway, the main road, the railway line and the pylons were coming together like the inevitable merging of river tributary and main river, and we were joining them, as if streaming towards an escape route.

To my complete surprise we came across the building works of a second bridge over the Severn. I had no idea about this, and my imagination started to run away with me. *Perhaps no one else knows it's being built. Perhaps they've kept it really quiet because the old bridge is unsafe?* My melodramatic daydreams continued to the point of a massive disaster — today.

Our next problem was to negotiate the building site without being squashed or arrested. I decided to be brash and walk straight through

the middle. No sooner had we squeezed through the particularly inse-
cure fence when a van appeared. The two men looked at me as though I
had just escaped from the men in white coats.

Nevertheless, we were soon sandwiched between them, and I briefly
hoped that they weren't about to kidnap me. My mind was making up
incredible stories today. I told my friends about my wild bridge
imaginings, but luckily they didn't return me to the men in the white
coats. Instead, they set us on our way with a cup of very milky tea
which gurgled in my stomach all the way to the bridge.

We had come to the end of the 588.6 mile stretch of Welsh coastline,
and the roar and shudder of the Severn Bridge was upon us. There is no
sign here to say 'Welcome to England' or 'Farewell from Wales', so we
posed with the Mayor of Chepstow beneath the motorway exit sign.

The Mayor was looking immaculate in a blue blazer, tie and his two
tiered chain, and at full stretch Tess could easily reach his nose. 'I think
she likes me!'

'Certainly does,' I humoured.

In front of us the Severn Bridge ran for over two miles, rising gradually up and down in a gentle hill so that I couldn't see the other end. The
other end was England. I wanted to reach England now, and to know
that I would be home and would not be leaving it again during the
Walk. Scotland and now Wales were really behind us — we had walked
their coastlines.

I tried telling myself this, but it produced no result. I had eight hours
per day to think about these things, but I still couldn't grasp the fact
that we had now walked 3,416.9 miles.

It wasn't that I never thought we would make it this far, I just hadn't
allowed myself to think about crossing back to England, in the same
way as I never let myself think about any section of coast beyond the
current week's. The trouble was that now we were here I was still blocking it from my mind; I had mastered the art of 'one day at a time' so
successfully that when the future arrived I wasn't with it. I wondered if
I ever would be.

Owen and Tony (Shelter Bristol) declared their intentions of joining
us across the bridge. In a masochistic sort of way I wanted to be on my
own — or be with Tess. I wanted to revel in the sensation of crossing yet
another country boundary. But I also liked the company. Sometimes it
seemed that I was hard to please.

I dipped in and out of their conversation, but it was as though they
were two people we had just fallen into step with. I tried to sound on
the ball, but failed dismally.

Tony continued with us for the afternoon. Unlike many of the Shelter staff we met, most of whom work on the administration side, Tony's work at Shelter is grass roots. He is the force behind a Rough Sleepers Initiative and every week dispenses hot food to homeless people. He also provides a listening ear, and his sympathetic and staunchly dedicated nature must have helped a good many people.

The section of coast he witnessed made me feel ashamed, as if I was tour guide to our coastline. The railway line beat us and we were forced onto the frantically busy and pavement-less road. I apologised to Tony at a shout.

'What do you mean sorry! You must have walked a good deal of this. It makes it all the more amazing,' came his reply. 'I think a lot of people think that all your walking is along beautiful cliffs and beaches.' Perhaps they did.

Avonmouth docks arrived, and our five day holiday started. But first we had to visit the Bristol Cable TV studio, and put faces to the voices we had talked to during live phone-ins every Monday afternoon over the last eight months.

Tony, Tess and I squeezed onto a narrow wicker sofa. Behind us was a large map of Britain with ribbon marking our progress. Femmy the person, instead of the always cheery phone voice presenter, sat on the other side of the wicker table. Tess fell asleep on my lap. We were live on cable TV.

During the interview Femmy showed photographs of us on the screen. They were photos I had been taking with a disposable camera and sending back; a deserted Lincolnshire beach, Tess playing in the snow, Llandudno, Tess welcoming a Mayor to his own parlour.

Then came the self timed photos I had taken in the wilderness of the Highlands. Even in that clinical studio I felt the happy but humbling solitude I had experienced there; and was sad that that time had come and gone.

The interview was coming to an end, and Femmy was reaching down to the other side of her chair. 'Here's a contribution from us here at Cable,' Femmy handed me a jar full of money. 'But we couldn't forget Tess!'

Femmy produced a chewy bone, but Tess slept on. I waved it under her nose. 'Here Tessie!'

She woke up with a start, took one look at what was on offer, grabbed the bone, and leapt off the sofa. In her eagerness she took the wicker table and two pot plants with her — the whole lot went flying and Tess was out of the shot, leaving a scene of devastation live on Cable TV.

CHAPTER FIFTEEN

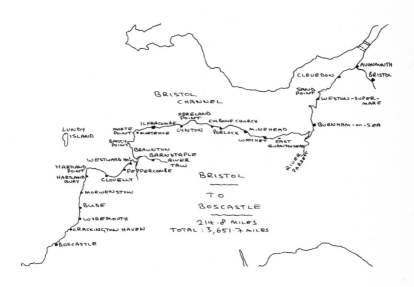

An insignificant river south of Clevedon left us with no option but to resort to the M5 hard shoulder for fifty yards. The lorries belted past to Bristol, Manchester or Edinburgh, and their roar stayed with us on the other side, as we stuck religiously to footpaths which were the only way of negotiating the mass of drainage ditches. A hill shaped like a door wedge rose up at the coast, and heralded the end of the day; the first day back walking after five days off.

The car park was emptying of day visitors to the hilltop Roman settlement, and David had the kettle on. 'Good day?' he asked.

It was good to have David back. I knew the chemistry was there, and he would provide a bit of spice to my one track life. I had decided that he was good fun, good looking, willing to give foot massages, intelligent and a good cook. He was also single. What more could one want?

'Yes thank you 'darling'!' I crooned. 'Except for my hamstrings which pulled; and my head which throbbed.'

We had shaken the collecting tins round the clubs and pubs of Bristol the previous night, and now David told me he had banked £200 from this ordeal. He also told me that Beetle was turning up that evening — an old friend who I hadn't seen for eight years, and who was now sponsored to come and walk with us for a day.

We chatted away while David cooked a curry, and kept our ears open for Beetle's arrival on this dead-end road. 'I wonder what Beetle's like now?' I reflected. 'I hope he doesn't mind the chaotic Spudtruck.'

'What does he do?'

'He was in the army. Maybe he'll turn up in combat gear, you know, all that camouflage stuff!' I laughed at the image.

'And survival pack!'

'He might pitch camp in the bushes -!'

'And eat grubs and dehydrated food, rallying his men!'

'And he'll lie in wait all night. 'Freeze. Don't move!' David held up a carving knife in an alarming manner, and pretended it was a gun. The tears of laughter were beginning. 'He'll march into the Spudtruck, lay down his regulation sleeping bag and polished boots!'

The images went on and the tears streamed. David sat down, unable to cook any more. I had never seen anyone cry when they laugh as much as our family do, but David easily equalled us. My cheeks ached and my belly muscles hurt.

Headlights swung onto the windscreen of the Spudtruck, and David hung out of the door by one hand and still waved the carving knife around in the other, while I peered over his shoulder. 'Hi Beetle!' we called, and grinned like mad into the dazzling lights, our eyes piggy from laughter.

The car took off with a squeal of wheels and flying dust. 'Look what you've done! Beetle thought he'd come across the mad murderer of Somerset!' The laughter started again. 'We must have looked a right sight! You waving a knife around with that inane grin, and calling out greetings to beetles!'

So much of David's and my relationship was based on such laughter; and how important was that laughter in shedding my Walk shell.

Luckily or otherwise it hadn't been Beetle. Someone, somewhere was probably still shaking from that vision in Sand Point car park. Neither was Beetle anything like the ridiculous picture we had painted. He had only been in the Spudtruck a few minutes when we were trying to tell him about our description of him; of course, it just sounded pathetic.

The next day Beetle and I caught up on eight years of gossip.

Around Worlebury Hill, with its wind stunted but still elegant beech trees, Weston-Super-Mare appeared. Like Clevedon, Weston has a traditional charm, and hotels, B&Bs and cafes were just opening their doors and blinking blearily out to the grey March day.

Just below the pier, with its centipede legs, was a wooden rail, such as you might find outside a Western Saloon Bar — only it was thigh high and had sunk into the mud. A painted sign nailed onto the rail read 'D Trapnell. Donkey Rides. 50p.'

A seven mile beach took us to Burnham-on-Sea. Again the tide was out and the sand was hard. Beetle walked in good army length strides, and his walk was bouncy and energetic compared to my shuffling, legs apart walk. People said it looked as though I'd just wet myself; but my body had found its natural position which is with the hips and ankle bones in a straight line. My walk may have been comical, but it was balanced.

We met David in Burnham, and I noticed Beetle shedding his boots fairly promptly. Beetle had blisters.

On March 26th I wore my shorts with no leggings for the first time in 1994; we were well into our fourth season and were nearing the full circle. The trouble was that the circle of the coast had so many detours. South of Burnham-on-Sea the River Parrett wiggles and winds inland, forming textbook meanders which will one day, I'm sure, become textbook ox-bow lakes.

On the flat horizon beyond the opposite bank, Hinkley power station was four miles from us. We had to walk over twenty five miles to reach it.

The sun evaporated the salt on the mud flats, and they gave off a warm, saline smell which I had once hated and now enjoyed. The flats looked still and mirror-like, but I knew now that they teemed with life underneath. Why else were the shelduck, curlews and oystercatchers strutting around the mud, leaving their fossil-like footprints and occasionally dipping their bills into the shiny surface?

A snoozing heron rose into lugubrious flight, its neck tucked between its shoulders and its legs flailing behind as though he had no control over them; and in a flat and drained field to our left, a gaggle of barnacle geese were devouring precious grazing, stocking up on food reserves before starting their long migration.

Slowly the hills began, starting with low cliffs comprised of fantastic strata of mudstone, limestone and shale which took us past East Quantoxhead towards Watchet; and then at Minehead the real hills began. These were the hills which signified the start of the South West Coast Path.

The clocks went forwards that night, and the next morning we congregated under the entrance to Butlins, Minehead, where a large bill board depicts scenes of roller coasters and nightclubs, and reads 'Butlins Welcomes You to Somerwest World. Let yourself go . . . and you won't want to leave.' Good old Sir Billy Butlin.

We were joined by various important and not so important people, and I was being presented with an enormous cardboard cheque — but I couldn't concentrate. The hills ahead were slowly being revealed in a damp and mysterious glory. They were dark green from thick vegetation, and the cloud diffused through the trees as it might in a rain forest. My hamstrings twitched just to look at them. What would happen if I suddenly said 'I can't do it! I can't go any further!' It was a fleeting thought, which served only to amuse me as well as push us into action.

I concentrated on my walking up the first steep hill through the cloud shrouded woodland. *Take small strides. Don't lean forwards, sit back on your bum so that your legs stay under you. Small strides . . .*

The oaks, hazels and rhododendrons were saturated from the drizzle, which barely seemed to be falling. At the top of the hill we popped out of the woodland and crossed bracken smothered moorland to Porlock Bay, on the other side of which the path again weaves its way up and down through woodland. Every so often it crosses small streams which gambol over the rocks, producing noise levels far above their size and emitting white water produced negative ions.

Perhaps it is because of the negative ions that there has been a church in one such tranquil combe since 630AD. Culbone Church is situated four hundred feet above sea level, and is accessible only by foot or by rough track; it is a magical and serene setting for this, the smallest Parish church in Britain.

The mellow stoned church with its toy looking proportions measures thirty five feet long and seats thirty two people. During its lifetime it has been a place for convicts, leper colonies and American charcoal burners. It is now frequented by colourful goretex layered walkers such as myself, as well as those seeking inner enlightenment. Next door to the plastic coffee mugs and bowls of damp sugar in the goodwill refreshment shed were a range of books with titles such as *Know Your Inner Self* and *The Art of Meditation*.

I called Tess away from the sticky table and rejoined the path, which occasionally popped clear of the woodland, but then ducked back in again. When we came entirely clear of the trees the full force of the escalating wind and rain made itself known. This was the wild moorland of Exmoor, and it was so wild here that everything apart from the ground a few feet in front of us was obliterated. We found the Spudtruck alone on the exposed road.

We were found here by cousin Beth, a whispy figure in her late fifties who had come to walk with us. She was wearing a tea cosy hat, a new looking waterproof and walking boots. In fact she was suitably attired for the weather which had done nothing to improve its image. If anything the wind had strengthened.

The path was terribly muddy now, and while my boots dug in from sheer experience, Beth's didn't. I decided to avoid Foreland Point lighthouse, and cut straight over the top of a mist topped hill. Perhaps it was the wrong decision. Every now and again I stopped to wait for Beth, and the wind got stronger with each step nearer the top. We couldn't see more than a few steps in front again, and I knew that a few yards from us were sheer cliffs dropping straight down to the invisible sea.

Beth was struggling. I saw her willowy figure being swayed by the wind, and really thought she was going to be blown over. 'Hang on to me!' I virtually yelled, as though we were on the top of a huge mountain in a blizzard.

I grabbed Beth's arm and we balanced each other. A particularly strong gust nearly took us both off our feet, and I contemplated lying flat on the ground. The strength of the wind terrified me. It was something I was going to have to get used to, though at the time I was still blissfully convinced that spring was with us — somewhere.

As we battled over the saddle of the hill, keeping an eye on Tess' white snout, the path gradually began to drop again, until a white line of breakers appeared out of the murk and signified Lynmouth Bay. We trudged down like companionable adventurers.

Luckily the next day bore no resemblance whatsoever to that wild day. The sun pacified the country and subdued the sea; and Lynton, clinging limpet-like to the wooded Lyn valley, began its day with the cliff railway shuttling from the harbour to the town. David and I were the first two customers.

I had to take the cliff railway for the novelty factor. It was built at the end of the last century and is run by using water as weight, to hoist the carriage up and down. There was certainly no danger of a water shortage here.

The road south is a toll road which weaves its way this way and that, past a Christian Community and down into a shingle bay, before leaving the sea again and returning to the sesile oaks, which are twisted and gnarled from the gales, every branch a victory against the elements. It is a stunning and virtually car-less road. I began a new book, Dervla Murphy's *Ireland to India on a Bicycle*.

Wheel wobble had always got the better of me as a child, and I am far better on my own two feet. But now, the thought of riding a bicycle was rather nice; free wheeling down the hills, and watching gently undulating landscape pass by. There were no uphills in my daydreams.

However, it wasn't long before I was pleased to be on my own two legs, and in England. As I dropped down the bracken hillside into Heddon's Mouth Cleave, crossed the river, and began the slalom uphill path; Dervla was carrying Roz (her bicycle) up through passes of tremendous altitude in Afghanistan, rising from 1000 feet to 7000 feet over 21 miles, and enduring temperatures ranging from over 100°c to sub zero.

I pushed myself to the top of Holden Down, from where one gets a feel for the expansiveness of real Exmoor. In the distance, Exmoor gives way to patchwork fields with black hedges acting as untidy seams, and a rocky coast beckoned. High clouds were combed across the blue sky like carded wool, and I felt momentarily guilty that there were people working in offices; but then I reminded myself that they wouldn't have been so jealous yesterday.

After Great Hangman Hill, and its sibling, Little Hangman, each progressive hill got smaller, until I was forced onto the road to Ilfracombe. I plugged back into Dervla Murphy.

The cars went by in ones, twos and threes; the ones behind jostling to overtake the ones in front, and pulling out at the first possible opportunity. But when I reached Ilfracombe the cars which had whizzed past now sat idling in a road work bottleneck. They farted black smoke, all of which appeared to be aimed at me, and revved impatiently as if trying to compete with the already deafening sound of a pneumatic drill. I scowled at the drivers.

The mayhem made me irritable; irrationally irritable. The noise defeated Dervla, and I turned it off until Ilfracombe became a thing of the past and we found farm tracks and footpaths to Mortehoe. The country stuck out its tongue at Ilfracombe.

We crossed clear streams edged with the deep green leaves of wild garlic, whose smell indicated its presence long before I sighted it. Banked up behind the garlic were numerous grasses, rich in spring growth; and I saw my first cow parsley in flower.

The leafless and thorny blackthorn hedges were becoming white with flowers. Stinging nettles seemed to be sprouting lime green as I watched, and the other villain of the plant world, cleavers, was scaling the still flowerless hawthorn hedgerows.

Safe from such villains, celandines, marsh marigolds and daisies were just coming out in flower low on the ground. Like a child stretching to hold out its hand as flat and tight as possible to receive a treat, the daisies held up their heads as they made the most of any sun which briefly broke through.

My feelings for the hills and countryside were not dissimilar to Dervla Murphy's — the joy of nature's embracing seclusion, and the euphoric isolation of the wide open spaces; compared to the suddenly nerve shattering and hectic arrival in a built up area — however small or large.

Where towns had rejected me, the natural world had accepted me. I understood my own place. I felt in time with the ebb and flow of the sea as it mirrored my struggle; I felt a closeness to the seasons — to the new growth around us with its involuntary joy of living after the huddle of winter; and I felt accepted by the wildlife, as though by being on my feet we all became equal.

Also, through her incredible journey, Dervla was discovering the good and generous people who make up the large proportion of the world; as I was. A phrase from J B Priestley's *English Journey* summed up my feelings. 'Men are much better than their ordinary lives allow them to be.'

In a way, the Walk was withdrawing people from their own lives, and I had been overwhelmed and just a little surprised by the easy generosity and support we were shown. But there was one thing which stuck in my mind now.

At Christmas time there had been an article about us in the Scottish Big Issue. At the end of the article we had put an address for donations — the address being Jo's (who had joined us in Arbroath). A couple of weeks after the article had come out, Jo had received three Scottish pound notes wrapped up in a piece of paper and shoved in an envelope. There had been no note.

Several weeks later the same thing happened with five Scottish pound notes; and again, after another time lapse, more notes arrived. By now Jo had received a little over twenty pounds. There was never any note, and the paper and envelope were always crumpled. Whoever was sending them was clearly not affluent.

'Men are much better than their ordinary lives allow them to be.' I was learning lessons from them all.

Morte Point signified the end of the Bristol Channel and the start of the Atlantic. There is clearly tremendous tidal conflict here, and the white horses were confused as to which way they should be going. They raced and stalled from trough to crest, and skittered in a child's game of tag. From here we walked round Baggy Point, and through Braunton Burrows to Barnstaple.

David was parked in the sports centre in Barnstaple. I began my first cup of tea and doodled on the side of David's crossword. 'Right. What about this one. 'Appropriate type of dog for Jason.'

'Think of a type of dog,' David coached.

'Bullterrier, Lurcher, Pointer cross (Tess)!'

It was too much for my mind, and I made fun of it instead. But I had expressed a desire to learn how to do the cryptic crosswords and David was taking his role of teacher a little more seriously. 'Now, come on Spud. What did Jason and the argonauts sail off in search of?'

'You should ask me this sort of thing when I'm walking — oh, I know. The golden fleece!'

'So, what's the dog?'

'A fleecy terrier!' I wrote 'Golden Retriever' in the space.

'Neatly!' He could be so fussy.

Tess watched our movements. She came between David and I at any opportunity, sensing that she had competition for my affections. Really, there was no competition and I told her this.

'Right, I feel better now. Another clue,' I said after a shower among the swimmers in the sports centre. 'This sounds interesting. 'Hark: A sexual perversion (5,2,3,4)'! Sounds a bit filthy for such an erudite paper!'

I rolled myself a cigarette and we sat smoking and thinking about the clue — or rather David thought and I made intelligent noises. 'I've got it!' David exclaimed triumphantly after a while. 'Prick up the ears!' The tears of laughter filled our eyes again.

On the south side of the River Taw we joined the old railway line. A group of egrets looked dazzlingly white compared to the world around them, and after a while we fell into step with two ladies.

'Wow! Have you walked through Newquay?' they asked when they heard what we were doing. 'Newquay Wales?'

'Yes. We've been there on holiday.'

'If it's on the coast we've walked it!'

I had told them it was a coastal walk already. 'What about Threecliff Bay — on Gower?'

The duo kept asking me about places on the coast, and whether we had passed through them. It is like pressing an already illuminated lift button; every one of us has sought reassurance and pressed it more than once. Like so many others they pressed and pressed until TING — the lift arrived and the penny dropped.

We accompanied the duo to Northam bridge, where I branched off up the embankment in an undignified scramble, hotly pursued by Tess who thought this was some sort of game. Even short detours like following the slip road round were to be avoided! We were making for the coast, via Westward Ho! which is the only town in Britain to have an exclamation mark after its name! But the exclamation mark was doing nothing to make the town look cheery on a cold March day.

The path from here runs through rich grassland, along almost uniformly peaked and troughed cliffs. It was raining and there was no one else using the increasingly muddy path; there were no road accesses for over seven miles.

The temptation to drop onto the shingle beach, and skirt round some of the relentless hamstring-nagging hills, was very appealing. The tide was far out enough, but shingle was hard going and there was no proper access to the cliffs at the other end. We might have to retrace our tracks. Still I decided on the beach.

The shingle was in fact boulders the size of footballs, washed clean and slippery as well as naturally ankle breaking. From sea level the suck and blow of the boulders was deafening. I hoped the tide was on its way out.

The more we hurried, the more we slipped; and the more I realised that if one of us did hurt ourselves here we would be in trouble. Tess was miserable. She was talking now and glared at me with all four paws on different boulders; 'Why the hell did you bring me down here. I want to go home!'

We did manage to scramble up the cliffs, and rejoined a wooded and very muddy track at Peppercombe. Now I was slipping down every hill! I grabbed hold of the lichen thick oak branches to prevent several slides, and squeezed the water out of the lichen just for fun. It was staggering how much it held.

We didn't see anyone for ten wet and hilly miles, and when I reached the Haven Camp I was fed up and wet through to my knickers.

It was Easter weekend and the camp was full. But that night the electricity packed up throwing the camp into pandemonium; fraught parents, over excited children (now rechristened Tygers), and a stressed out manager. David and I resorted to an enforced game of murder in the dark in our chalet, which did wonders for our relationship . . .

Winds of over 100mph blew through the night, and the scene in the still powerless camp resembled the aftermath of a natural disaster the next morning. The scene on the path wasn't much better. Trees of every size had fallen and were blocking the track, and when we had passed Clovelly the full strength of the still gale force winds hit me like a physical blow from the south west. We fought our way along the edge of fields, enclosed by beautifully constructed dry stone walls.

Even the already short grass was being flattened by the wind, as was Tess' non-existent hair; and my coat and shorts flattened themselves against my body, reminding me of Flat Stanley.

The path began to run through brambles and bracken. I kept up the pace, but was soon clutching desperately onto any twig which was there,

and falling either right or left at every stride. The wind was one thing —
but the pathetically narrow path was another thing.

The path was a single, deep, muddy groove, only wide enough for
one foot, so that it was necessary to tightrope walk with arms outstretched. If you fell there was no safety net, only brambles, bracken,
rocky walls or the angry sea. The path must have been made by
monopeds. There was no other explanation.

I watched Tess in front of me, keeping all four paws neatly enclosed
in the groove; then I briefly watched the sea, which resembled a heaving
blackcurrant jelly made much too strong under the gigantic clouds. I
looked back at my feet again, as the sticky, red mud worked its way up
the insides of my legs.

The wind stung my face and dried out my eyes, so that I blinked
permanently; and all the time I tried to ignore a niggling pain in my left
knee.

The entire force of the Atlantic was hitting the land at Hartland
Point. Spray flew up and over the rocks to the lighthouse, and met the
next wave as it fell back again. The sea was competing with the wind for
noise levels, until they became one mass of thunderous power which
threatened my fragility.

Now the path was steep — and often stepped. We were on a roller
coaster of Disneyland proportions. I powered up the hills without thinking about stopping, felt exhilarated at the top, and set off down hill at a
lop-sided jumping gait, desperately ignoring the pain which shot through
my knee at every step.

It is fairly incomprehensible to think that anyone should build a
quay on such an exposed and hostile coast, but there are relatively few
estuaries or natural harbours on the north coast of Cornwall and consequently Hartland Quay was sculpted. It imported lime and coal until
the end of the last century, and two buildings remain; a seaspray-spat-
tered pub, and a wave-cleaned museum which bears witness to the large
number of ships wrecked on these lethal rocks.

We were an hour and a half late and David had been worried — at
least he said he had been worried. He looked fairly happy mixing
fundraising with pint swilling; but then at what point do you decide to
call the coastguards, as David had just contemplated? Or do you walk
back to look for a red body and a faithful dog? I wasn't sure, nor was
David. But we had made it.

Nevertheless I felt depressed. I tried to explain to David over a large
plate of chips. 'The wind's determined to stop you. The mud's ankle
deep and sticky. The hills are relentless; and the path's so narrow that
you can't keep balance. And —'

'What?'

'My knee.'

It hurt as I sat there, but I hated admitting it because in a way it was succumbing to it.

I couldn't decide what to do. We had to keep going; but then tomorrow things might be better. So far I had never not completed the day's planned mileage. But from here it would be another ten miles before there was a road access. I wasn't sure if I could face that. 'Well, it's up to you,' David said helpfully.

Of course it was up to me. Everything was up to me; but I didn't want it to be now. I wanted someone else to say 'do this' or 'do that'; even if it wasn't the right decision. 'Right. We'll call it a day,' I finally said. We had walked sixteen miles anyway. Someone had to make the decision, and it could only be me.

But the next day was no different. I strapped my knee up in an elastic bandage which was still blood spattered thanks to Tess' Scottish cut, but this only made my knee very hot and did nothing for the pain.

The clouds were skidding across the sky, throwing shadows over the sea. At intervals I could see Lundy Island, and when the sun briefly broke through it cast spotlights on the milky water. But then the world became dark again, and columns of rain flattened patches of sea, occasionally drenching us in sleet. The radio that morning had told of snow throughout Britain, and of temperatures plummeting to -2°. So much for the arrival of spring.

The water from streams was being blown back onto the cliff in a mass of spray and foamy spume, and I scuttled past these. The wind made listening to tapes impossible, and made communication with Tess hard, except by telepathy. We walked with the sound of the sea and the wind; yet despite everything it was hard to ignore the splendour of this coast.

I felt so high and invincible on reaching the top of a hill that nothing would have been capable of putting me down. I was alone with the hills. It was impossible to ignore the endorphins which pumped through my body, regardless of the pain. Reaching the top of a hill was like reaching a crescendo; a pinnacle of euphoria and well being which made me deliriously light headed, and coursed through my body. I recommend endorphins above any manufactured drug.

We only saw two people on the path in two days, and we stayed the next two nights on my aunts dairy farm, which was in danger of being washed away. On Easter Day David shared the delights of the continuing gale force winds and rain with us.

Within a mile from Widemouth we were soaked through and were on some of the highest cliffs in Cornwall. My knee still twinged, but I didn't slow down. I wanted to get this Easter ordeal over and return to the warmth of the wood burner.

The hills undulated inland, smooth and green as though washed clean. There wasn't a tree in sight. The cliffs slumped below us down to the sea, covered in gorse and bracken. Higher and higher we climbed over the fields, while Tess ran ahead and took refuge behind gorse bushes.

I joined Tess at the top of Long Cliff, and waited for David. He was walking his bow-legged walk, steadily and surely — but slowly. I dug out my camera from under my bin-liner rucksack cover and took a picture of him. 'That's mean,' he gasped. 'I can't walk any faster. I can't keep up!'

David stood bent over, breathing heavily. I put my hand on his chest and through the soggy layers of waterproofs I could feel his heart pounding and pounding. It made me frightened to find how much strain this was putting on him. It was ridiculous, but I had never realised until then just how fit I had become.

I felt completely responsible. There were no road accesses, and there was no way David could stop now. He caught his breath and we dropped down, and then back up the next hill. The hills weren't as steep as the previous day, but they were long and relentless. Tess and I waited again, and again David gasped for breath. 'Alright?'

'Mm. Wish I'd had breakfast though! And don't say "I told you so" —' David was losing his sense of humour.

On top of Rusey Cliff we waited again. I wondered whether David would have stopped if he had been able to, or whether pride would have got the better of him. It was silly to think that you could come out and walk fifteen miles of this terrain, and at this pace, without being very fit. It would be like trying to run a marathon without any training.

After fourteen memorable miles, there was Boscastle's long and twisting harbour, squeezed between two rugged headlands. We caught The Cobweb pub just before it shut, and dripped buckets of water on the flagstones. Another soaked set of clothes. 'Remind me never to come walking with you again!' David said.

'If you do, remember to have breakfast!'

'And don't give me that rubbish about 'one more hill'. It makes it much worse.'

We shared our pints with Tess. David was leaving the next day. I was sad to see him go, but pleased to be having new people driving. They all added to the Walk and stopped me from getting too complacent about all that they did for us. If nothing else, David and I had got the tongues wagging.

CHAPTER SIXTEEN

BOSCASTLE
TO
PLYMOUTH

265.1 MILES

TOTAL: 3,916.8 MILES

For the first time I felt defeated. My normally dehydrated eyes became filled with tears; tears of frustration and tears of weakness. My entire body felt as though it had been through a wringer and was now deflated and lifeless. 'Piss off wind. Just go away,' I screamed with an energy I didn't feel.

Tess came running back at the commotion, and the sight of her worried face brought fresh tears to the backs of my eyes. I didn't dare sit down for fear that I'd never get up. I bit my lip again. I had broken my rule of never stopping half way up a hill.

The jeering wind had been sending me back two steps for every one forward along the higgledy-piggledy monopeds' path from Boscastle, and a particularly strong gust had brought me literally to a standstill. It was a battle of the wills; the wind against my body, and my body against the *boss*. I wondered which would crack first.

The wind would never crack. So it was between my body and the *boss*. Would there come a time when my body simply felt that it couldn't put one step in front of the other? When a combination of pains and external factors just became too much? Or would my mind push me until I literally ground to a halt?

The *boss* was still in charge, and somehow got me to my feet. We had no choice but to get to the Spudtruck. So, see-sawing with my wooden knee, and thinking of the mega dose pain killers which sat in my rucksack until the time came that the pain was *really* unbearable, we took each hill as it came until Port Isaac came into view.

A fishing boat heading into the harbour was being carelessly tossed about on the huge waves, this way and that, up and down. It disappeared from view and then reappeared again on the white crests of the opaque sea, bobbing and curtsying and seemingly making no progress at all. If nothing else, walking the Cornish coast in such weather brought history alive.

Of all the counties that we walked through, Cornwall has the largest sea frontage. For this reason, the coast offers more insight into the county; its past and its present joined by the one common factor upon which this land has relied — the sea. From the smallest cove, to the largest city, maritime activity of some sort is visible. Above all, the sea has provided transport for Cornwall's thriving mineral industry.

During the nineteenth century Cornwall was the most important source of copper in the world. On a more local scale, it was exported to South Wales for smelting, and in return the boats brought coal back to fire the steam engines. Cornwall also mined tin, and became a leading slate and granite exporter; London Bridge and Chelsea Embankment were built from Cornish granite.

To avoid the added danger of negotiating Land's End when exporting all these, small harbours, (or porths), were laboriously sculpted along the inhospitable north Cornish coast. Where a porth was out of the question, beach trading sufficed. But mining and fishing declined, leaving a once self-sufficient county now reliant on outsiders. Car clogged lanes and clotted cream theme parks obliterate history in the summer; but under winter's cruel coat the little wave-tossed fishing boat turned back time. If these men and women could survive on this beautiful yet hostile coast, I could surely manage to keep my two feet moving on the more stable terra firma.

A steep hill led us out of empty Port Isaac with its narrow streets, and back to the fray. The sea was mesmerising in its power, and its intense pressure was illustrated by the wave formed cauldron of Lundy Hole. I peered down into it with a sort of masochistic pleasure, and the spray and spume reached us high up on the cliffs.

I hummed 'For those in peril on the Sea,' and thought of all the wrecks and their aquatic inhabitants. Where a path branched off from the main one, Tess stopped and waited. Five months previously she would have trotted off down any old path, but now she knew. I teased her, making to go one way and then going the other. 'Which way Tessie Too?'

'I don't mind. You're the one who makes these decisions.'

'But don't you know the sea's always on our right?!' No answer. She was off to Padstow.

Out beyond the disorderly breakers of Padstow Bay, the occasional glimpse of a colourful sail indicated a thrill seeking windsurfer, while to our left, the small spire of St Enodoc Church just poked through the dunes. It is easy to believe that it was once drowned by the sand. It was unearthed in 1836, and I feel sure is now safe from such perils because it sits in the middle of that most sacrosanct of land — a golf course.

As we rounded the final corner towards Rock a small boat came into sight ahead. It was the ferry bound for Padstow and its gang plank was down in a very tempting manner. Tess was off at a gallop.

Having barked ferociously at the very first marine monster she had been in, she was now very fond of boats. But still I watched in amazement as she trotted straight up the gangplank, stopped at the perfectly positioned and open window of the wheelhouse, gave the Captain a large lick of appreciation, and continued into the packed boat, her tail beating like mad against the legs of the passengers. The captain thought she was worth her fare in entertainment, and waived both our fares.

In sheltered Padstow I turned my attention to my stomach. I bought a curry pasty, and we ensconced ourselves on a central bench overlooking the harbour. Here, in central Padstow, on a Tuesday lunchtime, we were part of a mass pasty eating ritual.

We sat on bollards, benches, kerbs, windowsills or the edge of the harbour. We ate with great concentration, searching for meat (which often likes to disguise itself as potato or swede), and tasting for pastry quality, filling, stodge factor, bouquet, nose or aftertaste. But, although mine ranked pretty highly in the pasty stakes, everyone else's looked much better. I wasn't the only person thinking this. Everyone else was looking at everyone else's pasties.

The trick was to take glances at everyone else's pasty without being caught. Every so often someone was caught, and the two parties would look away simultaneously, immediately embarrassed. Those with flakes of pastry or onion on their chin were to be avoided completely, because this only hinted at their affliction. (A petit lady with several bags of shopping at her feet was being ostracised by a stubborn piece of swede.)

Then the hail started. With one mad dash the pasty eaters made for the octagonal shelter, each trying to look as though they weren't desperate for a seat when everyone knew they were. I secured a seat squeezed between the lady with the swede (she had lost the swede, and was having a post-pasty cigarette); and a small boy and his pasty-eating mother.

Tess got the rest of my hail soaked pasty, and a rustle caught her attention. An elderly man was just finishing his pasty. He was scrunching up the paper bag in one hand and held his final morsel in a thoughtful fashion in the other hand. Positioning herself at his feet, Tess bottom-shuffled closer and closer, and pricked her ears harder. Reward. I was still hungry and wondered if I could try a similar tactic.

The wind returned with full force at Stepper Point, but from here the walking was easier along low headlands and intermittent beaches.

After thirty six hours we were reunited with the Spudtruck in Porthcothan. Its starter motor had decided to go in the middle of a farmyard river on gale force, rainy Easter Monday; just at the moment that Kari, the new driver, had arrived. She had stepped out of her car and straight into a pool of swirling cow shit, and her immaculate white sneakers had been immediately brown. Despite watching her son drive away with a look which said 'Don't leave me here!' she was now still with us.

I clambered into the Spudtruck after Tess, negotiating Kari's seven bags which ranged from plastic bags to wicker baskets and little red suitcases, and through which Kari was already rummaging. 'I know I had another packet of cigarettes somewhere,' she said, starting on the third bag. 'Oh, by the way. Linda phoned. From Lancashire? She's arriving in Newquay today.'

We met up with cheery Linda (with the chickens in her Leyland garden) more by chance than planning, and heaved her monumental rucksack into the Spudtruck, where it competed with Kari's seven bags. Kari and Linda had never met each other, but they had two things in common: the Walk; and rummaging.

Back in Porthcothan they took turns in jumping up to 'find something,' but the required article was always in the wrong bag, and the right bag was always in the wrong place, and the wrong bag was in the right place. None of this was very conducive to successful rummaging; but one thing was a certainty — if one bag came down for a rummaging session, the others would closely follow.

Kari finally settled down once she had her vodka (drowned with coke to 'disguise the taste of the vodka'), her cigarettes and her handbag within reach. Linda replaced the contents of her rucksack for the fourth time, and the two of them began to chatter.

The peace in the morning sounded like music. I pulled open the curtains to watch an equally ecstatic musical blackbird. I savoured the moments until I could bear to be inside no longer, and didn't even notice the probably knee deep melée of bags.

A gentle path ran along the low grassy cliffs, which appeared to have been smoothed off with a plane before being sliced off at the edge. The sea was gentle, gracious, and unrecognisable. After two miles we came to Bedruthan Steps — three large rocks just offshore which have been the scene of many a shipwreck. The last one was a boat called The Samaritan in 1846. It was carrying fine clothes, and the locals descended on the wreck before it had hardly broken up. They were soon dressed in finery and nicknamed the rock the Good Samaritan — and it is called this to this day.

Linda was walking as though her life depended on it. She is one of the world's enthusiasts, even managing to assemble the Spudtruck bed as though indulging in some longed-for treat. We talked of New Zealand, where I had first met Linda, and continued to talk of travel. Linda asked the natural question. 'What d'you think you'll do afterwards Spuddy?'

'Haven't thought that far. Well . . . I have as far as how I'll live.'

'How's that?'

'Sometimes it's all settled — you know, a cosy home. I thought that way near the beginning of the walk.'

'And now?'

'Well, now . . . I'm into this existence. Sometimes I yearn to stop for a few days. But then, when we've spent two nights somewhere, it feels like an age! I think perhaps man needs to keep moving to retain interest, keep alive the imagination.'

I thought this more and more. It doesn't have to be large scale travel; just movement to prevent stagnating like a lifeless pond. Whether it be between houses, jobs, towns, villages, countries or planets! The newness of things is stimulation — new people, places, ideas. It might only mean travelling to your neighbour whom you never knew existed.

Wherever you find it, the stimulation can only be beneficial. The quote at the front of the book, by Danish philosopher Søren Kierkegaard, sums up my feelings.

Linda had blisters. She joined Kari, while we rounded the River Gannel from Newquay and walked through rich pasture from West Pentire to Perran Beach. We had now had the calm before the storm, and that night I was woken by the wind and rain, which was even stronger and more determined to defeat us.

We crossed a long since deserted airfield to St Agnes, and the wind stung my face, whistling over the thistles and octopus-tentacled brambles. Even the nettles and gorse struggled to survive, while grass in its first year looked tired and worn out. The curled up vegetation took on the end-of-summer brownness — but this was only April.

The path left the airfield and entered an area which stands as a memorial to Cornwall's bygone days of mining. Chimneys rise up from the copper coloured shingle; mine shafts disappear into the brambles; slag heaps are evident from gorse smothered hummocks. But it is the engine houses which provide the most distinctive headstone, rising up from the horizon like giant twenty first century tarantulas.

Unnecessary paraphernalia has been swept clean off this landscape, leaving only the indestructible memorials and most resilient vegetation. The wind nearly swept me clean off the landscape. It knotted my hair into dreadlocks and was making my hands swell. Over the next few days they took on the form of air-filled marigold gloves, and eventually they blistered. The Weather God was illustrating our mortality.

The soft sand of St Ives Bay brought on my end-of-day knee pain, and I tried to amuse myself with the limerick about St Ives: 'As I was going to St Ives, I met a man with seven wives —' but I couldn't remember any more. I contented myself with silly additions, all of which cursed the wind. After twenty-eight miles St Ives finally landed in our path.

The cafés and galleries lining the maze of narrow St Ives streets were shut in the early morning, and the Tate Gallery was bracing itself for the next onslaught. The gallery, which draws art enthusiasts from all over the world, was just about to celebrate its first birthday. But it too was shut, and for now Land's End beckoned; it filled my mind like a long awaited reunion with an old friend. As a final insult, my number one enemy blew harder and harder as we rounded the left hand corner of Britain.

There were no road accesses for eleven miles. There was just Tess, myself, my endorphins and the wind. The streams were still defying gravity, and the sea was more wild and furious than I had seen it during the entire eight months. It threw itself against the cliffs and I could feel the salt on my lips and the spray on my back. It was exhilarating but menacing. It roared, but encouraged. It, too, was defying us to reach Land's End.

Through my tunnel-vision, the door-wedge shaped Cape Cornwall came into view, and from here a small cluster of white buildings shone out in the murk to the south. They were the buildings of Land's End; the old friend.

But there was still five miles to go and, as if to put me to the final test, the path became strewn with ankle breaking granite boulders. They lay in piles resembling rock cakes, and I tried to negotiate each stretch of rock cakes when the wind had momentarily eased; but each time the wind noticed and blew harder. Each step took concentration.

We dropped down onto Whitesand Beach, and up through Sennen. At the top of the final hill the shy sun came out for a few very brief minutes. It blinded me after the ten days of darkness, and faded the black sea into a mixture of opaque blue and phosphorescence. I had won my private battle, and this was the reward.

In the hotel, which was putting us up, Linda and Kari bore great gifts. A bottle of bubbly; a fluffy pink pig; a plastic sunflower (to signify the spring we hadn't witnessed); and a sex patch to be attached to an unspecified part of the body to bring on immediate orgasm! It seemed I was set for all occasions.

When our thoughts turned to food, we discovered that the restaurant had dress regulations. The skirt which had travelled 3,760 miles because 'you never know who you might meet,' and which had caused much mirth from the drivers, would be put to use after all.

The skirt was damp and smelt of onions, but I felt like Cinderella as we headed downstairs. This feeling didn't last long. On the final carpeted stair I missed my footing, and landed in a crumpled heap. Kari and Linda burst out laughing but came to my rescue. 'She's pissed already!'

'Give her a pair of walking boots and leggings!'

The walk had almost come to an undignified end on a carpeted step.

I couldn't help comparing Land's End to John O' Groats. They are both treeless and bleak; but they are also both famous for being nothing. There are no quays, castles, ancient churches — there is not even a mine in sight. Instead there is a stretch of coast, beyond which are the Scilly Isles and then America.

Having said that, the sight of Land's End had brought tears to my eyes. It was enough to experience the euphoria of having walked the length of the country (covering 2,420 miles), and I for one will remember Land's End — whatever the reason for its fame. We took a purposeful left turning to begin a route which could only take us daily closer to our destination.

Walking east was instantly different. Apart from the gale, which now blew us along, the sun, when it appeared, hit us from the right rather than face on as it had done for 2,250 miles. There are also plenty of shelter giving bays which allowed spring growth and bird song.

At Porthcurno there is a remarkable open air theatre built into the cliffside. At the time it was closed, but I have been there since and it is the most fantastic setting. The seats are cut into the cliffs, and the stage is on a rocky platform below. The backdrop consists of the sea in a 180° vista.

Around the next bay from Porthcurno lies Logan rock — a seventy ton rock sitting precariously balanced on a rocky outcrop. During the end of the last century a band of sailors managed to dislodge it completely. The story goes that they were immediately told to put it back! They clearly succeeded.

We ran down the final hill into Mousehole, ignoring the strong complaints from my knee which thought that downhill, tarmac and running were too much. We found a pub with minutes to spare. I was determined to watch the Grand National, which was another sign of spring.

I was hot and sweaty, and my rolled-up leggings exposed legs thick with Cornish mud. I went up to the bar. 'A pint of Tinners please, and —' I turned to Tess, but checked myself just in time. Tess ignored the abrupt cut off and said 'same for me please.' She was panting heavily.

We found a seat and Tess took big slurps from my pint and dropped pieces of ready salted crisp into it, while I watched my horse come in somewhere near the end. Around us the locals put their empty pints on the bar, which were re-filled without any eye contact with the barman. They were all freshly scrubbed fishermen. Another few plastic bottles bobbing on the seas.

While the fishermen were drinking to their wins or losses, their boats sat so densely in Newlyn harbour that they couldn't even bob on the swell. We passed the swilled out fish market, and the Spudtruck was parked on Penzance harbour. Since Penzance was the first big town we had hit for two weeks, we set off fundraising that Saturday night.

But the donations from Penzance's macho drinkers were scarce for two reasons. The first was a tin shaking Seventh Day Adventist who beat us to every pub and, no matter how compassionate, people will only give to one charity in a night. The second was the attitude 'fend for oneself'. Cornwall has the largest discrepancy between wages and house prices in the whole country, thanks largely to holiday homes.

Several days later I met a young guy called Steven, who was working on a youth training scheme with BBC Cornwall. Two days before Christmas he had been kicked out of his home by his mother, and had spent Christmas on the streets. For the time being he was staying with friends but, with the prospect of his temporary job coming to an end, he faced a bleak future.

Even sleepy Marazion isn't free of problems. The next day a newspaper headline caught my eye — 'Sex and drugs concern in Marazion.' I couldn't believe that such a small and picturesque place could be a village of such disrepute, but the teenagers of Marazion were turning to these activities from boredom and disillusionment. It doesn't bode well for urban areas.

I returned to the place where I felt at home. Like the seasons, I too was completing a full circle; and now each bud, emerging bee, courting fulmar and nesting gull encouraged us. I felt guilty of the amazing relief that the natural world gave me. 'Solvitur ambulando' — 'it is solved by walking'. If only it was.

We walked the two mile bar of Porthleven Sands in ankle shaping sand which held my boots like sticky mud, and I turned round and walked backwards for the last part of the beach to Lizard. Walking backwards was like swapping a heavy bag from one arm to the other. The relief was temporary, but was a relief all the same.

The Lizard Peninsula lived up to its name, as we strode across its lounging back in long awaited still sunshine the next morning. Its sheer cliffs and flat top make it appear to have been cut out of a large land mass with a pastry cutter. We walked through the hidden villages of Church Cove and then Cadgwith until gentle hills, serviced by meandering lanes, took over.

A small gift shop in Coverack allowed me to use their phone for my Cable TV interview. I ran through the week to Femmy, watched with interest by the browsers. '— and now we're in Coverack,' I concluded. There was a commotion outside followed by a loud bark which sounded dangerously close. 'Is that Tess?' Femmy asked.

'Yes. Oh . . .'

I had tied Tess up to a plastic guide dog of about her height outside the shop, but she had clearly had some sort of falling out with her new friend, and was now dragging the dog into the shop. They were stuck in the doorway. Tess was wagging her tail ecstatically at the sight of me, and was causing more chaos than a masked intruder; the customers were trapped and the proprietor was flustered.

Unlike better behaved dogs, Tess refuses to wait for me outside shops, and dashes in the moment the next customer opens the door. So far she had made off with ice cream signs and plastic rubbish bins. On one occasion I had tied her to a supermarket trolley which I thought was securely fastened to its neighbour — but wasn't.

I replaced the guide dog and gave it an involuntary pat. The Helford River beckoned that afternoon, as did the thought of my first day off for three weeks, since Bristol.

The water of the wooded Helford estuary was strangely calm, and on every turn I expected to see Daphne Du Maurier's Frenchman aboard La Mouet; dark suave and pirate-like, as he sat smoking his pipe and sketching a nearby heron or curlew. There is certainly a romanticism to the hidden inlets and muddy creeks.

In Helford village small cottages jostle for a water-side position. The rest of England might be another world away, and the only mode of transport might be one of the few boats tied to trees or small jetties. One such boat took us across the Helford after our day off.

The path to Falmouth was dry, gently undulating and wooded; and the hedgerows were jam packed with wild flowers. My favourite was stitchwort, with its small and delicate white flowers which can smother an entire bank. Mixed with the red of red campions and the blue of bluebells, the banks appeared in a blaze of patriotic colour.

From the wilderness and colour of nature's garden, I watched the gardens of Falmouth's suburbs unfold. Lawns had already been mown and were free of a single stray piece of grass; while annuals were planted like strategically placed troops. There was none of the carefree abandon of nature's garden.

People's gardens mirror their lives so that passers-by can spy on strangers' lives; from the concrete gardens, to the meticulous garden, to the flamboyant garden, to the couldn't-care-less garden. I wondered what kind of garden I would ultimately have; or whether I would have one. At the moment I was sold on the stitchwort and red campion.

Falmouth suburbs didn't last long. I bought the best pasty I had so far had, and boarded the ferry to St Anthony.

We had a leisurely afternoon and took our time. The path was easy and ran along the edge of grass fields empty of any stock. Dividing up the fields were more large turf and stone walls. Finding a particularly comfortable looking one I clambered up and called Tess after me. I found some dry tobacco and rolled a cigarette. The act of rolling alone is therapeutic.

Tess sniffed the smoke in a resigned manner. Then I saw her prick up her ears and wag her tail in a way which said 'goodie, there're people coming'. Sure enough, a solitary man came into view with a Border Terrier. Tess leapt off the bank and raced towards the man, her whole body in paroxysms of delight.

The usual doggy exchanges began, while the Border Terrier followed Tess with great interest. 'Oh, Marcus loves big bitches!' the grey haired man proudly explained. 'It all started when he was a pup and used to play with a Wolfhound pup.'

I continued to sit on my bank like a Buddha, while the big bitch and her idolater fought over a stick. 'Yup, any big bitch and Marcus is in his element. He doesn't like small bitches you know. He was in a kennel with a big black Doberman lady once. They cuddled up together all the time.'

I listened to more stories of Marcus' amorous antics with big bitches, and was still smiling over the Great British Dog Walker as we got down and walked on to Pendower Beach.

The duo of Linda and Kari had been replaced by the duo of Harriet and Jo. Harriet is a friend who also played secretary of the fundraising committee. It was she who had introduced me to such alien things as meeting minits and agenda, and was soon to introduce me to yet more frighteningly efficient terms. She had lost her driving licence several weeks earlier, so had brought Jo along, (who had driven through Arbroath).

Harriet greeted us at the Spudtruck door, clutching the clipboard in one hand and a packet of Marlboro in the other hand, and Jo appeared from the nearby vegetation, enthusing about the flora.

'Jo's been teaching me the names of all the wild flowers,' Harriet said knowledgeably. 'Alki . . . alkisomething!'

'Alkanet!' Jo corrected.

'That's it. And nipplewhatsit!'

'Nipplewort!'

'That's it. Nipplewort.' Harriet put on a funny accent and laughed another secret squirrel laugh. Jo joined in. 'I tell you Spud. H has been bossing me around all day!'

'I've just been trying to stop you getting lost!'

'But you scream directions just as we've passed the turning!' Jo winked at me.

They were like a couple of naughty schoolgirls, but Harriet was highly organised. 'So. What's your ETD, Spud?' she asked the next morning, clipboard at the ready.

'You what?'

'ETD? Estimated time of departure!' Jo winked, and Harriet laughed.

'Oh. Any minute!'

'What about lunch? And your ETA?'

'Estimated time of arrival?!'

Harriet wrote on the clipboard; 'Gorran Haven seafront. ETA 1pm.'

My day thus planned, I set off through flowering gorse which emanated heat and a sweet honey smell which sent the bees wild. Areas of the hedgerows were so colourful that I couldn't take my eyes off them. *Why had I never noticed such abundant spring plant life before?* I was learning the flowers' names, and enjoying them all; alkanet, bluebells, forget-me-nots, sweet cicely, ramsons, speedwell, common vetch, sainfoin and my other two favourites — sea campions and sea pinks.

I scaled the hills and dips. The hills aren't high, but they are continuous from Gorran Haven, and every so often they are broken up by beautiful villages such as Portloe and Mevagissey; where it is possible to buy anything from Cornish pasties, to fine art, to buckets and spades to precious rocks. But I enjoyed the harbours more, with their salt stained boats and buoys, and the air full of the smell of dried salt on wood and fish ingrained pots.

From Mevagissey I couldn't help noticing the white hills on the horizon. Rather than a freak localised snow storm, this is the site of large china clay works. Further evidence of the china clay works are at Pentewan, where the river is as white as milk.

Pentewan is now a one pub village but, during the eighteenth century, china clay was transported from here around the world. China clay is decomposed granite and, unlike the other mineral industries in Cornwall, it is still in abundance.

On the coast, however, it was still green, lush and undulating. The sea in St Austell Bay was calm and indifferent. It lapped at the small beach in Duporth, lazily entered the harbour in Charlestown, and caressed the cliffs which make up Gribbin Head.

Twisting streets took us down into Fowey, which outstares the equally sloping village of Polruan across the River Fowey. A ferry shuttles between the two. From Polruan the path runs along the top of steep and dramatic cliffs, and after a mile we came to one of Britain's hidden gems — Lantic Bay.

An expanse of white sand was being lapped by almost imperceptible waves, behind which the sea was azure blue where the sand shone through it; before it became mottled by the addition of rocks beneath. Further out, sheer depth extinguished all features completely.

The sea's unnatural calmness gave it a wonderful feeling of space; a vast openness stretching away and away, and wrapping the world in an immense blueness highlighted only by the addition of a single white triangle of a yacht's sail.

Lantic Bay now came second in my league of beaches; and Polperro rated top for fishing villages. Many of the jostling pink and blue houses on the small river are built so that at high tide the view from the window would suggest you were on one of the many boats stranded by low tide. One house had a dinghy suspended from a veranda on a special hoist, while the walls of others drop down at cheeky angles suggesting foundation movement that no one really worries about.

Tess wasn't a great admirer of such views, and stretched now in a lackadaisical greyhound manner, prompting me into action.

Back on the path, a National Trust sign said 'Talland 2 miles'; but by my thumb reckoning, which proved correct by the pedometer, it was barely a mile. I was completely confused as to the length of a mile; no one seemed to know. My guide book underestimated the miles drastically; while locals to an area never had a clue. Nearing Talland a guy jogging said Looe was four and a half miles away. I made it three.

The following day I tested my pedometer to a road sign, and it proved to be correct — or we were both wrong!

Talland was comprised of a PC and a car park, in which there was a small kiosk. 'Where are you off to?' the lady asked, as she filled up my water bottle. I told her.

'My son's a walker. He was the youngest child to walk Land's End to John O' Groats. He was nine,' she told me. I had seen his photograph in the Land's End hotel. 'But,' the lady went on, 'he's about to have the record taken from under his nose! His brother, who's six now, wants to do the walk when he's eight!'

To complete the family of fitness, father was in training to run the Cornish Coast Path (about 250 miles). I thought of the hills and mud which I had negotiated, and offered my advice; 'Look out for the knees!'

Cornwall ended with a cream tea overlooking the River Tamar. This was the way to arrive in a city. One minute we were walking round the clifftops of Rame Head, and the next minute Plymouth had appeared, flanking the many inlets of the River Tamar which make the ideal situation for a port.

The ferryman waived the fare, and the local MP welcomed us back into Devon. He was clutching a plastic bag which looked distinctly like a bottle. Lyn from Shelter Plymouth presented me with an engraved flask, and the MP thrust the bottle into my hand saying; 'The Shelter grapevine's been working!'

The following day, Tess and I appeared in the local papers, sitting on the quay with a flask in one hand and a bottle of House of Commons whisky in the other.

Battling Cornwall's incessant wind; mining landscape near Perranporth.

CHAPTER SEVENTEEN

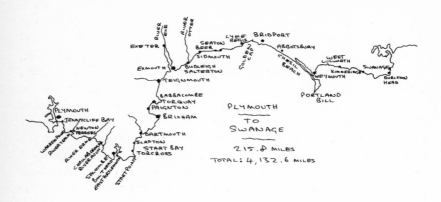

It was a Sunday in Jennycliff Bay, the first undeveloped piece of water-front in the suburbs of Plymouth, and the world joined us in the front stalls of the car park. It was to set a precedent for what was to become my weekly diversion of Another Sunny Sunday on the South Coast.

With early morning enthusiasm, the Reliant Robins and Metros were first. They looked driver-less, until two grey heads bobbed like feeding chickens just above the dashboard. They ground slowly to a halt, and squeezed into spaces rather than be exposed.

Once successfully parked, the thermos of milky tea would appear, followed by a tantalising array of scones and sandwiches. Throughout this snack he would look seawards through his binoculars, while she produced a book of crosswords. When the time came for them to leave, they reversed apprehensively and revved clutches, causing momentary pile-ups in the car park entrance, and setting off down the road in first gear.

Next came the families. Clutching fishing nets and picnics, they slowly descended to the shore. Normally they returned empty handed, and clearly tired and emotional, while often the threat 'if you don't behave, we'll go home without having the picnic' had been carried out. Father was bored, and mother was at the end of her tether.

After lunch, fathers monopolised amateur kites while sons had the important job of rescuing the kite each time it hit the deck. It is true British grit which allows enjoyment to be gained from such stubbornly unaerodynamic machines.

In late afternoon the lovers appeared, released from Sunday lunches and frolicking in courtship. They ran down the hill hand in hand, and fell over with careless abandon as if enacting a scene from *Love Story*. Here they engaged themselves in the foreplay ritual of mock fighting which, without exception, resulted in a major love scene for the whole car park to see.

The car park began to empty. Kites were landed; couples sat like Siamese twins on benches; children were carried back up the hill; thermos' were packed away and crossword books closed; solitary figures walked pensively back to their cars; and dogs were led reluctantly home.

In place of all these came the lads. A packed Mini was pushed into the empty back row, so joining a Ford. Thick smoke billowed from all their windows as it had from the professor's factories, and each one's music competed with each other. As the day ended, and my fifth newsletter was written, I joined them in the back row. Not to be outdone, I played trendy music and puffed smoke from my window. So passed my third night on my own in eight months.

Even on a Monday morning the Jennycliff Bay car park was filling up, as I went in to Plymouth to pick up Gaynor.

Gaynor and I were at college together, but our lives couldn't be more different. She works in the city and her 'buy, sell, buy, sell' life suits her hyperactivity and her notorious affinity for red wine. She scuttled out of the station, with her feet at ten to two. 'Hiya darling,' she said, giving me a hug.

She climbed into the driver's seat, lit her first Silk Cut, shoved her glasses up her nose, pulled her yellow peaked cap firmly down and said 'Right, where to doll?'

'Jennycliff Bay. Gently!'

The sea stayed busy with boating activity, even after we had rounded the corner away from Plymouth Sound, and the military presence was both onshore and offshore. We dodged in-use rifle ranges, and soldiers with faces blackened in camouflage, to arrive at Warren Point on the River Yealm.

There is as much to Warren Point as the name implies. It is a wooded promontory, served by a rutted track and home to a handful of cottages. Across one arm of the River Yealm is Newton Ferrers, and across another arm of the river is the other uninhabited point which I hoped we would get to. It was clearly optimistic to hope for a ferry.

But an array of yachts and dinghies were moored on the water, and I was sure that someone would give us a lift. I dumped my rucksack on the cracked step and settled down to wait.

After a few minutes I heard an outboard chugging up the river. I yelled and waved and yelled and waved, but they could neither see nor hear. We waited again.

Tess stood right on the water's edge, peering into the water and the perfectly defined rocks below as though by concentrating very hard she would will us both across the water. When a second dingy putt-putted up the river, and I waved and yelled again, it also avoided us, either accidentally or intentionally.

After an hour I had eaten my sandwiches (after only five miles), had counted the boats, had watched for fish and dreamt of Frenchmen, and had waved manically at three boats. I was now reluctantly preparing for the twelve mile road detour.

In the distance a toy looking dinghy came into view, and began to weave through the boats towards Newton Ferrers. Before I had time to think about whether we would actually fit into this boat, the dinghy had responded to my waves and was heading in our direction. It reminded me of the plastic boats that we played with in the bath as children. It was orange and white, and had double layered plastic.

The man beamed at us. 'Couldn't leave you stranded here!' Tess eyed the dinghy with contempt, and I could see what was going through the mind of the dog who had originally had to be manhandled into boats; 'We started off in a yacht in Essex, and since then we've regressed. Now she expects me to get into this pudding bowl!'

I bundled her in on top of my rucksack and clambered in after her. The sea was less than an inch from the top of the boat, but our Captain was quite unconcerned. He rowed with confidence and luckily no other boats passed us, whose wakes would surely have tipped us up.

We watched as our Captain rowed over to his yacht and waved us farewell. 'Tess the Cabin Boy, and Able Seaman Spud! Hey Tessie?'

'Yes, yes Mum. Now let's get going in case someone saw us!'

I followed Tess along a track which wound up hill through coniferous woodland, and then popped out to more open country. Five miles further on we came to the next river — the River Erme.

The distance across was slightly less than the Yealm, and this one was more sandy. It had crossed my mind that we might be able to wade across it, but I wasn't prepared to play guinea pig to quicksand.

As we loitered around the river mouth, investigating plastic Spanish cleaning bottles, listening to *Ring O Bright Water*, and wondering whether Gavin Maxwell's otters really enjoyed long plane flights, never mind living in London and being taken for walks in the park on a lead, a man appeared and assured me we could wade across the river at low tide. As luck would have it, low tide was any minute.

Avoiding the two river detours in one day was like winning the lottery, and I covered the final few steep miles to Challaborough Haven Park in good humour.

That evening we met Indie, who was trying to persuade the Haven receptionist to let him park his technicoloured passion wagon in their car park for the night. He was a loner who refused to fit any pigeon-hole.

He came to the bar with us, and we asked him what brought him to Challaborough, (a village which is only comprised of the Haven Park.) 'I had several signs,' he told us. 'They were all connected with a place called Belle Vue! I knew these signs meant something and I've discovered there's a Belle Vue Farm round here! I'm off to find out if I can stop there for a while.' The farmer was still unaware of this plan.

Indie drank pints of Guinness and smoked dry tobacco. He was clearly pleased to have some company, and we soon learnt of his professed range of occupations — journalism, a stint in the Navy, and commerce, of an unspecified sort. We asked him what his current project was; 'I've really come to Belle Vue to work on a book.'

'What type of book?'

'It's a trilogy. A trilogy on life, the universe and religion,' he said. There was a pause. 'I've started work on it,' he repeated, as if to add credence to the fact.

I could see Gaynor raising her cynical eyebrows: Indie changed the subject. 'Do either of you need any clothes? What about walking boots, Spud?'

'Not really.'

'You see, I've got heaps of stuff in the van. You can have this jersey if you want.'

He was already starting to take off his violently coloured jersey, which declared the fact that it had had many homes. 'No, honestly, Indie. It's alright —'

'Yup, we're fine,' Gaynor backed me up, and I couldn't help laughing at the girl who once worked for Ralph Lauren now being offered Indie's cast offs.

'I've salvaged amazing things from tips. Would you like a bicycle? I've got one in the van?' We declined. 'What else do you need? I've got shoes, clothes, pots and pans, chairs, brooms . . .'

Gaynor and I went to shake collecting tins round the scarce holiday-makers, and Indie declared that he'd leave 'right now' in search of Belle Vue Farm. He wanted to meet up again 'somewhere on the road,' and asked where we would be the next night. 'Somewhere between here and Brixham,' I said rather vaguely, and a look of relief swept over Gaynor.

Indie thought he had found kindred travelling spirits. The lure of the travelling life was certainly getting to me, and so long as I had the Spudtruck as home I was happy. But at the end of the day I also still had the friends who I knew and loved, and trusted would be there for me when needed, as I hoped I would be for them. The difference with our life was that it would one day come to an end — or would it? Could it?

Later on there was a knock on the door of our chalet and Indie appeared like a lost soul. 'I found Belle Vue Farm, but there was no one there just now. I liked your company and . . .' Indie trailed off.

Gaynor went uncharacteristically quiet and we both began to summon large yawns which would have been impossible half an hour earlier. 'We were just on our way to bed,' I lied, and then felt terrible.

I hoped that somewhere Indie had some good friends to return to. Friends like Gaynor. And after Indie had taken the hint and left us, I went to bed thinking how lonely a life on the road can be, as people come and go in the various chapters of that life. A loneliness that I had myself experienced.

The next morning we were ferried across the River Avon by the local boatbuilder, and took to the red soiled path bordered by fields harrowed into stripes of light green and dark green swathes. The countryside was its flawless patchwork; and all around us was the primeval surge which brought the country out in search of a mate.

The path was littered with furry black flies fully absorbed in the joys of copulation, and I had to watch my step to avoid putting an abrupt end to their joyful union. Joining them were beetles, and I suddenly realised the disruption I may have caused in my effort to play the Good Samaritan. For three days now, the path had been littered with these beautiful blue/black armoured beetles; only they had been predominantly on their backs, waving their legs frantically in the air as though screaming for help.

Dutifully heeding their pleas, I had been stopping to set each one back on their feet. But now; now they were also in the full throws of reproduction on our path, and I couldn't help wondering if the 'waving the legs in the air' ploy wasn't all part of their courtship. Perhaps I had successfully managed to put a stop to a lot of lady beetles' fun? And if the beetle population of the South West Coast Path was dramatically reduced in 1994, then I will be held responsible.

The oystercatchers were frantic in activity. I saw one great black backed gull giving relentless chase to a juvenile one who was threatening to steal his female. In the morning I had seen courting herons, aloof and clearly playing hard to get, and a pair of powerful swans joined them.

I wondered what was going on out of sight in the sea. Was the humble and inert limpet becoming gallant in courtship? Were the mackerel chasing each other through the seaweed and rocks? Were the sea urchins displaying some unique and prickly fornication? Were the mussels fighting each other over partners? And were male crabs locked in duels, their eyes wary and their lethal claws poised?

All this was hidden by a sea so calm that only a narrow band of white water was visible around the base of the rocks. We rounded Bolt Head and arrived in Salcombe.

Salcombe lies on the hillside overlooking the Kingsbridge Estuary. It is very popular as a yachting venue, but I was convinced that most people I saw striding around Salcombe advertising the expensive chandlers had never set foot on a boat. The only boat which moved among the impressive array of yachts on the estuary was the ferry to East Portlemouth.

A wonderfully higgledy-piggledy coast runs east from East Portlemouth, consisting of rocky bays and promontories with names such as Pig's Nose, The Bull, Shag Rock, Ball Rock and Ham Stone.

Tess came up behind me on the narrow path, whacking the backs of my knees with her stick as she tried to pass. I bullied her into giving me the stick and threw it for her. As she went back to get it, I hid behind a large rock. She sniffed me out, and when she found me her body became rubber bandish. This was our game of hide and seek.

It was, however, a one sided game, because whenever Tess hid I just yelled, and if she didn't come I got irate. This game was most unfair on Tess; but she got plentiful revenge with her game of 'grab the lead off Spud, retrace our steps, then drop the lead.' This brought in a few more pennies for Shelter and, needless to say, wasn't my favourite game.

At Start Point we turned left at the lighthouse into Start Bay, a sweeping bay which offers none of the rocky protection of the coast we had just walked, and has consequently lost many villages. Probably the most famous village is Torcross, which has been repeatedly flooded.

From Torcross, the fine shingle bar of Slapton Sands runs for a little over two miles, from where we followed lanes and tracks to Dartmouth with its vertically stacked houses, and noticeably less pretensions than Salcombe.

We were then on one of the steepest parts of the entire South West Coast Path, between Kingswear and Brixham. The red hills are so condensed that there isn't enough room for them all, and they are concertinad like the folds of a squeeze box. When we arrived in the conurbation of Torbay, we were red and sweaty.

Except for Brixham's small fishing fleet, the remainder of Torbay is given over to tourism. But it was still too early for life. We walked down Torquay High Street and out onto the red cliffs of Babbacombe Bay. I felt distracted that day. Human life had left its evidence everywhere, and most of all I noticed the deterioration of the sea. It too showed evidence of human life; it was murky and dull. I couldn't help thinking that we had left behind for good the unspoilt coves, the non-conformist Atlantic waves, and the miles of washed sand.

I felt a physical stab of regret. Although we still had the Dorset coast, I felt that it could never live up to these areas. Above all, I knew that we had many miles of urban walking to come.

At a nameless point somewhere between Mackerel Cove and Labrador Bay we crossed our 4,000th mile. I might as well have been watching a car speedometer notch up that amount; and after sixteen miles we reached the designated 'P for Parking' on the River Exe. We gave Tess a 4,000 mile bone, and stuck a new sticker on the back of the Spudtruck which read 'Spud and Tess have walked 4,000 miles.' The next one would be 4,500 miles.

As we were putting the sticker up, a couple passed us and said 'Spud looks as though she's enjoying her bone!' In many people's eyes we had now become one and the same person. It had even been suggested that we might win 'the dog most like its owner.'

Another Sunny Sunday on the South Coast was not very conducive to taking a fast passage along Exmouth Esplanade. Children, dogs, kites, windsurfers, canoes, roller skates, windbreaks, ice cream, hot dogs, even the wide boys who cruised the dead end road with their tinted windows and music blaring — they were all there.

At the end of this sea of humanity a path took us up through some downland, and through the Sunday walkers. I was keeping to myself when I felt a tap on my shoulder. 'I couldn't help seeing your sign. It's something I've always wanted to do —' the man said, coming closer as he spoke, and showering me with a fine spray of spittle.

He was wearing shorts which revealed skinny and rather bandy legs, and his grey hair was plentiful for his age, which was sixty. 'Well, actually,' he continued. 'I'm thinking of running the coast of Britain,' he said, as though saying he wanted to run round the block.

I stifled a look of incredulity, and tried to wipe away the droplets of spittle without embarrassing him. 'How long do you see it taking?'

'I reckon I can do it in a hundred days.' That was forty five miles per day — every day. 'I'm keen,' he grinned an inane grin.

Without trying to dampen his enthusiasm, I told him that he may need a little more time, or several sets of knees in Cornwall, or both. He didn't seem unduly daunted and continued to smile and spit. If you ever hear of a sixty year old who is running the coast of Britain, cheer him on but whatever you do don't get too close.

Up on the cliffs the red land declared 'Devon' in its strongest accent. Fields were neatly ploughed, and the red tilth was so fine that it looked as though the finest breeze would blow it away. In other places red rivulets of water headed across our path and out to sea, which was also red around the base of the cliffs.

We dropped down into Budleigh Salterton and walked along the seafront, to pass the scene of my first camping holiday ten years ago, with a boyfriend. Knee Cracker cider had lived up to its name when we tried to crawl out of our tent; beware of the cider they call Cripple Cock.

The River Otter ran past our old camping spot and we stopped on the bridge to watch a pair of male shelduck fighting over a female. Tess watched them with indifference and yawned noisily by my side. 'Come on Tessie May. Lunch in Sidmouth!' Lunch wasn't a word that meant much to Tess though. Not like 'hello' or 'home' or 'supper' or 'who's that' or 'piddle' or, for some inexplicable reason, 'scrabble!'

From Sidmouth, a dreary and damp mist was settling on the tops of the daunting looking hills ahead, and by the time we got to Branscombe it had descended to sea level. I watched the mist as it swirled slowly, while other drops sat in motionless suspension, and felt our way down to Beer and then Seaton, where we joined bingo week in the Haven Park.

After the bingo, the entertainments hall remained packed for the Most Glamorous Granny contest. A row of grannies formed an orderly queue running off the stage. 'Ladies and gentlemen. The competition you've all been waiting for . . . and here are our nineteen gorgeous ladies —' the red coated ents. manager announced, and there were flattered giggles from the grans. The competition began. 'What's your name darling?'

'Mavis.'

'And where are you from?'

'Basingstoke.'

Eighty two year old Mavis, dressed in blue befitting the Queen, clasped her hands together in front of her and smiled self consciously. But her eight grandchildren and two great grandchildren were no competition for the next competitor, who walked confidently on stage, glittering jewels. 'And what's your name my darling?' The ents. manager put his arm round the lady.

'Oh, I like that,' she laughed, and put her arm round him. 'My name's Millicent. But my friends call me Milly.' She gave a saucy smile and the audience laughed. 'Whoa! And how old are you Milly?'

'Eighty nine. But I'm younger at heart!'

Milly was an old hand, and was clearly out to win the contest — which she did. She flirted outrageously with the ents. manager and told the audience that she had fourteen grandchildren and seven great grandchildren. She loved dancing, and gave a cha-cha on stage, twirling her black dress and glittering jewels.

Among others, there was Dee from Cardiff, who liked horse racing; Marge, who sung a perfectly tuneful rendition of Vera Lyn's 'There'll be bluebirds over the white cliffs of Dover'; and Phil from Northampton who announced she was after a toy boy. They were an outrageous lot; but not without competitiveness.

Beetle (who had walked with us for a day in Somerset) was now driving, and we watched all this from the back of the hall, consciously reducing the average age of the room dramatically. Before long we left them to party.

Apart from the fact that I was suffering a bout of Devon Belly, the fact that I had less stamina than the grans almost three times my age hit a nerve. I longed to have the energy, or opportunity, to party; I longed to feel lively, to play squash, tennis, ride a horse, run for a train or a bus, without feeling a good deal older than those octogenarians acted. I wanted to stop being Mrs Walker (as someone had recently phoned and asked for), and do normal things — clean a windowsill or change a lightbulb! I craved normality.

Two days later we visited some friends of friends. I had only entered two private houses since leaving Bristol five weeks previously, and it was like entering a museum of life; paintings, plants, photographs, mantlepieces heavy with treasures, thick floor rugs, many years worth of interesting magazines, and jam packed bookcases. It was a far cry from the mobile home we returned to.

As if to add perspective to our time span, I also heard at this time that my sister Poopa (in Laos) had had a baby boy. I had learnt that she was pregnant on the Northumberland coast; and now she had had the baby and we were still walking.

The path from Seaton to Lyme Regis is one of the most spectacular stretches of the South West Coast Path. For six miles it runs along chalkland which slumped during several monumental landslips in 1839 and 1840. The vegetation has regenerated magnificently: beech, sycamore, hazel and rhododendron smother the slips and enclose the path; while thriving below them are endless mosses, lichens, ferns and other nameless plant species. I could have sworn there were lianas, and from time to time a strange bird call could be heard.

When the mist partly cleared, and a break in the thick vegetation allowed, escarpments and pinnacles of the white chalk offered the only diversion from the blanket of green. This is one of nature's most ambitious English gardens; and is the closest thing to rainforest you will find in Britain.

From Lyme Regis the coast ahead rises and falls until it culminates in the highest cliff on the south coast of Britain — Golden Cap. But the mist obliterated all of this, as we felt our way along the fossil hunters paradise of Charmouth Beach. Tess was instantly in her element. Each rock which I picked up with great anticipation that it might be the mother of all fossils, was instantly presumed to be for her enjoyment. Her ability to sniff out the exact pebble I threw for her on a shingle beach never failed to amaze me!

A scramble up the cliff, followed by a network of footpaths, led to the six hundred foot summit of Golden Cap. This was one of the first pieces of coastline to be acquired by the National Trust through Enterprise Neptune. I now know that the views from the top are superb; back to Lyme Regis and ahead to Chesil Beach and to Portland Bill. But at the time I saw nothing, and had only avoided getting lost on the ascent by using the compass.

The mist made the walking placeless and surreal. We could have been in Yorkshire, or even Suffolk, so obliterated were the hills; or we could have been drifting through some make believe world. People, houses, birds and trees came and went from sight like out of focus photographs. By day three of this I felt very claustrophobic.

To avoid the ten mile shingle bar of Chesil Beach, we walked inland and met Beetle at Abbotsbury swannery. The mute swan colony has been here since the fourteenth century and we found ourselves wandering along the designated paths literally stepping over and picking our way through nesting females.

The nests ranged from carefully built cushion-like thrones, to hastily built scrappy affairs — (the sort of swan which would have a couldn't-care-less garden.) The occasional protective swan manoeuvred its long neck to attack our feet.

I saw the swans again in the afternoon, along the shore of the Fleet lagoon formed by Chesil Beach. The mist made the water and the sky merge into one grey mass, but from out of the greyness emerged four brilliantly effortless and very white swans, making only the slightest ripple on the water's surface. The scene came straight off the cover of *Swan Lake*.

The swans were joined by common terns, which whizzed and darted in and out of view, their heads tilted downwards in their search for food; and also by a mass of shelduck. I had also seen the first housemartins of the year.

The mist finally cleared in Weymouth where, beneath the esplanade Clock Tower, a gathering of dogs waited for us. At the ends of their leads was a gathering of Weymouth animal welfare supporters, overseen by the local dog warden.

I could see a Chihuahua jealously eyeing up Tess, who jauntily flaunted her freedom; and a Labrador cross with a curly tail was wrapping its owner up in its lead, a middle aged lady with slacks and sensible walking shoes. She was telling me about Josie's eating habits.

'Well. I tried Josie on complete food, but . . . now she gets her way, you know how they do . . .'

'Mindy was the same . . . I buy her offal.'

Mindy was a bored Yorky Terrier, whose owner had the same nondescript brown hair and small features. Then there was Max the long, low Dachshund; and Meg the compulsory Collie mongrel. These three were straining to sniff Tess' bottom. Their owners were unaware. They had moved on to discuss the rescue dog which had been newly acquired by a mutual friend of theirs, and who was '. . . from a broken home . . .' We all agreed this was awful.

We then moved on to the merits and drawbacks of flea collars, flea drops, and shampoos; and then various photos, so that I was soon admiring the entire population of Weymouth's rescued dogs and cats. The dog warden rescued me.

'We'd like to wish you luck on your way, and we've got a little something for you.' He handed me something in a plastic bag — a poopa scoopa. I looked round to see Tess eyeing me from behind a low walled-in flower bed.

As we left, Tess strutting a hip-waggling walk, I saw the Weymouth dogs look up at their gossiping owners in a hopeful manner, and I was sure that if they had been off their leads we would have left like the Pied Piper.

It was a beautiful day and the sun was surprisingly hot. I made a tape to Poopa, and this brought us to Ringstead Bay where the coast takes on the features typical of this limestone area. 'The rolling hills so weedless,' I told Poopa. 'More like a neatly kept lawn. The cliffs are sheer and white. Ahead of us are Durdle Door, Lulworth Cove and various stacks and arches pointing out from the sea. But sadly the army are playing games today, so we'll have to stick inland. They're looking for unexploded mines which disappeared overboard from a boat, and are being washed up on shore!'

I stopped talking on a long slow hill to East Lulworth, and walked backwards nearing the top. This hill was our lunchtime goal, so that our reward was that it was downhill after lunch. I found a grassy patch with a view overlooking another untouched grassy MOD hill which separated us from the sea. The MOD may own some beautiful parts of the country, but at least in their hands it will remain beautiful. Afterwards we snoozed for while. *This is the life* I thought.

I was brought back to life by Tess. 'Well. This isn't going to buy the dog a new collar is it Tessie?' I said getting to my feet. It was my equivalent of buying the baby a new dress. 'I don't know, Mum. But you've been saying that for nine months and I'm still wearing this grotty old thing with the stitching coming undone.'

'Sorry Tessie. One day!'

The coast we returned to east of Kimmeridge Bay is a continuation of the dramatic and erosion prone limestone. The path is also terribly eroded, so that smooth white slides took us down the steep hills, making it tempting to walk on the grass either side. It is easy to see how such paths become pedestrian motorways and, though I cursed the irregularly sized steps, they definitely alleviate the problem.

We sped past our diverse companions that Saturday, but there was one couple I admired enormously. Two midgets were climbing the steep Hans-tout Cliff. For every one of my strides, they were probably taking three, and their progress up the cliff was slow but steady, and very cheery.

Guillemots nested on the cliffs below and near Durlston Head a school of dolphins rewarded my months of sea watching. They leapt joyously in the wake of a yacht, then disappeared and reappeared somewhere else.

It was a beautiful evening when we reached Swanage. Beetle had left and David had taken over until the next driver arrived in two day's time. David sat me down outside his family's house with several pints of water and a glass of wine, and we looked beyond the flighty terns and contemptuous gulls to Old Harry and his wife. But I was feeling completely shattered. I had had swollen glands for four days, Devon Belly, and long days and late nights of fundraising. It was to be another late night in Swanage.

By the time we returned from the pubs of Swanage and Corfe I was having trouble keeping my eyes open, but they soon opened when I saw shattered glass outside the Spudtruck. The passenger window had been broken and my rucksack was gone.

My rucksack had become an integral part of me. It was my identity. The valuables were replaceable, but the moulded shape of that faded and worn form, and the sentimental valuables in it, weren't: pebbles, driftwood, my notebook, most listened to tapes, poetry book, and other nick nacks. My walkman/dictaphone had also gone — my vital thread to sanity.

What would anyone want with a smelly dog's coat decorated with the Berghaus logo? Or a notebook full of illegible thoughts? Or a film which showed ten dogs idolising Tess under the Clock Tower of Weymouth? Or tape twelve of Iris Murdoch's *The Severed Head*?

I knew what they might do with the spare set of Spudtruck keys, and we spent a long time fastening the window for the night. But I felt sad for the people who had broken into a van plastered with charity signwriting. What on earth had gone through their minds?

This started one of cynical David's and mine pet argument. We sat at the kitchen table into the night, drinking coffee and whisky. 'But, Spud, there will always be a proportion people who do this sort of thing —'

'But if you accept that, the problem will just get worse. The problems are deeper than 'an accepted proportion'. It's to do with the break down in values, the lack of communication, understanding between us. Each one of us can help change that in our own small way —'

'No, but . . .'

The argument went on and on, and in the morning nothing had changed. I still had to take the Spudtruck to Poole to have the window fixed and locks changed; and I still had to come back and walk, in a semi-daze, to Bournemouth.

CHAPTER EIGHTEEN

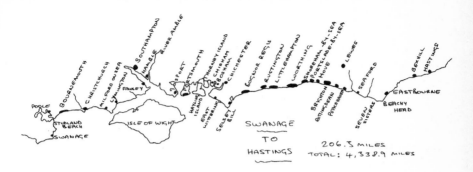

Studland Bay meant one thing — a geography field trip aged ten. We had spent a day in the dunes where we had been told to make up a play. Our group's was about a boy called Lofty who climbed aboard a moored goods ship, fell asleep, and unwittingly set sail for Africa. In Africa he had encounters with lions and cheetahs; and lived off peanuts.

At some point in the play (Lofty's Dream) I had remembered a piece of information obviously picked up from my sisters, and declared victoriously 'peanuts make you randy!' The teacher, Miss Reynolds, had not known what to say; Lofty woke up to discover the whole thing was a dream; and we had won the competition.

We stopped for a drink of water on the mouth of Poole Harbour. The water bottle was the only thing banging around in the base of a freeby Esso rucksack, but still the narrow plastic straps cut into my shoulders. It felt absurdly uncomfortable; like a new haircut, or someone else's clothes which are not your style. I missed my identity.

But after the hassle of the previous night I found comfort in the quiet freedom of our own world. There was no need to talk, and no need to explain. Tess understood, and if she didn't then she never questioned.

We caught the ferry across Poole Harbour, and said farewell to the South West Coast Path which we had followed since Minehead — 617.8 miles of rain, wind, mud and pain; yet I had still found masochistic enjoyment this path. It was now back to finding our own route.

After a while on the empty beach to Bournemouth, a loud speaker shattered the peace. 'That dog's not supposed to be on the beach. You —' the voice boomed in Big Brother fashion from somewhere. 'You! Come here!'

The man appeared with his loudspeaker. 'But the beach is empty!' I tried to reason.

'It doesn't matter. It's not allowed here,' he said. 'I could give you a £100 fine if you like!' The fines were getting progressively higher.

'No thanks. We'll take to the unforgiving promenade won't we Tess!' I wiped my brow in mock martyrship, but the warden was dead pan. Beach wardens and I would always disagree.

The groynes came and went. Unlike Swanage, Bournemouth hadn't woken up to summer yet, and the bulk of Bournemouth's population were wandering among the High Street stores as though they were nowhere near the sea. It was all so featureless yet familiar and we (Chris, who had got us lost in Wales, had come to drive) followed our peers through their doors in search of a new dictaphone.

We then retired to a pub for phone calls, where we found the third side of Bournemouth so far removed from deckchairs and beach wardens; or Boots and M&S.

The dark pub had frosted windows with tatty red curtains hung over their bottom half, and the bar hadn't seen a broom or cloth for many a day. Empty beer glasses were stuck firmly to the table by means of old beer turned glue, and our boots stuck to the once blue flecked floor in the same way.

Between the three locals hunched over the bar, there were always at least two cigarettes on the go, and the ashtray was suitably heaped. The barman was clearly there 'because it was a job.'

The other customer in this uninspiring scene was on some Monday lunchtime binge, and had been ostracised by the three locals at the bar. He was in his sixties and wore brown baggy trousers slipping slowly down his legs. He swayed over to us. 'On holiday here then?'

'Sort of,' we replied, noticing the red lipstick kisses all over his face.

'Popular with tourists you know, Bournemouth. Always has been. Mind you —' he waved his pint around as he spoke, adding substantial glue to the floor. 'Mind you, it's a different thing in the winter. Sora like peaceful.'

He went thoughtful for a few minutes, then came back to the present, only to dig up the past. 'Lotta people come here you know . . . Mind you . . . it's not what it used to be. They're all off to the Costa del whatsit now —' he broke off again.

The nostalgia treatment of Bournemouth could take all afternoon, and as we got up to leave our friend came back to the present. 'Youoffthen?' he slurred. Standing behind sturdy Chris, our friend's shoulders sagged so visibly that it looked as though he was trying to get into his pint.

The pub was one of a chain which appear in almost every coastal town in Britain, in which days gone by are dwelt on while the present passes by behind frosted glass and red curtains. Some of the aged customers try to align past with present, but then the 'mind you, it's not what it used to be's' come into play. These pubs and their customers wear cobwebs from the fifties and sixties when seaside towns such as Bournemouth thrived. People pilgrimaged here annually, staying in guest houses run by draconian landladies: you had to be out of the guest house by 10am, and weren't allowed back until 5pm — which left a long day if the weather was bad. So enter Sir Billy Butlin.

From Bournemouth's peopled promenade with its defensive blockade of accommodation offering ample parking, spa baths, H/C, A/C, or TV, we branched through a residential area to find the bridge over the River Stour. Tess nipped into any gateway which was open, but otherwise stuck to the pavement. When she came to a road, I told her to 'wait' and she stood on the kerb like the green cross code model. A brief patch of land so far free from development signified our crossing into Christchurch.

The heavily developed coast from Christchurch is unstable. Caravans, golf course greens, roads and beach huts disappear regularly; but valiantly we fight on with groynes and promenades. Around the corner from Milford on Sea are Pennington marshes, left to the tide and the birds.

We found Chris in Lymington, where the boats stretched away down the estuary; gin palaces with names such as Crack On and Mary Lou moored alongside fishing boats whose names, such as Dobbin, implied that they worked for their keep.

I was soon answering the unimaginative questions for the local reporter. I answered the boring questions with equally boring answers, and we came to other category. 'Have you ever nearly been run over?'

'Have you ever felt threatened by people? What bad experiences have you had?'

Did they want me to be hit by a passing bus, mugged on a lonely road, or raped on a back of beyond path? Why didn't they ask about all the good experiences? Their attitude always brought me back to the supposed *real* world — where papers sell.

I thought about this as we set off in drizzle the next morning, following a series of yellow roads marked as 'The Solent Way'. They were the closest lanes to the coast and were quiet and banked up with vegetation. Through a gap between two oak trees I saw a family of Canada goslings sticking close by their mum in Sowley Pond. But I felt unusually depressed.

We had gone fundraising around the pubs of Lymington the previous night, and in the Black Cat I had met Barry. Barry had been kicked out of his home by his mother when he was sixteen, but, as he said 'my mother's now dead — thank goodness.'

He had gone to London in search of work, and ended up with a cardboard box as a bed. At first life on the streets was fun. 'I felt the sense of freedom after home and its turmoil. I drunk lager with the other guys, and felt relief.'

He stayed like that two years, then; 'That feeling wore off pretty quickly. I had no work, and no prospect of getting work. I knew no one apart from the other guys on the streets, and was going nowhere fast.'

Barry finally returned to Lymington, and found voluntary work. He was helped out by friends, but was largely his own saviour and is now a social worker. He had a frankness found in so many similar people. Although Barry's story spurred me on, I was still despondent.

From the day's total mileage of twenty-five we could only walk two miles of footpath along the shore of the Beaulieu River, where the trees were freshly washed in the dampness, and the chestnuts were out in their grand candelabras, but it was then back on the straight road skirting the New Forest. I wanted anything to take my mind off the road and the greyness, but without my poetry book, talking books, tapes or music there was nothing to do but watch the chimneys of Fawley oil refinery coming closer.

Everything was huddled in the damp. In Fawley, the trees were silent; the shops were shut and grey; the mothers picking up children were huddled and glum; and even the straggling lines of children were miming their gossip. What an entirely English phenomenon drizzle is!

Within twelve hours spring returned. Instead of cardboard cut-outs, people became human once more. We walked through their lives: 'The thing is, Brian never sees the kids. He's working till seven o'clock these days . . .' Another pair of mothers chatted outside the same school gate. 'So I said "we just won't get away this year," I said, "we'll just stay here . . ."'

The schoolchildren watched us with audible interest, and by the time they were all ensconced in classrooms Tess and I had reached the retirement end of Marchwood, where Grandpa cleaned his shoes in The Ferns, and a lady was hanging her washing outside Copse Side. The sound of the vacuum cleaner came from The Village Bells in Rooksgreen.

In the space of two hours we had passed through the lives of countless people, or they passed through ours. Either way it was similar to watching a stream of people passing by your window.

Noise and confusion enveloped Southampton station where I waited for Chris. Every time the pneumatic drill stopped my senses relaxed a little, but then it would start up again. I looked up to a few resilient plane trees and began watching a pigeon making its nest. Back and forth flew the urban pigeon with its bill-fulls of twigs, undisturbed by the racket below.

While I sat, pigeon watching, the sniggering school children of that morning were probably having secret lunchtime fags, and ash and beer would be undoing the work of the vacuum cleaner of The Village Bells. Grandpa would be wearing his clean shoes, the pigeon nested, the 1.40 train left for London and we ate lunch. Everyone was getting on with their lives.

I thought of the ignored gypsy with his dead horse by the River Neath. There was so little interaction between so many people living in such close proximity, and I was even more of an outsider; an onlooker passing through the spectrum of life, but not involved. Involvement takes time; and time, these days, is a precious commodity.

We skirted Southampton centre and crossed the River Itchen to re-join the Solent Way, where a gravel track gave way to ragwort, thistles and broken glass. The track then regained its dignity in the Royal Victoria Country Park where the dog walkers were out. You can rely on dog walkers for involvement.

There were the Collies who would take fright at the sight of sheep, and then there was a fat Spaniel which came straight up to say hello. Its owner was immediately by my side. 'That's George Withajay,' the suited middle aged man said proudly.

'George Withajay?'

'That's right. George Withajay.'

'Oh, you mean 'Jeorge', with a J!'

George Withajay clearly enjoyed the mention of his aristocratic sounding name, and panted as he wagged his stubby tail. 'He's fifteen you know?' George Withajay's owner told me in the same proud way.

We moved on to George Withajay's recently removed lump, vets bills and sleepless nights. Again the potential was limitless. *Perhaps I should change Tess' name to Tess Withatee*, I thought as we finished the miles to Hamble and crossed the River Amble.

The following day we took the ferry across Portsmouth Harbour. It was a Saturday morning and a steady stream of yachts were motoring out of the harbour, crossing the paths of a spectrum of aquatic vessels. As soon as they had negotiated the harbour traffic, they put up their sails and took on a more carefree air. At the end of Portsmouth promenade another ferry took us across the mouth of Langstone Harbour to Hayling Island and Another Sunny Sunday on the South Coast.

Ponies, mountain bikes, sun worshippers and ice cream eaters all joined us along the indented coastline until the real sea was some five miles out beyond muddy marshes, and Hayling and Thorney Islands. Of all the miles of beautiful sandy beach we had walked, and after some four thousand two hundred miles and eight months of the sea as company, Tess decided to swim — in the muddy, stagnant water which could hardly be called sea.

My jaw fell open. In and out she ran through the marshy seaweed, as though she had always had a deep affinity for water. How much enjoyment she had missed!

The marshy margin grew wider, so that the water's edge was out of reach, and we crossed flat country to Chidham and then Bosham; hopping from one row of red tiled rooves broken up by the greenery of woodland, to the next; and from one church spire to the next. This was England.

The country lanes, bordered by sycamore, chestnut and poplar throwing their shadows over the road, ran alongside fields of deep green wheat in the full throws of growth, and occasionally the bright yellow of oil seed rape. The peacefulness here belied our proximity to main roads and towns. The truest indication of all was that I could hear my pedometer, 'one, two, one, two, one two . . .' regular and familiar. Twenty four flat miles had brought us to Chichester.

On the east bank of the Chichester Channel, we followed quintessential English footpaths. Cow parsley and hawthorn were smothering the banks in white, and filling the air with their summer smells. It was a lazy hazy summer's day.

We found the Spudtruck at Selsey Bill, a low lying resort stuck out on a shingle headland. The Spudtruck was spotless. The fridge had been cleared of ageing organic matter, and even the windowsills were no longer covered in a sticky dust. The new driver, Angie, mother of three, had the Spudtruck looking and feeling like a cared for home.

Between mouthfuls of Selsey Bill crab, I suggested Angie went on to Butlins. 'It's so exciting. Butlins! Wow!' Angie's eyes sparkled. 'It's such an adventure. I've been looking forward to this week since I put my name down for it last year!'

A year previously, Angie had introduced me to the world of computer screens, mice and Wordperfect when I put together the Walk literature. She had been unphased by my complete rural ignorance of such things, and was now witnessing the result of her endeavours.

The tide was out in Bognor, and shingle was backed up at the back of the expanse of gently shelving sand/mud, into which the groynes were sinking. One groyne was unsuccessfully disguising the sewage outfall. Also sinking into the mud are the skeletal remains of the central pier.

Not only are there therefore no pier attractions, but there isn't even a promenade to speak of in Bognor.

I missed the garish bustle of the old piers in their new get-up. Bring back the screaming children, fat ladies, hassled husbands; bring back the crazy mirrors, the bingo, the dirty postcards, the candy floss, the windbreaks, the space invaders, the cuddly toys, the two penny games, the Jolly Fishermen cafés; bring back the donkey rides, the fortune tellers, the funfairs and the end-of-pier theatres. Without all these, and more, Bognor felt sad, and just a little embarrassed at its decline from fashionable Victorian resort to twentieth century town which just happens to be on the coast.

It then became clear that Bognor is Butlins, or vice versa. In Butlins High Street the money machines jangled, and a bingo session was starting. The Cockney Pride pub was full, and the fat, faceless lady painted onto a board was causing riotous mirth, as children and adults of all shapes suddenly developed a fat and swimsuited body. In the street-lit pedestrian precinct we passed Sweeney Todds, the Piano Bar, the Broadway venue, and a large board advertising — 'Freddie and the Dreamers — Live tonight — 10.30pm.'

Angie was being entertained by Drew, the PR Manager. He was in his thirties with heavily brylcreamed hair and a suntan which hinted of Tenerife. He was clearly being charmed by Angie's harmless flirting and twinkling eyes; an outcome which was doing wonders for the mother of three's ego. Such was Angie's charm that Drew forfeited his gym session that evening and entertained us instead.

Or rather he entertained Angie. I left them to it and, like a good child, only spoke when I was spoken to. I felt shattered and drained. My joints felt like those of the Tin Man in *The Wizard of Oz*, and at four the next morning I woke with terrible cramp in my legs, which was becoming more common. I slept again and dreamt of being suspended in water.

Counting £220 in coppers kept Angie busy for a good deal of the next morning, while we found a grassy track between the shingle beach and the row of houses, where anchors, glass fishing weights, rusty ships lanterns and the occasional hull of a wooden boat adorned the gardens. They gave the impression that retired naval officers lived behind every door.

The odd person sat on benches, gazing out to sea in a way that only the sea or open fires make you do; as though the solution to life might well be found through that gaze.

The grassy track became a narrow path enclosed by vegetation. When we came level to the first couple of fellow walkers, they politely stepped to one side of the path, while I stepped to the other side. Tess kept to the path and trotted straight between us, wagging her tail and looking up at us saying, 'you humans are funny. You've got a perfectly good path but you insist on scrambling into the vegetation. Well, if you won't use the path, I will!' Dear Tess with her unreserved audacity.

Tess was my best friend, and I loved her beyond comprehension. Her's is such an unconditional love. I had frequently despaired with her; I had beaten her in no uncertain manner for her sheep chasing and lack of obedience, and I had vented tired frustration on her at times when nothing was even her fault — yet still she was faithful and affectionate. I gave her a big cuddle on a garden wall in Rustington, and couldn't have cared less who was watching.

A short stretch of grass indicated the end of Rustington, and then we were straight into Worthing. 'Left .. left .. left .. right .. left. My pack's too heavy, my boots . . .' My legs swung mechanically and I hummed *Yellow Submarine* as Worthing unfolded itself in front of us, and I began map number one hundred. *Only four more maps to go.*

Worthing has a three lane promenade, and a nightclub on the pier. I wondered how many late night revellers had taken midnight dips among those wooden millipede legs. Next door to the pier, small fishing boats were winched up onto the shingle, where padlocked boxes held the fishermen's tackle. Flags protruded from the blue and red boats and helped give Worthing some colour.

We steered inland a little to negotiate the River Adur, and the chaos of Shoreham and Portslade-by-Sea docks, to reach Hove promenade. The buildings gradually became taller and more important, indicating Brighton.

The sun came out. The sea looked remarkably clean, and the beach took on an orange hue. The promenade, with its several levels, has gaily painted railings, arches and underground openings which house cafés and arty shops. In many ways it is spacious and clean; but in other respects things aren't quite so prim. Other cafes were boarded up and graffitied, while shabby bus shelters were decorated with litter. They were also home to numerous sleeping bodies.

I found Angie parked near the severed West Pier, and nearby was one such body. We made some sandwiches and a cup of tea, and I ventured over.

The guy was breathing heavily, sprawled out on his side with his arm half shielding his face. An overcoat was scrunched up into a makeshift pillow, and his clothes were filthy and his face covered in shiny stubble.

He was still asleep, and I awkwardly said something very British like, 'excuse me — er, would you like a cup of tea?' No reply. I tried the Good Samaritan line. 'Are you alright?'

Of course he wasn't alright. He had a shocking hangover and probably the last thing he felt like was a cheese and pickle sandwich! I left him sleeping it off. So what if my back hurt, my legs were crampy, my hamstrings pulled and my bum felt as though it had been in a saddle for weeks?

One mile from the pier, and the sleeping, sweaty, drunk, homeless bodies, we came across the Brighton Marina. Nowhere on the coast had I seen such an extravagant show of wealth. Its exclusive developments opening straight onto private moorings, home to gin palaces and yachts which were larger and whiter than I had seen, came straight from an exotic location for 007.

This world would have no need to know that Brighton existed just round the corner. Even the water looked too deep blue and clean to be real, as if those sleek looking launches were incapable of discharging anything as dirty as oil.

We set off along the clifftop, hemmed up against the edge by the main road, to Rottingdean. From Rottingdean we went inland to Lewes for a day to stay with my Godmother, Sue, who is Beetle's mother. While Beetle worked on the Spudtruck's badly failed MOT, (he had even discovered that the spare tyre, which had remained untested, didn't fit!), Sue had rallied her unsuspecting friends into action on Shelter's behalf.

In the evening we set off to an old people's home, and it soon became clear they were expecting more than just an informal chat. The old dears took their seats.

Now, I may have been able to walk, and often talk the back legs of the most flighty of horses, but to stand up and talk to a room full of the deafest of old people was enough to send me running. It is the same fear of interviews.

I told Tess to lie by my feet, sipped nervously on a glass of wine, and strung the usual speel together into monologue. I wanted to shrink from their gaze. I was wearing a grey t-shirt — and grey t-shirts and sweat do not go together.

It was a ridiculous fear, and I survived the ordeal; but it made me realise that the Walk would not simply come to an end. I was doing something that other people thought about, but rarely did. How many times had people said 'I'd love to do something like that'? — too many times to remember.

For the first time I tried to think about the end of the Walk, and what it would bring both in terms of my character and in terms of a future. But, however hard I tried, the end of the Walk was still not something that had any place in my head. The Walk was probably changing my life, though to what extent I still wasn't sure. For the past nine and a half months I had blocked out any such thoughts, and had concentrated on one day at a time; but Tower Bridge was no longer an unconnected place. It was a goal within reach. The previous day Angie had produced an Evening Standard, and a postcard of Tower Bridge. The evidence that we were nearing the end had started with a signpost to London which had drawn me up in my tracks in Southampton; and now it was drip feeding — and chipping away my carefully constructed exterior shell. I was beginning to relax.

With the mental relaxation came the physical relaxation, and it was this which was bringing to the surface all the ignored aches and pains. It is like getting flu the minute you go on holiday. You begin to relax, and all the tension, stress, bugs, viruses etc. just under the surface now make their presence known. Already the final weeks were proving to be the hardest of the lot.

My lower back felt rusty when we left Lewes on a muggy morning which was bringing out hundreds of sticky black flies. The clifftop path was fenced in by one continuous conurbation — Rottingdean, Saltdean and Peacehaven, and at some point during this sprawl we came across a signpost to the world.

London was forty eight miles, and Delhi was a mere 4,172. I had never realised it was so close — or so far. I couldn't work out which. We would be nearing Calcutta by now.

I tried to push away all the thoughts which these endless signposts were bringing on, but they flooded my mind the minute I stopped walking. My fuses were getting shorter and shorter, as the distance left became shorter and shorter. I was fed up with the questions. I wanted to be sitting on a mountain top on my own, wallowing in my own solitude far from the need to talk, listen, communicate, organise, listen and talk again. Walking was still my escape.

Beetle's sister, Sarah, walked with us over the green-topped, chalk roller-coaster of the Seven Sisters (though we counted eight), and we rounded Beachy Head to arrive in a drizzle deserted Eastbourne.

Huddles of blue and white striped deckchairs were stacked up against the railings, and the beach-dividing groynes slid into the sea, giving no indication where they stopped and man's interference ended. Just visible at the end of the beach was the pier, on which sat several featureless and lump-like buildings. There wasn't a stick person in sight. 'Welcome to Eastbourne!' chuckled Cousin Guy, resident of Eastbourne.

Despite the murk, Eastbourne has an air which declares itself several stations above resorts such as Bournemouth, certainly Bognor and even Brighton. The people of Eastbourne were saying 'there's no need for us to show British grit in such weather, we know our worth.'

Or perhaps it is simply because Eastbourne is largely an old person's place? It was clear from Guy that nightlife is limited; 'The place shuts down at 11pm. The lights go out along the promenade, and everyone is tucked away.'

The first thing I noticed about Hastings on May 15th was that all the clocks were wrong. I am used to relying on public clocks, but Hastings is not the place to be if you need to be punctual. The next thing I noticed were black people on the streets, and it was only then that I realised how parochial much of Britain's coast is. I felt as though we had arrived in London.

But to show us we weren't in London, posters announced the coming season's entertainments: 'Star Guest — Barbara Dickson' or 'Coming soon — The George Formby Show' or 'John Byrd — Britain's most famous Medium.' One venue was after the younger clientele and advertised 'The Chippendales' and 'Kevin Bloody Wilson.'

Angie, who had born the brunt of my burnt out body, had left and the next day we were to be joined by David. We were to have one brilliant, luxurious, longed for night on our own, and I hoped it would help recover some of my good humour. You can rely on Havens.

The Tyger Club children sung at top voice, prompted by the ever cheery red coats:
'We're looking for tygers
We're looking for cheetahs,
We're looking for rhinos
And big alligators;
Gorillas and panthers
And little bear cubs, 'cos
We're having fun in the TYGER CLUB!'
There were tears, screams, wails, tellings off, and laughter. It was a grand pantomime, and was followed by the Kiddies Laughing Competition.

Each competitor stood on stage, had a policeman's hat thrust onto their head, and was subjected to the Laughing Policeman song. At the moment when the policeman began his 'ha ha ha ha ha ha ha ha, ho ho ho ho ho ho ho', the music was turned down and the child had to laugh.

Well, it is hard to laugh on cue at the best of times, but to be plonked on stage with a too large hat falling over your eyes, and several hundred pissed parents expecting you to find nothing in particular very very funny, must be nigh impossible. But they were game. Some mumbled 'he he he' into the floor, or the hat; and others laughed a staccato 'a a a a' as if their lives depended on it. Some went on and on and had to be stopped; and others went off before they had started.

The children ranged in age from toddler to teenager, and all performed differently. But they all had one thing in common — they all looked deadly serious. I for one cried enough tears of laughter to make up for them all.

Shedding my walking gear . . . Butlin's, Bognor.

CHAPTER NINETEEN

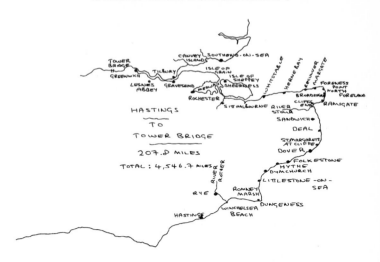

I was sitting outside a café in a French town square, sheltered from the sun by an umbrella, and tasting local wines. The table cloth was red checked, and we were eating crusty baguette, unsalted butter, ripe cheeses, salamis, olives and tomatoes. I could taste the cheeses and wine; then looked right-handed to France, thinking with regret that the only problem with going anywhere would be the smuggling of Tess.

Whatever we did in the future, I had come to the conclusion that the wandering life, with all its unsettling and sometimes lonely disadvantages, suited me. The term 'home' was now symbolised by people, rather than materialistic paraphernalia, and it was this that we were walking for. 'Homeless' doesn't simply mean people living in cardboard boxes, but arises too from the lack of security, family, friendship or trust — to feel neglected by society. Wandering tribes do not feel 'homeless' because they have the companionship and security of the rest of the tribe; members of our tribe are lost.

One's own space is also vitally important, but this may be anything from a tent to a treehouse or palace — it is still one's 'home'. Many people in Britain are experiencing both types of homelessness.

I thought of the Spudtruck, or as it had recently been called in an article The Spudtrap. That white rectangular, damp, shoebox on wheels. It filled my mind with its connotations — shelter, food, laughter, warmth and friendship.

From Winchelsea Beach we followed the River Rother inland to Rye, which was originally on the sea. It was connected with the Cinque Ports of the south east coast, towns which were bound, in exchange for certain privileges, to equip ships for the royal fleets. But the sea receded and left Rye high and dry. Instead of eroding, the coast here is being silted up. Perhaps some of the material for this comes from the crumbling cliffs of the Seven Sisters? Or from the ungroyned beach at Hastings? Perhaps there would be more silting if Eastbourne or Bexhill weren't so heavily groyned? A few metres lost here would mean a few metres gained there. The coast is dynamic; surely we cannot enforce our own modern inertia on such natural movement?

The flat land of reclaimed Romney Marsh stretched away from us on each side of the road, stealing any sense of perspective. A haze sat on the land, making it still flatter, and the only thing which rose up from the sparsely vegetated country were pylons from Dungeness power station. They strode across the country, planting their feet confidently in the shingle and waving their arms at their sides like air traffic controllers.

From the new lighthouse at the tip of Romney Marsh we followed the road northwards, which seems to have been rolled onto the mottled green and cream landscape, and near Littlestone-on-Sea, sand replaces shingle. A group of greenshank flew up in start when we passed. I had been noticing that the birds here are far more flighty than elsewhere on the coast. They weren't so companionable. They were wary, as were many of the people.

There was an 'eyes in the back of your head' reserve here. Even in Littlestone-on-Sea that night we were suspiciously questioned by the hotel owner, near which we were parked. In the end she offered me a bath, but the trust did not come so naturally.

David was knocking up fresh plaice. The last time I had seen him was in Chichester, nursing a hangover brought on by a lonely booze binge. I had been unsympathetic and too wrapped up in my world to discover any reasons. But now I had taken time; time to realise that there was still a world out there.

Many of David's and my initial nights in the Spudtruck had been spent discussing the deaths of our respective mothers. Since the death of his mother, less than a year previously, he had felt a rootlessness, a loss of a home. Chichester had involved my family, and that of Chris, and this had struck close to the bone.

We talked and talked about this, and laughed and felt at ease in each other's company. David saw me as Spud, and this was a balancing factor in my life. We could balance each other.

'How's the meditating?' David teased.

'It's moved on to more mundane things now. Words like 'shingle' — which just come to my head!' (Weird!) 'Then I had a long conversation with someone today about how I'll 'cope' at the end of the walk, and —'

'How will you cope?'

'That's what everyone asks! You just do, don't you? You tell yourself to walk, and you walk. You tell yourself there will no longer be a map in your hand day in and day out, and then you do it. It's in the mind.'

'It's not always that easy.'

'People cope with far worse things than coming to the end of a walk!'

As we were nearing the end, the knowledge that I was completing something was satisfying. I often felt that I had flunked out of things. I had been asked to leave school (politely expelled); I had been rejected from every university; I had abandoned an agricultural degree; I had even left a three month cooking course half way through! Finally, I had left a longstanding and perfectly happy relationship in New Zealand, to go in search of I knew not what.

My body now took some cranking up. Even the front of my legs hurt, so that from my back down was one continual complaint; I was conscious of the most simple movements, such as climbing one of the endless groynes.

In Dymchurch I was offered a five hundred pound fine, or to take Tess of the beach. I chose the latter and was bombarded by swifts on the sea wall. The radar systems of the housemartins were working better, and they swooped and fed on the wing without nearing me. There was a stretch of busy main road with a scrubby rough verge; and in Hythe there was another promenade, another shingle beach, another amusement arcade — and then there was a flier of the local paper. 'Hythe teenager finds dead body.' It could easily have read 'Traffic jams in Hythe.'

By the time we had fought our way through the exhaust fumes into Folkestone, I felt ready to disown my body, and indeed the world.

The Spudtruck was parked behind a cage fence of the Seacat terminal. I lay flat on my back on the floor with my feet poking into the cab. The matted carpet stank of squashed banana, dog, garlic and dampness — despite the fact that it really looked remarkably clean.

'I don't think we'll be able to fundraise here anyway,' David was saying. 'Everyone says the same thing — "You can try, but you won't get much". There's a lot of unemployment. The ferries no longer go from here, and the Channel tunnel. That's why we're parked in here!

Everyone warned me there's a fair bit of crime.' He had been advised correctly.

It didn't take long to leave Folkestone and climb onto the North Downs Way. Once up on the cliffs, I was aware that beneath us the first commercial trucks ever were using the Channel Tunnel that day. We were walking above a little piece of history.

Over the next rise Dover came into view, dominated by two things; the dual carriageway and the ferry terminal. Roads, people, cars, trucks and bicycles were either scurrying towards the terminal, or belting away from it. Tess and I blazed a trail through the middle of them and stumbled onto the White Cliffs.

Poor Dover. To the majority of people it means 'ferry terminal'; or perhaps lucky Dover? Perhaps the town centre is so neglected that it is beautifully quiet and happy. I didn't know, and wasn't now prepared to turn back and find out.

The downland was brilliantly colourful. I hunted for orchids, but found none. Instead I came away with a bunch of the most prolific wild flowers to identify, staggered back to sea level at St Margaret's at Cliffe, passed the closest pub to France, and climbed what I decided must be the last hills before flat Kent took over. It was a struggle.

With the last proper hill negotiated, we joined the Deal dog walkers along the flat land of a shingle/grass path. A puce faced girl was yelling at her gloriously disobedient Golden Retriever; while further on a Pekinese thought Tess was the best thing since retractable leads. Ignoring its elderly female owner, it followed Tess with its uplifted nose stuck firmly to her bottom. At this angle it couldn't see where it was going, and repeatedly stubbed its already blunt nose on Tess' bottom when she stopped. Its owner was also snub nosed and short legged, and began calling for it so softly that it was as if she didn't really want it.

'William! Honestly. Naughty —' she said, with little emphasis on anything. I had noticed that Pekineses are often very determined, or else it is that they are owned by elderly ladies who prefer to have something to complain about.

Although I took to the fishing town of Deal, there is one eyesore it is hard to ignore — the pier. Built in 1950, after the old pier was demolished by a ship, the present one is a poor fifties attempt at replicating history's charm. This pier is concrete! It is as sacrilegious as the concrete beach.

The concrete theme continued to our parking spot at the end of Deal, where a pier-like wall obscured both sight and sound of the sea. Yet I knew it was there as I slept that night. I could sense its presence. How I was going to miss the sea!

My emotions started to play havoc. I was physically and mentally exhausted, and was ready to stop walking; yet at the same time I wasn't. I was overcome with a sadness, and the two emotions tugged and pulled so that I wasn't sure whether to laugh or cry. I tried telling David; 'I'm going to miss all this. The sea. The birds and bees and trees —'

'Sure,' he replied. 'I love the sea too. I hate leaving Swanage.'

'No, but —' I broke off each time.

'I know, the life too. I enjoy this life. Why do you think I've been back so many times?!' he laughed casually. It was useless. David hadn't even been at Tower Bridge at the beginning.

It had been the best part of a year of my life. During this time I had controlled everything within me to ensure that we could keep going; and now it was all about to break through like a tidal wave of emotions. Gratitude, relief, euphoria, tears of sadness, tears of happiness, frustration, love, hate, fear, anger and humility. They were all in there somewhere, like randomly chosen ingredients of an emotional cake which might or might not turn out.

I needed to be alone to make sense of all this; but at the same time I wanted to share them with someone. But no one understood. There was only one person who had experienced the whole lot — Tess.

Tess had waited on the muddy paths of Cornwall when I had thought I could go no further; she had experienced my Highland euphoria, and leapt the peat gullies with sheer joie de vivre; she had pounded main roads, being sprayed by polluted puddles; she had walked hundreds of miles of empty beach; she had fallen in rock pools, and communicated with foxes; she had learnt the laws of nature, and had learnt to love the sea; she had played in the snow, and sweated many miles; she had walked through numerous eight hour long deluges; she had chewed Mayors' ears, and eaten their teas; she had despaired with photographers and wrestled with policemen; she had made homeless people smile; she had loved the drivers and made them each feel special; she had slept in Castles, Butlins, grand hotels, haunted spare rooms, mobile homes, guest houses and top floor flats.

She was a star.

Four thousand four hundred and forty miles had not made me much wiser in some respects. I was still convinced that if I walked through the puddles on the road, the tarmac was softer. The road to Sandwich had ample puddles, and ample trucks hurling the dirty water up at our faces. Tess scowled.

The detour of the River Stour ended at Cliffs End, and we found a small path down to Ramsgate, which began the conurbation of Broadstairs, North Foreland and Margate. Small sandy beaches interrupt the sweep of low cliffs accommodating the towns, and in places there is a coastal path, but in other places it was back to residential streets and garden watching.

We arrived at the final left hand turn — Foreness Point. A melancholy grey sea was hitting a rocky ledge at the base of the cliffs. *My sea. My poor, tainted, polluted sea. My volatile companion.* Today my personified sea was sad, and I felt sad too. The thought of watching it deteriorate with each step closer to London made me more sad. Like watching a gradual death. How I was going to miss the sea!

We turned left and walked in silence to Margate.

The sea was indeed grey, but it still curtsied and bowed merrily, slapping against the concrete wall which runs along the base of the cliffs from Margate, before retreating and declaring 'you can't catch me.' Even so, the concrete wall gave it the feeling of a swimming pool. I looked further out and thought of Essex and Suffolk. *Sea walls. Hpmh.*

A track took over and led us along the edge of flat drained countryside. The sun came out and Another Sunny Sunday on the South Coast began. Nearing Reculver the skinny figure of David came into view, and a small rise took us up to the remains of St Mary's Church. At the top David pointed out to sea and said casually 'Essex.'

'What?'

'That's Essex.' I stared out to sea in disbelief.

Sure enough, there was a distant landmass suspended between the grey sea and the clear blue sky. *Could it really be Essex? No. Surely not. Yes! No. My God! Essex. We've come a full circle: Well, almost. Imagine if something happened now? Don't think like that!* Silly thoughts went through my mind, and I called them back and tried again, eventually letting out a scream. 'My God. Essex!'

Somehow, now that I had seen that landmass I felt more relaxed. It was as if it had been so long coming that my irritability had been caused by impatience instead of fatigue. Whatever happened, we had at least seen the coast that we had set out on so tentatively ten months previously.

I rolled my socks over the top of my boots, and rolled up my t-shirt sleeves to get the maximum sunshine, and set out through Herne Bay. We sped through push chairs, whining children, berating mothers and overhung fathers. The centrifugal force was again flinging everyone to the coast, and in Whitstable the row of mellow coloured weatherboard beach huts displayed the usual seaside paraphernalia, overseen by granny sitting in the doorway. Lowry figures on Whitstable Street were colourful against the grey sky.

Whitstable itself was quiet. The shingle beach is divided by almost antique groynes which enhance Whitstable's character. An array of lovely old houses stand on the beach, so that at very high tide the sea almost laps their doors. We stayed in one such house, and that night I fell asleep to the sound of the sea on the pebbles. 'I'm here, I'm here' it said. How I would miss it!

We left Whitstable on May 25th in the knowledge that in six days time we would be home. Chris joined us for these last days.

We followed The Saxon Shore Way; a raised turf wall grazed by ewes and enormous lambs. The mudflats were being exposed by the retreating tide, and beyond them the Isle of Sheppey came closer until it ran parallel to us.

It was a humid and overcast day, which threatened a thunderstorm, and all day the birds flew around in such a noisy and lively fashion that I was sure they knew something I didn't. The black headed gulls were raucous in their guidance. Then there were the lapwing calling out their 'pee-wit' in voices that sounded magnified on the flatness. Joining in from time to time were the 'smart men going out to dinner,' but they didn't stay long. They often deemed themselves above us.

Common terns were acrobatic; and the occasional turnstone flew up. I remembered the first time I had seen them perform this quest for food on the shore of the Moray Firth.

There were nesting shelduck, and a pair of mute swans had built a throne-like nest in a waterlogged dip. They weren't silly the swans; they had prepared themselves a perfect castle complete with wide moat.

Every way I looked, our new friends were coming out to cheer us home.

I was amazed by the isolation here, when the map marked habitation in every direction and chimneys marched closer. I refolded the map; map number two — the same map which had got us stuck on Fobbing Marshes and safely through Southend-on-Sea. It now got us to Sittingbourne.

Our background music that night was cars, lambs and larks; but no sea. It already felt like a million miles away and, as if to try and assure myself that the sea was still somewhere, we walked round an island the next day. The Isle of Sheppey did not sound as if it would be an idyllic wilderness of dunes, beaches and crashing waves, but it was to offer a few surprises.

To reach Sheppey, we followed a marked path down Milton Creek. The first thing the path did was to disappear into a sewage works. Tess and I followed it, and wandered among the circular tanks, trusting my sense of direction as to where the path should resume, and holding our breath for as long as possible. There was no one around.

At the furthest end of the works a tall fence and a padlocked gate blocked our way. We were trapped in that stinking place, and only the ignominy of being found here stopped me from wailing and made me rattle my brains. I rattled and rattled, but it was too late. A surly looking man was marching towards us. 'What are you doing here?'

I smiled sweetly, 'Trying to follow the path.'

'It doesn't go through here.'

'I can see that,' I laughed to try and butter him up, but the smell made me realise why the man had such a surly look on his face. Anyone who has to work with the smell of the nation's sewage up their nose would be the same. 'You'll have to go back,' he said.

The thought of going back to Sittingbourne, and then following the main road, was distinctly unappealing. I then realised that at any minute (if we could get out of here) we were about to cross our 4,500th mile. This worked; 'I'll let you through. But don't come back this way again!' Perhaps I could write a book on coastal walks NOT to do?

On the other side the scene was no more cheery. The 'path' was more like virgin jungle of ragwort, docks, thistles and nettles. Pylons buzzed and threatened; and after a mile the path opened up into a patch of wasteland where sheets of rusty corrugated iron, strips of wood, lumps of concrete, broken glass and discarded pieces of machinery showed that there had once been a factory.

My over-riding thought was just to get out. Out of that destructive mess and carelessly abandoned man made shit. But it was another rainy mile and a half before we did. My socks squelched in my boots. There was a power station, and a paper mill, and another demolished factory; and then there was an old port, and more tangled pylons, and more wasteland. Finally there was the bridge.

As if to add the finishing touch to one of our worst mornings, a truck driver slowed up, wound down his window, gave me the V sign, and told me to 'fuck off off the road' — and he meant it.

Now I was depressed. Everything cried 'Stop!' and I wanted to cry 'Stop!' too. 'Stop this destruction: stop this hate and aggression and rush; stop this distrust and this egotism; stop all this which is obliterating all that is good and true and beautiful. Because there is goodness, truth and beauty on our doorstep. But we can be so blind to it. We should see it now, before our increasingly warped perspectives turn the whole lot irrecoverably upside down.'

I felt tears in the backs of my eyes, but the *boss* took us on to flat, grassy and empty Isle of Sheppey. I was walking like a robot, thinking and saying all these things and more. It was one of Britain's problems which had got me here, and it would take more than 4,550 miles to provide homes (let alone the rest), but if we each chip away at the base, the top will topple.

The world is like a wide and busy road. When we are small we are taught to hold hands and stick together when we cross such roads, but for some reason, when we grow up, we let go of each other's hands. If we crossed life's wide and busy road with a little more awareness of each other, perhaps there wouldn't be so many casualties; and perhaps we may gather back some of our wandering, despairing tribe who are straying off course.

While I contemplated the dirt, decay and 'V' sign which had brought this to a head, we were threatening the nesting sites of hundreds upon hundreds of Sheppey's birds. The sky became so busy that I feared there would soon be a collision

I looked right handed and took a double take — there was a group of avocets — and, yes, I recognised them. They are so graceful; their long legs, their slender, upturned bills; their black head and stripy black and white body. I watched and thought *Tom, you'd be proud of me*; and I felt my mental equilibrium returning to some extent. It was as if I was dealing with the ingredients of the emotional cake one by one.

But there was still one part of me which was screaming 'Stop,' and that was my body. From my lower back to my toes felt as though it had been deflated by a steam roller; as though every particle of energy had been squeezed out, leaving lifeless empty blood vessels and brittle and unlubricated bones and joints. I felt continually crampy. My legs quite simply wanted to stop at every stride, and were being left behind by the top half of my body. I regretted the fact that I had ever seen the signpost to London, or all the other signs. I knew that if we had just stumbled across London things would have been easier.

Once back on the mainland we were forced on to normally quiet but now frantic yellow roads. There was no verge, and the cars came so close that I could have easily touched them. The noise and fumes screeched through my ears and teeth, and resonated through my highly sensitive body, each one like a dentist catching an exposed nerve.

This is the Saxon Shore Way, along the muddy network of the Medway River. It is hard to imagine this estuary as anything but full of cars, towns and chimneys; but one and a half thousand years ago the Saxons settled here, using the salt to preserve food and the alluvial flood plains to grow food. It was the perfect place to settle, and settle we did.

My upper body led me through Lower Halstow, Upchurch, Lower Twydall, all of which merged together to form linear settlements, and finally to Rochester.

With three nights left it was reward time, and in Rochester we filled our supermarket trolley with goodies; bubbly, pringles, olives, squidgy bread.

At the fruit section a young guy was filling the shelves. I gave him a cheery 'hello,' and he almost dropped the box he was balancing. 'What did you say?' I repeated the greeting. 'Oh —' he looked confused.

'It's a word two people sometimes use to greet each other,' Chris said.

'Mm. Hi!' he said hurriedly, and then smiled.

We parked for the night in a vacuum of peace on the Isle of Grain. It was a warm evening and the windows and the doors of the Spudtruck were open as we drank bubbles, ate pringles and looked out across the lush early summer verges and growing wheat, to the chimneys of the refinery and the pylons escaping the power station. A wild rose had pride of place on the table.

We talked about our daydream farms, and both came to the conclusion that we wanted Belted Galloway cattle; we talked about relationships, and both built the perfect partner; we talked about Africa and we talked about New Zealand. We talked about mundane things, and never mentioned the Walk. This was real life.

The following morning, Southend pier and the chimneys of Canvey Island greeted us as clear as a bell four miles across the Thames. To say it was strange to see a landmark for a second time would be a dramatic understatement. It was an indescribable feeling of shock. It was as though I had not actually expected them to be there; as though they might have moved in the last ten months.

Tower Bridge was only thirty miles away (in a straight line), but we walked for ten miles without seeing a single person or passing a sign of habitation. The chaffinches, wrens and tits had woken us at 4am that morning, and now the teal, swan, heron, shelduck and the rest were calmer today; as I was too. I held the time to myself smugly. I knew that I could find it again; like I knew that I would find the sea again. I had made up my mind to go and live in the Western Highlands of Scotland.

The other side of the Thames was getting closer, and we swung left handed on its first bend. On our left a black and white field materialised into hundreds of piebald horses. There was one foal which had been born a matter of hours before, and was drunkenly tottering after its mother, who had decided that the experience had left her starving.

Chris appeared and walked with us. I voiced my thoughts. 'People keep asking if I'd do anything like this again. At the moment I don't want to walk anywhere, well, not with this body! But I'd like to do a trip with a pony. It could carry stuff, or Tess, or me when I got tired. It's something I've often dreamt about.'

Chris had stopped at my side and was looking left, blinking through his persistently troublesome contact lenses. 'It's a bloody flamingo!'

'You what?' I laughed, but followed his gaze. Sure enough, standing on a strip of land running between two reservoirs, was a flamingo. 'It must be plastic —' But it wasn't. It was the crowning glory to a twitcher.

The final stretch of Saxon Sore Way was another raised and grassy bank, but now the isolation was disappearing. Roads, railways and pylons began to converge on the shore, channelling into Gravesend; squeezing out the countryside and bringing with them people, piers, fences, factories, cranes, noise and bustle. I clung to this last piece of greenery. We passed a fisherman, then another and another. We walked under a skinny jetty, then another. More and more tugs faced upstream in the river.

Five hundred yards, fifty yards, and then the grass stopped. We had come to the end of the greenery. I turned round, and Tess came back to me. 'Are we going back now mum?'

I looked back at the fishermen — sitting on stools or checking their lines. Beyond them the raised bank curled itself round the brown water, and ran away from us into the distance. Miles and miles. Miles of mud, sand, shingle, marsh, cliffs, promenade. Miles of all this which would take you ultimately to Sandwood Bay in Scotland, then to Cleethorpes and all the other places which now ran through my head like a string of beads linked by the shore, and ultimately back to Tilbury which now lay opposite.

I turned to face London, and Tess and I funnelled into the fenced-in concrete path. Some token greenery clung stubbornly onto the shore, but then that too disappeared, and gave way to a series of foreboding and rat infested alleyways. Gravesend was how it sounded.

I dug out map number one. There it was, the route we had taken through West Ham, Barking and Dagenham, highlighted in yellow. The map was crumpled from the endless nervous folding and refolding that first day. Scrawly writing across the map read Wapping High Street and Woodward Road.

Now I didn't need road names, and set off along the network of smaller roads, sometimes finding scrubby and well thistled paths, or empty expanses of land offering 'Exclusive Development Potential'; but most of the time it was pavements.

Left here, right there . . . two children were clearly skyving school; a starling was helping itself to grapes outside a green grocer; two ladies stood gossiping outside a mini-mart. We interacted with no one that day. We just walked. Walked and walked on those square paving blocks, avoiding the lines when I remembered, and consciously lifting my leaden legs to step up a curb. *This time tomorrow* I looked at my vomit green, one pound watch, *this time tomorrow there'll be no more pavement and no more map.*

Lesnes Abbey Woods Caravan Park is a haven of countryside in the midst of Greater London. The Spudtruck was parked under a large squirrel frequented plane tree. It was being spruced up by Chris, and that night it was scene to the final nostalgic spaghetti Bolognaise. I had no doubt that we had eaten our way through several thousand miles of spaghetti.

David and Chris were decorating the Spudtruck with balloons as Tess and I prepared to leave — our final morning to ourselves, our final self indulgence. I gave Chris and David a hug, put on my rucksack and pedometer, and set sail for Tower Bridge feeling calm and in control.

I drifted off into mundane but contented thoughts, occasionally voicing them to Tess, and occasionally being dragged from them by a stalking photographer who popped out from behind furniture stores, garages, and blocks of flats.

After six miles we arrived at the Cutty Sark. This was where our splendid isolation ended, and standing under a huge banner reading 'Spud and Tess have walked 4,500 miles for the homeless' was a party of twenty five supporters who were joining us the rest of the way. There was no time to think anything now. It was all easy. If we had come to a grinding halt I am sure that they would have carried us. I had handed over the responsibility, and all I did was walk mechanically.

After a mile, and then another mile, we met the Spudtruck. At each stop the corks flew out of bottles, and bubbly was sprayed and drunk with equal abandon. Tess received her quota in a plastic bowl, slurping it back as though her life depended on it. She knew the reason.

Her one time co-pilot, Florence, rode high and mighty in the Spudtruck, along with the less energetic of the group. Faces cheered and smiled out of every window when it passed us, hooting and trailing its colourful decorations. It was one moveable street party. 'Go go!'

'Whoops, whay hay!'

Toot Toot Toot.

'Yahooo!'

We rounded Rotherhithe. More bubbles, more photos, more streamers. The sun was shining fiercely and it was as hot as the day we had left. I lifted my eyes upwards to the clear blue sky, and quietly thanked everyone. I was calm. It didn't matter if I felt pain and fatigue; but I didn't. I was being swept along by the gaiety of the occasion, and felt incredibly in control. I had sorted the emotions into their proper places; the cake had turned out alright.

The column stopped at a corner and Tess and I weaved our way to the front where the road turned sharp right. Round that corner would be Tower Bridge. I looked up to the sky again, holding my breath. *Thank you. Thank you.*

I took a deep breath and turned right.

The sight ahead opened the floodgate of emotions in a way I had never thought possible. From the tips of my toes to the tips of each strand of hair, it welled up in an instant. A minute ago, just round that corner, I had been calm; but now I was possessed. Every part of my body which had been numb for an age, was now coming to life with a surge which could easily prove to be too much. Without thinking anything I began to run.

Tess' lead dropped from my hand and I shook a bottle as I ran. I felt deranged, hysterical. I watched Tess ahead of me. Her ears were flapping as they did when she ran, and now she had spotted Chris and Pops and goodness knew who else.

Then, all of a sudden, I deflated. It happened as fast as I had inflated. I collapsed to the ground and spurted tears and spumante. The circle had come round.

I felt arms round me and got to my feet, calling Tess. Her body was elasticated in her sheer ecstasy at so many people, and I bent down and scooped her up in my arms, nestling my face in her wonderful, and still almost puppy smelling fur. As far as I was concerned we were the only two people on Tower Bridge for those private moments of thanks. She licked tears, sweat and spumante from my face, and I could feel her tail going hammer and tongs against my legs. *Yes, Tessie. We've done it.*

Epilogue

One month after reaching Tower Bridge, Tess and I realised our day-dream and returned to the old crofter's cottage in Glenuig. It was here that the bulk of the book was written. Since then we have maintained a semi-nomadic existence in Scotland, Cornwall, Northumberland, Devon and Wiltshire. The sea is never far.

I keep in touch with all the drivers, though our various homes have been somewhat inaccessible. They still talk about the Spudtruck with a certain masochistic nostalgia. The two pregnant drivers, Ruth and PC, gave birth to Charlie and Paddy respectively — the whisky and Spudtruck life did them no harm at all. They were joined by a third, Lettice, born to my other sister, Charles, and her husband, Will, as a result of the excessively long queue to the Cavern Club in Liverpool!

David and I split up eight months later. We still see each other. He still does the Guardian crossword, and still swears that he never drinks spirits.

As for the initial reason for the Walk, we raised almost £44,000 for Shelter. The money went to Housing Aid Centres throughout Britain, and was spent on various projects aimed at young people. The last time I went to Oban I heard that Margaret was still in the area and still on the road. I didn't find her, but plan to on the next visit.

And then there is Tess. The main thing she couldn't get used to was living in a house. The Spudtruck remained at home for a month after the Walk, as it underwent a series of home made repairs, and during that time Tess treated it as home. It was only when it was sold to a Country and Western couple that she accepted four more solid walls. Since then she has taken on a variety of roles, from sheepdog during lambing, to sea dog. She still loves ears, and still suffers from wind.

My body recovered over time, and we continue to walk. I still find it therapeutic, meditational and essential for my well being. I have no doubt this will remain the case, and that my restlessness will take us elsewhere.